TOGAF® 9 Certified
Study Guide 4th Edition

The Open Group Publications available from Van Haren Publishing

The TOGAF Series:
The TOGAF® Standard, Version 9.2
The TOGAF® Standard Version 9.2 – A Pocket Guide
TOGAF® 9 Foundation Study Guide, 4th Edition
TOGAF® 9 Certified Study Guide, 4th Edition

The Open Group Series:
The IT4IT™ Reference Architecture, Version 2.1
IT4IT™ for Managing the Business of IT – A Management Guide
IT4IT™ Foundation Study Guide, 2nd edition
The IT4IT™ Reference Architecture, Version 2.1 – A Pocket Guide
Cloud Computing for Business – The Open Group Guide
ArchiMate® 3.0.1 – A Pocket Guide
ArchiMate® 2 Certification – Study Guide
ArchiMate® 3.0.1 Specification

The Open Group Security Series:
O-TTPS - A Management Guide
Open Information Security Management Maturity Model (O-ISM3)
Open Enterprise Security Architecture (O-ESA)
Risk Management – The Open Group Guide
The Open FAIR™ Body of Knowledge – A Pocket Guide

All titles are available to purchase from:
www.opengroup.org
www.vanharen.net
and also many international and online distributors.

TOGAF® 9 Certified

Study Guide

4th Edition

Preparation for the TOGAF 9 Part 2 Examination
Prepared by Rachel Harrison of Oxford Brookes University and
Andrew Josey, The Open Group

The Open Group

Van Haren
PUBLISHING

Title:	TOGAF® Version 9 Certified - Study Guide 4th Edition
Subtitle:	Preparation for the TOGAF 9 Part 2 Examination
Series:	TOGAF Series
A Publication of:	The Open Group
Author:	Prof. Rachel Harrison and Andrew Josey
Publisher:	Van Haren Publishing, Zaltbommel, www.vanharen.net
ISBN Hard copy:	978 94 018 0292 5
ISBN eBook (pdf)	978 94 018 0293 2
ISBN ePUB	978 94 018 0294 9
Edition:	Fourth edition, first impression, April 2018
Layout and Cover design:	Coco Bookmedia, Amersfoort –NL
Print:	Wilco, Amersfoort – NL

Copyright © 2010-2018, The Open Group
All rights reserved.
No part of this publication may be reproduced, stored in a retrieval system, or transmitted, in any form or by any means, electronic, mechanical, photocopying, recording, or otherwise, without the prior permission of the copyright owner.
The views expressed in this document are not necessarily those of any particular member of The Open Group.
In the event of any discrepancy between text in this document and the official TOGAF documentation, the TOGAF documentation remains the authoritative version for certification, testing by examination, and other purposes. The official TOGAF documentation can be obtained online at www.opengroup.org/togaf.

Study Guide
TOGAF® 9 Certified, 4th Edition
Document Number: B181

Published by The Open Group, April 2018.

Comments relating to the material contained in this document may be submitted to:
The Open Group
Apex Plaza
Reading
Berkshire, RG1 1AX
United Kingdom
or by electronic mail to:
ogspecs@opengroup.org

Contents

Chapter 1 Introduction 1
1.1 Key Learning Points 1
1.2 The Open Group Certification for People Program 1
    1.2.1 Certification Document Structure 2
    1.2.2 TOGAF 9 Foundation 3
    1.2.3 TOGAF 9 Certified 3
    1.2.4 The Certification Process 4
    1.2.5 Preparing for the Examination 6
1.3 Summary 6
1.4 Recommended Reading 7

PART1: TOGAF 9 ARCHITECTURE DEVELOPMENT METHOD (ADM)

Chapter 2 Preliminary Phase 11
2.1 Key Learning Points 11
2.2 Objectives 12
2.3 Inputs 13
    2.3.1 Architecture Frameworks 13
    2.3.2 Business Principles, Business Goals, and Business Drivers 13
    2.3.3 Pre-Existing Architectural Inputs 14
2.4 Steps 14
    2.4.1 Scope the Enterprise Organizations Impacted 15
    2.4.2 Confirm Governance and Support Frameworks 15
    2.4.3 Define and Establish the Enterprise Architecture Team and Organization 16
    2.4.4 Identify and Establish Architecture Principles 16
    2.4.5 Tailor the TOGAF Framework and, if any, Other Selected Architecture Frameworks 20
    2.4.6 Develop a Strategy and Implementation Plan for Tools and Techniques 22
2.5 Outputs 22
    2.5.1 Architecture Principles 23
    2.5.2 Organizational Model for Enterprise Architecture 23
    2.5.3 Tailored Architecture Framework 24
    2.5.4 Architecture Repository 24

		2.5.5	Business Principles, Business Goals, and Business Drivers	24
		2.5.6	Architecture Governance Framework	25
		2.5.7	Request for Architecture Work	25
	2.6	Summary		26
	2.7	Exercises		26
	2.8	Recommended Reading		27

Chapter 3 Phase A: Architecture Vision 29

	3.1	Key Learning Points		29
	3.2	Objectives		30
	3.3	Inputs		31
	3.4	Steps		31
		3.4.1	Establish the Architecture Project	31
		3.4.2	Identify Stakeholders, Concerns, and Business Requirements	32
		3.4.3	Confirm and Elaborate Business Goals, Business Drivers, and Constraints	37
		3.4.4	Evaluate Capabilities	37
		3.4.5	Assess Readiness for Business Transformation	38
		3.4.6	Define Scope	40
		3.4.7	Confirm and Elaborate Architecture Principles, including Business Principles	40
		3.4.8	Develop Architecture Vision	41
		3.4.9	Define the Target Architecture Value Propositions and KPIs	42
		3.4.10	Identify the Business Transformation Risks and Mitigation Activities	42
		3.4.11	Develop Statement of Architecture Work; Secure Approval	43
	3.5	Outputs		43
		3.5.1	Statement of Architecture Work	44
		3.5.2	Capability Assessment	45
		3.5.3	Architecture Vision	46
		3.5.4	Communications Plan	47
	3.6	Summary		47
	3.7	Exercises		48
	3.8	Recommended Reading		50

Chapter 4 Phase B: Business Architecture 51
4.1   Key Learning Points 51
4.2   Objectives 52
4.3   Inputs 52
         4.3.1   Business Principles 53
4.4   Steps 54
         4.4.1   Select Reference Models, Viewpoints, and Tools 55
         4.4.2   Develop Baseline Business Architecture Description 57
         4.4.3   Develop Target Business Architecture Description 58
         4.4.4   Perform Gap Analysis 60
         4.4.5   Define Candidate Roadmap Components 60
         4.4.6   Resolve Impacts across the Architecture Landscape 60
         4.4.7   Conduct Formal Stakeholder Review 60
         4.4.8   Finalize the Business Architecture 61
         4.4.9   Create the Architecture Definition Document 61
4.5   Outputs 62
         4.5.1   Architecture Definition Document 62
         4.5.2   Architecture Requirements Specification 64
         4.5.3   Architecture Roadmap 65
4.6   Summary 66
4.7   Exercises 66
4.8   Recommended Reading 67

Chapter 5 Phase C: Information Systems Architectures 69
5.1   Key Learning Points 69
5.2   Objectives 70
5.3   Considerations for the Implementation Order 70
5.4   Inputs 70
5.5   Steps 70
5.6   Outputs 70
5.7   Summary 71
5.8   Exercises 71
5.9   Recommended Reading 71

Chapter 6 Phase C: Data Architecture 73
6.1   Key Learning Points 73
6.2   Objectives 73
6.3   Inputs 73
         6.3.1   Data Principles 74

6.4	Steps		75
	6.4.1	Select Reference Models, Viewpoints, and Tools	76
	6.4.2	Develop Baseline Data Architecture Description	77
	6.4.3	Develop Target Data Architecture Description	78
	6.4.4	Perform Gap Analysis	78
	6.4.5	Define Candidate Roadmap Components	78
	6.4.6	Resolve Impacts Across the Architecture Landscape	78
	6.4.7	Conduct Formal Stakeholder Review	79
	6.4.8	Finalize the Data Architecture	79
	6.4.9	Create Architecture Definition Document	79
6.5	Outputs		80
	6.5.1	Components of the Architecture Definition Document	80
	6.5.2	Components of the Architecture Requirements Specification	80
6.6	Summary		81
6.7	Exercises		81
6.8	Recommended Reading		81

Chapter 7 Phase C: Application Architecture 83

7.1	Key Learning Points		83
7.2	Objectives		83
7.3	Inputs		83
	7.3.1	Application Principles	84
7.4	Steps		85
	7.4.1	Select Reference Models, Viewpoints, and Tools	85
	7.4.2	Develop Baseline Application Architecture Description	87
	7.4.3	Develop Target Application Architecture Description	88
	7.4.4	Perform Gap Analysis	88
	7.4.5	Define Candidate Roadmap Components	88
	7.4.6	Resolve Impacts Across the Architecture Landscape	88
	7.4.7	Conduct Formal Stakeholder Review	89
	7.4.8	Finalize the Application Architecture	89
	7.4.9	Create Architecture Definition Document	89
7.5	Outputs		89
	7.5.1	Components of the Architecture Definition Document	90
	7.5.2	Components of the Architecture Requirements Specification	90
7.6	Summary		91

7.7	Exercises	91
7.8	Recommended Reading	92

Chapter 8 Phase D: Technology Architecture 93
8.1	Key Learning Points	93
8.2	Objectives	94
8.3	Inputs	94
	8.3.1 Technology Principles	95
8.4	Steps	96
	8.4.1 Select Reference Models, Viewpoints, and Tools	96
	8.4.2 Develop Baseline Technology Architecture Description	98
	8.4.3 Develop Target Technology Architecture Description	99
	8.4.4 Perform Gap Analysis	100
	8.4.5 Define Candidate Roadmap Components	100
	8.4.6 Resolve Impacts Across the Architecture Landscape	100
	8.4.7 Conduct Formal Stakeholder Review	101
	8.4.8 Finalize the Technology Architecture	101
	8.4.9 Create Architecture Definition Document	101
8.5	Outputs	101
	8.5.1 Components of the Architecture Definition Document	102
	8.5.2 Components of the Architecture Requirements Specification	102
8.6	Summary	103
8.7	Exercises	103
8.8	Recommended Reading	103

Chapter 9 Phase E: Opportunities & Solutions 105
9.1	Key Learning Points	105
9.2	Objectives	106
9.3	Inputs	107
9.4	Steps	107
	9.4.1 Determine/Confirm Key Corporate Change Attributes	107
	9.4.2 Determine Business Constraints for Implementation	109
	9.4.3 Review and Consolidate Gap Analysis Results from Phases B to D	109
	9.4.4 Review Consolidated Requirements Across Related Business Functions	110
	9.4.5 Consolidate and Reconcile Interoperability Requirements	111

	9.4.6	Refine and Validate Dependencies 111
	9.4.7	Confirm Readiness and Risk for Business Transformation 112
	9.4.8	Formulate Implementation and Migration Strategy 112
	9.4.9	Identify and Group Major Work Packages 113
	9.4.10	Identify Transition Architectures 114
	9.4.11	Create the Architecture Roadmap & Implementation and Migration Plan 114
9.5	Outputs 115
9.6	Summary 116
9.7	Exercises 116
9.8	Recommended Reading 116

Chapter 10 Phase F: Migration Planning 117

10.1	Key Learning Points 117
10.2	Objectives 118
10.3	Inputs 118
10.4	Steps 119
	10.4.1 Confirm Management Framework Interactions for the Implementation and Migration Plan 119
	10.4.2 Assign a Business Value to Each Work Package 120
	10.4.3 Estimate Resource Requirements, Project Timings, and Availability/Delivery Vehicle 123
	10.4.4 Prioritize the Migration Projects through the Conduct of a Cost/Benefit Assessment and Risk Validation 123
	10.4.5 Confirm Architecture Roadmap and Update Architecture Definition Document 124
	10.4.6 Complete the Implementation and Migration Plan 125
	10.4.7 Complete the Architecture Development Cycle and Document Lessons Learned 126
10.5	Outputs 127
	10.5.1 Implementation and Migration Plan 127
	10.5.2 Architecture Definition Document, including Transition Architecture 128
	10.5.3 Implementation Governance Model 129
10.6	Summary 129
10.7	Exercises 130
10.8	Recommended Reading 130

Chapter 11 Phase G: Implementation Governance 131
- 11.1 Key Learning Points 131
- 11.2 Objectives 132
- 11.3 Inputs 132
- 11.4 Steps 133
  - 11.4.1 Confirm Scope and Priorities for Deployment with Development Management 133
  - 11.4.2 Identify Deployment Resources and Skills 134
  - 11.4.3 Guide Development of Solutions Deployment 134
  - 11.4.4 Perform Enterprise Architecture Compliance Reviews 134
  - 11.4.5 Implement Business and IT Operations 136
  - 11.4.6 Perform Post-Implementation Review and Close the Implementation 137
- 11.5 Outputs 137
  - 11.5.1 Architecture Contracts 137
  - 11.5.2 Compliance Assessments 139
- 11.6 Summary 139
- 11.7 Exercises 140
- 11.8 Recommended Reading 140

Chapter 12 Phase H: Architecture Change Management 141
- 12.1 Key Learning Points 141
- 12.2 Objectives 142
- 12.3 Inputs 142
  - 12.3.1 Change Requests 143
- 12.4 Steps 143
  - 12.4.1 Establish Value Realization Process 144
  - 12.4.2 Deploy Monitoring Tools 144
  - 12.4.3 Manage Risks 144
  - 12.4.4 Provide Analysis for Architecture Change Management 144
  - 12.4.5 Develop Change Requirements to Meet Performance Targets 145
  - 12.4.6 Manage Governance Process 145
  - 12.4.7 Activate the Process to Implement Change 145
- 12.5 Outputs 145
- 12.6 Summary 146
- 12.7 Exercises 146
- 12.8 Recommended Reading 147

Chapter 13 ADM Architecture Requirements Management 149
13.1 Key Learning Points 149
13.2 Objectives 150
13.3 Inputs 150
13.4 Steps 150
13.5 Outputs 153
       13.5.1 Requirements Impact Assessment 153
13.6 Summary 153
13.7 Exercises 154
13.8 Recommended Reading 154

PART 2: GUIDELINES FOR ADAPTING THE ADM

Chapter 14 Iteration and Levels 157
14.1 Key Learning Points 157
14.2 The Concept of Iteration 157
       14.2.1 Iteration to Develop a Comprehensive Architecture Landscape 158
       14.2.2 Iteration within an ADM Cycle (Architecture Development Iteration) 158
       14.2.3 Iteration to Manage the Architecture Capability (Architecture Capability Iterations) 158
14.3 Factors Influencing the Use of Iteration 159
14.4 Iteration Cycles 160
14.5 Classes of Architecture Engagement 162
       14.5.1 Identification of Required Change 162
       14.5.2 Definition of Change 162
       14.5.3 Implementation of Change 162
14.6 Mapping TOGAF Phases to Iteration Cycles 165
       14.6.1 Iteration between ADM Cycles 165
       14.6.2 Iteration within an ADM Cycle 166
14.7 Applying the ADM Across the Architecture Landscape 169
       14.7.1 The Architecture Landscape 170
       14.7.2 The Architecture Continuum 171
       14.7.3 Organizing the Architecture Landscape 171
14.8 Summary 172
14.9 Exercises 172
14.10 Recommended Reading 173

Chapter 15 Security 175
15.1 Key Learning Points 175
15.2 Introduction 175
15.3 Enterprise Security Architecture 175
15.4 Security as a Cross-Cutting Concern 176
15.5 Adapting the ADM for Security 177
15.6 Summary 181
15.7 Exercises 181
15.8 Recommended Reading 181

PART 3: THE ARCHITECTURE CONTENT FRAMEWORK

Chapter 16 Architecture Content Framework 185
16.1 Key Learning Points 185
16.2 Introduction 185
16.3 The Content Framework and the TOGAF ADM 186
16.4 Why do we Need a Metamodel? 186
16.5 Components of the Content Metamodel 187
16.6 Core Metamodel Concepts 189
      16.6.1 Core and Extension Content 189
      16.6.2 Core Metamodel Entities 191
      16.6.3 Building Blocks, Catalogs, Matrices, and Diagrams 193
16.7 Summary 194
16.8 Exercises 195
16.9 Recommended Reading 195

PART 4: THE ENTERPRISE CONTINUUM

Chapter 17 Architecture Partitioning 199
17.1 Key Learning Points 199
17.2 Introduction 199
17.3 Applying Classification to Partitioned Architectures 200
17.4 Applying Partitioning to the ADM 201
17.5 Summary 203
17.6 Recommended Reading 203

Chapter 18 Architecture Repository 205
18.1   Key Learning Points 205
18.2   Introduction 205
18.3   The Repository in Detail 206
          18.3.1   Architecture Metamodel 207
          18.3.2   Architecture Landscape 207
          18.3.3   Reference Library 207
          18.3.4   Standards Information Base 208
          18.3.5   Governance Log 208
          18.3.6   Architecture Requirements Repository 208
          18.3.7   Solutions Landscape 209
          18.3.8   Enterprise Repository 209
          18.3.9   Architecture Capability 210
18.4   Relationship to Other Parts of the TOGAF Standard 210
18.5   Summary 210
18.6   Recommended Reading 210

Chapter 19 The TOGAF Technical Reference Model (TRM) 213
19.1   Key Learning Points 213
19.2   Structure of the TRM 213
19.3   The TRM in Detail 214
          19.3.1   Application Software 215
          19.3.2   Application Platform Interface 216
          19.3.3   Application Platform 216
          19.3.4   Interfaces between Services 216
          19.3.5   Communications Infrastructure 217
          19.3.6   Communications Infrastructure Interface 217
          19.3.7   Qualities 217
19.4   Taxonomy of Application Platform Services 217
19.5   Taxonomy of Application Platform Service Qualities 220
19.6   Summary 221
19.7   Exercises 221
19.8   Recommended Reading 222

Chapter 20 Integrated Information Infrastructure Reference Model (III-RM) 223
20.1 Key Learning Points 223
20.2 Drivers for Boundaryless Information Flow 223
20.3 How the III-RM Fulfills the Solution Space 224
20.4 The High-Level Structure of the III-RM 224
20.5 Components of the III-RM 225
20.6 Summary 228
20.7 Recommended Reading 229

Chapter 21 Architecture Governance 233
21.1 Key Learning Points 233
21.2 Architecture Governance and the ADM 233
21.3 Key Success Factors 234
21.4 Setting up the Architecture Board 235
21.5 Operating an Architecture Board 236
    21.5.1 General 236
    21.5.2 Preparation 237
    21.5.3 Agenda 237
21.6 Summary 239
21.7 Exercises 239
21.8 Recommended Reading 239

Chapter 22 Architecture Maturity Models 241
22.1 Key Learning Points 241
22.2 Capability Maturity Models 241
22.3 Capability Maturity Model Integration (CMMI) 243
22.4 ACMM 244
22.5 Maturity Assessments and the ADM 245
22.6 Summary 245
22.7 Exercises 245
22.8 Recommended Reading 246

Chapter 23 Architecture Skills Framework 247
23.1 Key Learning Points 247
23.2 Purpose 247
23.3 Benefits 248

23.4 Enterprise Architecture Roles, Skills Categories, and Proficiency Levels 249
    23.4.1 TOGAF Roles 249
    23.4.2 Skills Categories..249
    23.4.3 Proficiency Levels 250
    23.4.4 Example Role and Skill Definitions 250
23.5 Summary 252
23.6 Exercises 252
23.7 Recommended Reading 252

Appendix A Test Yourself Examination Paper 253
A.1 Introduction..253
A.2 Instructions 253
A.3 Questions...254

Appendix B Bonus Questions 271
B.1 Introduction..271
B.2 Questions...271

Appendix C Test Yourself Examination Answers 279
C.1 Question 1 279
C.2 Question 2 280
C.3 Question 3 281
C.4 Question 4 282
C.5 Question 5 283
C.6 Question 6 284
C.7 Question 7 285
C.8 Question 8 286

Appendix D Bonus Answers...287
D.1 Question 9 287
D.2 Question 10 288
D.3 Question 11 289
D.4 Question 12 290

Appendix E TOGAF 9 Certified Syllabus 291
- E.1 Preliminary Phase 291
- E.2 Architecture Governance (Level 2) 292
- E.3 Business Scenarios Technique 292
- E.4 Phase A: Architecture Vision 293
- E.5 Architecture Content Framework 293
- E.6 Stakeholder Management 294
- E.7 TOGAF Content Metamodel 294
- E.8 Architecture Implementation Support Techniques 295
- E.9 Phase B: Business Architecture 295
- E.10 Phase C: Information Systems Architectures – Data Architecture 296
- E.11 Phase C: Information Systems Architectures – Application Architecture 297
- E.12 TOGAF Foundation Architecture: Technical Reference Model (Level 2) 298
- E.13 Integrated Information Infrastructure Reference Model (Level 2) 299
- E.14 Phase D: Technology Architecture 300
- E.15 Migration Planning Techniques 300
- E.16 Phase E: Opportunities and Solutions 301
- E.17 Phase F: Migration Planning 301
- E.18 Phase G: Implementation Governance 302
- E.19 Phase H: Architecture Change Management 302
- E.20 ADM Architecture Requirements Management 303
- E.21 Architecture Partitioning 303
- E.22 Architecture Repository 304
- E.23 Guidelines for Adapting the ADM: Iteration and Levels 304
- E.24 Guidelines for Adapting the ADM: Security 305
- E.25 Architecture Maturity Models 305
- E.26 Architecture Skills Framework 306

Index **307**

Preface

This Document

This document is a Study Guide for the TOGAF® 9 Certified qualification. This fourth edition is based on Version 3 of The Open Group Certification for People: TOGAF Conformance Requirements (Multi-Level) and is aligned with the TOGAF Standard, Version 9.2. It gives an overview of every learning objective for the TOGAF 9 Certified Syllabus beyond the Foundation level, and is specifically designed to help individuals prepare for certification.

The audience for this Study Guide is:
- Individuals who require a deeper understanding of the TOGAF 9 framework
- Professionals who are working in an organization where the TOGAF 9 framework has been adopted and who need to participate in architecture projects and initiatives
- Architects who will be responsible for developing architecture artifacts
- Architects who wish to introduce the TOGAF 9 framework into an architecture practice
- Architects who want to achieve a recognized qualification to demonstrate their detailed knowledge of the TOGAF 9 framework

This Study Guide assumes a prior knowledge equivalent to TOGAF 9 Foundation.

While reading this Study Guide, the reader should also refer to the TOGAF Standard, Version 9.2.

The Study Guide is structured as follows:
- Chapter 1 (Introduction) provides a brief introduction to TOGAF 9 certification and the examinations that lead to the TOGAF 9 Certified qualification, as well as how to use this Study Guide

- Part 1: TOGAF 9 Architecture Development Method (ADM) comprises Chapters 2 through 13 and consists of a tour of the ADM phases:
    - Chapter 2 describes the Preliminary Phase within the ADM
      This chapter covers the preparation and initiation activities required to create an Architecture Capability.
    - Chapter 3 describes Phase A: Architecture Vision
      This chapter covers the initial phase of an Architecture Development Cycle. It includes information about defining the scope, identifying the stakeholders, creating the Architecture Vision, and obtaining approvals.
    - Chapter 4 describes Phase B: Business Architecture
      This chapter covers the development of a Business Architecture to support an agreed Architecture Vision.
    - Chapter 5 provides an introduction to Phase C: Information Systems Architectures
      The next two chapters describe the details of the two parts of Phase C.
    - Chapter 6 describes the development of the Data Architecture within Phase C
    - Chapter 7 describes the development of the Application Architecture within Phase C
    - Chapter 8 describes Phase D: Technology Architecture
      The Technology Architecture is used as the basis of the following implementation work.
    - Chapter 9 describes Phase E: Opportunities and Solutions
      This phase identifies major implementation projects and groups them into work packages that deliver the Target Architecture defined in the previous phases.
    - Chapter 10 describes Phase F: Migration Planning
      This phase develops a detailed Implementation and Migration Plan addressing how to move from the Baseline to the Target Architecture.
    - Chapter 11 describes Phase G: Implementation Governance
      This phase ensures that the implementation projects conform to the architecture.
    - Chapter 12 describes Phase H: Architecture Change Management
      This phase ensures that the Architecture Capability can respond to the needs of the enterprise as changes arise.
    - Chapter 13 describes ADM Architecture Requirements Management, a process that applies throughout the ADM

- Part 2: Guidelines for Adapting the ADM consists of two chapters:
  - Chapter 14 describes how to apply iteration to the ADM, and how to apply the ADM at different enterprise levels
  - Chapter 15 describes security considerations during the application of the ADM
- Part 3: The Architecture Content Framework consists of a single chapter:
  - Chapter 16 describes the Architecture Content Framework and the TOGAF Content Metamodel
- Part 4: The Enterprise Continuum consists of two chapters:
  - Chapter 17 describes Architecture Partitioning
  - Chapter 18 describes the Architecture Repository, which is a model for a physical instance of the Enterprise Continuum
- Part 5: TOGAF Reference Models consists of two chapters:
  - Chapter 19 describes the TOGAF Technical Reference Model (TRM)
  - Chapter 20 describes the Integrated Information Infrastructure Reference Model (III-RM)
- Part 6: Architecture Capability consists of three chapters:
  - Chapter 21 describes the relationship between Architecture Governance and the ADM; it also describes how to establish and operate an Architecture Board
  - Chapter 22 describes Architecture Maturity Models
  - Chapter 23 describes the Architecture Skills Framework
- Appendix A provides a Practice Test for the TOGAF 9 Part 2 Examination
- Appendix B provides four bonus practice questions for the TOGAF 9 Part 2 Examination
- Appendix C provides the answers to the examination in Appendix A
- Appendix D provides the answers to the bonus practice questions in Appendix B
- Appendix E provides the TOGAF 9 Certified Syllabus

How to Use this Study Guide
The chapters in this Study Guide are arranged to provide coverage of the TOGAF 9 Certified syllabus and should be read in order. However, you may wish to use this Study Guide to study topics with which you are already familiar, and it is possible to select topics for review in any order. Where a topic requires further information from a later part in the syllabus, a cross-reference is provided.

Within each chapter are "Key Learning Points" and "Summary" sections that help you to easily identify what you need to know for each topic. Where applicable, a chapter has an "Exercises" section that will help you reinforce key learning points in the chapter.

Each chapter also has a "Recommended Reading" section that indicates relevant, additional sections of the TOGAF standard and other sources that should be read to obtain a full understanding of the subject material.

Finally, at the end of this Study Guide is a "Test Yourself" examination paper that can be used to test your readiness to take the official TOGAF 9 Part 2 Examination. This paper is designed to include the same question formats and a similar difficulty level to the official TOGAF 9 Part 2 Examination. In addition to the examination paper, four bonus practice questions are also provided.

Conventions Used in this Study Guide
The following conventions are used throughout this Study Guide in order to help identify important information and avoid confusion over the intended meaning.
- Ellipsis (…)
  Indicates a continuation; such as an incomplete list of example items, or a continuation from preceding text.
- **Bold**
  Used to highlight specific terms.
- *Italics*
  Used for emphasis. May also refer to other external documents.
- *(Syllabus Reference Unit X, Learning Outcome Y: Statement)*
  Used at the start of a text block to identify the associated TOGAF 9 Certified Syllabus learning outcome.

In addition to typographical conventions, the following conventions are used to highlight segments of text:

> A Note box is used to highlight useful or interesting information.

> A Tip box is used to provide key information that can save you time or that may not be entirely obvious.

About the TOGAF Standard

The TOGAF Standard, a standard of The Open Group, is a proven Enterprise Architecture methodology and framework used by the world's leading organizations to improve business efficiency. It is the most prominent and reliable Enterprise Architecture standard, ensuring consistent standards, methods, and communication among Enterprise Architecture professionals. Those fluent in the TOGAF standard enjoy greater industry credibility, job effectiveness, and career opportunities. The TOGAF standard helps practitioners avoid being locked into proprietary methods, utilize resources more efficiently and effectively, and realize a greater return on investment.

About The Open Group

The Open Group is a global consortium that enables the achievement of business objectives through technology standards. Our diverse membership of more than 580 organizations includes customers, systems and solutions suppliers, tools vendors, integrators, academics, and consultants across multiple industries.

The Open Group aims to:
- Capture, understand, and address current and emerging requirements, establish policies, and share best practices
- Facilitate interoperability, develop consensus, and evolve and integrate specifications and open source technologies
- Operate the industry's premier certification service

Further information on The Open Group is available at www.opengroup.org.

The Open Group publishes a wide range of technical documentation, most of which is focused on development of Open Group Standards and Guides, but which also includes white papers, technical studies, certification and testing documentation, and business titles. Full details and a catalog are available at www.opengroup.org/library.

About the Authors

Rachel Harrison, Oxford Brookes University

Rachel Harrison is a Professor of Computer Science in the Department of Computing and Communication Technologies at Oxford Brookes University. Previously she was Professor of Computer Science, Head of the Department of Computer Science, and Director of Research for the School of Systems Engineering at the University of Reading. Her research interests include systems evolution, software metrics, requirements engineering, software architecture, usability, and software testing. She has published over 100 refereed papers and consulted widely with industry, working with organizations such as IBM, the DERA, Philips Research Labs, Praxis Critical Systems, and The Open Group. She is Editor-in-Chief of the Software Quality Journal, published by Springer.

Prof. Harrison holds an MA in Mathematics from Oxford University, an MSc in Computer Science from University College London, and a PhD in Computer Science from the University of Southampton. She is a Member of the British Computer Society, an Affiliate Member of the IEEE-CS, a Member of the Association of Computing Machinery, and is a Chartered Engineer.

Andrew Josey, The Open Group

Andrew Josey is VP Standards and Certification, overseeing all certification and testing programs of The Open Group. He also manages the standards process for The Open Group. Since joining the company in 1996, Andrew has been closely involved with the standards development, certification, and testing activities of The Open Group. He has led many standards development projects including specification and certification development for the ArchiMate®, TOGAF®, POSIX®, and UNIX® programs.

He is a member of the IEEE, USENIX, and the Association of Enterprise Architects (AEA). He holds an MSc in Computer Science from University College London.

Trademarks

ArchiMate®, DirecNet®, Making Standards Work®, OpenPegasus®, Platform 3.0®, The Open Group®, TOGAF®, UNIX®, UNIXWARE®, X/Open®, and the Open Brand X® logo are registered trademarks and Boundaryless Information Flow™, Build with Integrity Buy with Confidence™, Dependability Through Assuredness™, EMMM™, FACE™, the FACE™ logo, IT4IT™, the IT4IT™ logo, O-DEF™, O-PAS™, Open FAIR™, Open Platform 3.0™, Open Process Automation™, Open Trusted Technology Provider™, SOSA™, the Open O™ logo, and The Open Group Certification logo (Open O and check™) are trademarks of The Open Group.

CMMI®, P-CMM®, SA-CMM®, and SE-CMM® are registered trademarks of the Software Engineering Institute (SEI), Carnegie Mellon University.

Energistics® is a registered trademark of Energistics in the United States.

Object Management Group® and OMG® are registered trademarks and BPMN™, Business Process Modeling Notation™, and SPEM™ are trademarks of the Object Management Group (OMG).

SABSA® is a registered trademark of The SABSA Institute.

Zachman® is a registered trademark of Zachman International, Inc.

All other brand, company, and product names are used for identification purposes only and may be trademarks that are the sole property of their respective owners.

Acknowledgements

The Open Group gratefully acknowledges The Open Group Architecture Forum for developing the TOGAF standard.

The Open Group gratefully acknowledges the following reviewers who participated in the review of this and earlier editions of this Study Guide:
- Beryl Bellman
- Geoff Burke
- Roger Cutts
- Jörgen Dahlberg
- Steve Else
- Bill Estrem
- Howard Gottlieb
- Joop Hoefnagels
- Paul Homan
- Andrew Josey
- Graham Neal
- Marleen Olde Hartman
- Simon Parker
- Mona Pomraning
- Felix Rausch
- Brian Selves
- Selvyn Wright

References

The following documents are referenced in this Study Guide:
- Bill Estrem: "TOGAF to the Rescue" (www.opengroup.org/downloads)
- Integrating Risk and Security within a TOGAF® Enterprise Architecture, an Open Group Guide, January 2016 (G152), published by The Open Group; refer to: www.opengroup.org/library/g152
- The Open Group Architecture Principles, Case Study by Darren Hawley on behalf of The Open Group Internal Architecture Board, October 2008 (Y082), published by The Open Group; refer to: www.opengroup.org/library/y082
- The Open Group Certification for People: Certification Policy for Examination-Based Programs, April 2016 (X1603), published by The Open Group; refer to: www.opengroup.org/library/x1603
- The Open Group Certification for People: Program Summary Datasheet, 2018, published by The Open Group (www.opengroup.org/togaf9/cert/docs/togaf9_cert_summary.pdf)
- The Open Group Certification for People: TOGAF® Conformance Requirements (Multi-Level), Version 3.0, April 2018 (X1810), published by The Open Group; refer to: www.opengroup.org/library/x1810
- The Open Group Certification for People: TOGAF® Program Configuration, June 2016 (X1401), published by The Open Group; refer to: www.opengroup.org/library/x1401
- The TOGAF® Standard, Version 9.2, a standard of The Open Group, April 2018 (C182), published by The Open Group; refer to: www.opengroup.org/library/c182
- TOGAF® 9 Certified Datasheet, 2018, published by The Open Group (www.opengroup.org/togaf9/cert/docs/togaf9_cert.pdf)
- TOGAF® 9 Foundation Datasheet, 2018, published by The Open Group (www.opengroup.org/togaf9/cert/docs/togaf9_foundation.pdf)
- TOGAF® 9 Foundation Study Guide, 4th Edition, April 2018 (B180), published by The Open Group; refer to: www.opengroup.org/library/b180
- TOGAF® Series Guide: Business Scenarios, September 2017 (G176), published by The Open Group; refer to www.opengroup.org/library/g176

- TOGAF® Series Guide: The TOGAF Integrated Information Infrastructure Reference Model (III- RM): An Architected Approach to Boundaryless Information Flow™, November 2017 (G179), published by The Open Group; refer to www.opengroup.org/library/g179
- TOGAF® Series Guide: The TOGAF Technical Reference Model (TRM), September 2017 (G175), published by The Open Group; refer to www.opengroup.org/library/g175
- Zachman® Framework, Zachman Institute for Framework Advancement (ZIFA) (www.zifa.com)

The following web links are referenced in this Study Guide:
- The Open Group TOGAF 9 Certification website: www.opengroup.org/certifications/togaf
- The TOGAF information website: www.togaf.info
- TOGAF 9 People Certification Overview presentation: www.togaf.info/sg01
- Introduction to the ADM presentation: www.togaf.info/sg02
- Sample Catalogs, Matrices, and Diagrams presentation: www.togaf.info/sg03
- TOGAF 9 Architecture Content Metamodel Overview presentation: www.togaf.info/sg04

Chapter 1
Introduction

1.1 Key Learning Points

This document is a Study Guide for students planning to qualify as TOGAF 9 Certified. This edition is aligned to the approved syllabus for the TOGAF Standard, Version 9.2. This document is a companion document to the TOGAF 9 Foundation Study Guide, and focuses on the learning outcomes beyond the Foundation level.

It gives an overview of every learning objective for the TOGAF 9 Certified Syllabus and in-depth coverage on preparing and taking the TOGAF 9 Part 2 Examination. It is specifically designed to help individuals prepare for certification.

> **Prerequisite Knowledge**
> This Study Guide assumes a prior knowledge equivalent to TOGAF 9 Foundation. This can be obtained by reading the TOGAF 9 Foundation Study Guide (see References).

This first chapter will familiarize you with the TOGAF 9 certification program, as well as give you important information about the structure of the TOGAF 9 examinations.

The objectives of this chapter are as follows:
- To provide an understanding of TOGAF certification
- To learn key facts about the TOGAF 9 Part 2 Examination

1.2 The Open Group Certification for People Program

Certification is available to individuals who wish to demonstrate they have attained the required knowledge and understanding of the TOGAF standard,

Version 9. The latest version of the Program is applicable to the TOGAF Standard, Version 9.2.

There are two levels defined for TOGAF 9 People certification, denoted *TOGAF 9 Foundation* and *TOGAF 9 Certified*, respectively. This Study Guide covers the second of these – TOGAF 9 Certified. Studying for TOGAF 9 Certified includes all the learning outcomes for TOGAF 9 Foundation, which are covered in a separate companion document (see References).

1.2.1 Certification Document Structure

The documents available to support the Program are as shown in Figure 1:

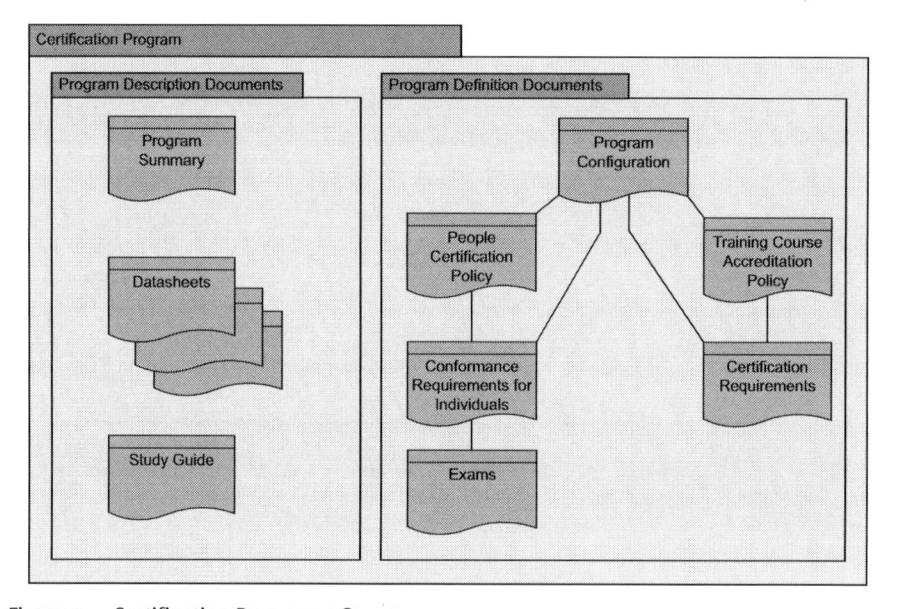

Figure 1: Certification Document Structure

Program description documents, such as this Study Guide, are intended for an end-user audience including those interested in becoming certified. The Program definition documents are intended for trainers, examination developers, and the Certification Authority. All these documents are available from The Open Group website.[1]

---

[1] Available at the TOGAF 9 certification website (www.opengroup.org/certifications/togaf), or The Open Group Library (www.opengroup.org/library).

1.2.2 TOGAF 9 Foundation

The purpose of certification to TOGAF 9 Foundation is to provide validation that the candidate has gained knowledge of the TOGAF terminology, structure, and basic concepts, and understands the core principles of Enterprise Architecture and the TOGAF standard. The learning objectives at this level focus on knowledge and comprehension. More information is provided in the TOGAF 9 Foundation Study Guide (see References).

1.2.3 TOGAF 9 Certified

The purpose of certification to TOGAF 9 Certified is to provide validation that, in addition to the knowledge and comprehension of TOGAF 9 Foundation, the Candidate is able to analyze and apply this knowledge. The learning objectives at this level therefore focus on application and analysis in addition to knowledge and comprehension.

Individuals certified at this level, in addition to the knowledge required for TOGAF 9 Foundation, will have demonstrated their understanding of:
- How to apply the ADM phases in development of an Enterprise Architecture
- How to apply Architecture Governance in development of an Enterprise Architecture
- How to apply the TOGAF Architecture Content Framework
- How to apply the concept of building blocks
- How to apply the Stakeholder Management Technique
- How to apply the TOGAF Content Metamodel
- How to apply TOGAF recommended techniques when developing an Enterprise Architecture
- The TOGAF Technical Reference Model (TRM) and how to customize it to meet an organization's needs
- The Integrated Information Infrastructure Reference Model (III-RM)
- The content of the key deliverables of the ADM cycle
- How an Enterprise Architecture can be partitioned to meet the specific needs of an organization
- The purpose of the Architecture Repository
- How to apply iteration and different levels of architecture with the ADM
- How to adapt the ADM for security
- The role of architecture maturity models in developing an Enterprise Architecture

- The purpose of the Architecture Skills Framework and how to apply it within an organization

Self-Study Paths

The self-study paths[2] to achieve certification for TOGAF 9 Certified are summarized in Figure 2. The chosen path depends whether you want to first become certified to TOGAF 9 Foundation or proceed direct to TOGAF 9 Certified.

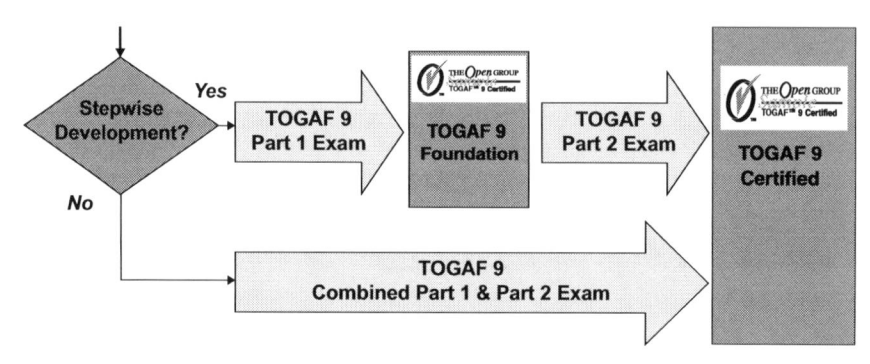

Figure 2: Paths to Achieving TOGAF 9 Certified

> **What is the Relationship between TOGAF 9 Foundation and TOGAF 9 Certified?**
> Candidates are able to choose whether they wish to become certified in a stepwise manner by starting with TOGAF 9 Foundation and then at a later date completing TOGAF 9 Certified, or bypass TOGAF 9 Foundation and go directly to TOGAF 9 Certified.
> For those going directly to TOGAF 9 Certified there is a choice of taking the two examinations separately or a Combined examination. The advantage of taking the two examinations over the single Combined examination is that if you pass Part 1 but fail Part 2 you can still qualify for TOGAF 9 Foundation.

1.2.4 The Certification Process

The TOGAF 9 Certified Syllabus is contained in Appendix D.

Readers are assumed to be already familiar with the syllabus for TOGAF 9 Foundation and its accompanying TOGAF 9 Part 1 Examination. Detailed

---

2   The latest information on the TOGAF 9 certification program can be obtained from the TOGAF 9 Certification website at www.opengroup.org/certifications/togaf9.

information is provided in the TOGAF 9 Foundation Study Guide (see References).

The TOGAF 9 Part 2 Examination
The syllabus for the TOGAF 9 Part 2 Examination consists of all the learning outcomes defined in both Level 1 and Level 2 of the Conformance Requirements document. At the time of writing this document, the examination topics are drawn from the learning outcomes with eight scenario-based questions.

The eight scenarios are drawn from the following major topic areas:
- ADM Phases: Project Establishment (Phases Preliminary, A, Requirements Management)
- ADM Phases: Architecture Definition (Phases B, C, D)
- ADM Phases: Transition Planning (Phases E and F)
- ADM Phases: Governance (Phases G and H)
- Adapting the ADM
- Architecture Content Framework
- TOGAF Reference Models
- Architecture Capability Framework

1.2.4.1 Format of the Examination Questions
The questions for the TOGAF 9 Part 2 Examination consist of eight complex scenario questions. Candidates must read a scenario describing a situation where the TOGAF standard is being applied. The question will then ask how the TOGAF standard would be used to address a particular point, and provide four possible answers. The answers are graded. One answer is more correct than two of the others, and one is incorrect for the situation. The aim is to select the best answer according to the TOGAF 9 standard. The correct answer scores five points, the second best answer three points, and the third best answer one point. The incorrect answer (or distracter) scores zero points. You may need to refer to the TOGAF document during the examination and a copy is provided with the examination (see below for more details).

The exact display format is test center-specific and will be made clear on the screens when taking the examination. Examples of these questions are provided in Appendix A.

1.2.4.2 What do I need to bring with me to take the Examination?
You should consult with the exam provider regarding the forms of picture ID you are required to bring with you to verify your identification.

1.2.4.3 If I fail, how soon can I retake the Examination?
You should check the current policy on The Open Group website. At the time of writing, the policy states that individuals who have failed the examination are not allowed to retake the examination within one (1) month of the first sitting.

1.2.5 Preparing for the Examination
You can prepare for the examination by working through this Study Guide section-by-section. After completing each section you should complete the exercises and read the referenced sections from the TOGAF documentation. Once you have completed all the sections in this Study Guide, you can then attempt the Test Yourself examination paper in the appendices. This is designed as a thorough test of your knowledge. If you have completed all the prescribed preparation and can attain a pass mark for the Test Yourself examination paper, then you may be ready to sit the examination.

> **Open-Book Examinations**
> The TOGAF 9 Part 2 Examination is open-book. The TOGAF reference text is provided as part of the examination itself.

1.3 Summary
The Open Group Certification for People: TOGAF Certification Program is a knowledge-based certification program. The current Body of Knowledge covered by the Program is based on the TOGAF Standard, Version 9.2. It has two levels, leading to certification for TOGAF 9 Foundation and TOGAF 9 Certified, respectively.

The topic for this Study Guide is preparation for the TOGAF 9 Part 2 Examination, leading to TOGAF 9 Certified. The TOGAF 9 Part 2

Examination comprises eight scenario-based questions to be completed in 90 minutes.[3]

Preparing for the examination includes the following steps:
- You should work through this Study Guide step-by-step
- At the end of each chapter, you should complete the exercises (where provided) and read the sections of the TOGAF documentation listed under Recommended Reading
- Once you have completed all the chapters in this Study Guide, you should attempt the Test Yourself examination paper in Appendix A and the bonus questions in Appendix B
- If you can attain the target score for the paper in Appendix A and satisfactorily complete the bonus questions in Appendix B, then you have completed your preparation

1.4 Recommended Reading

The following are recommended sources of further information for this chapter:
- The Open Group Certification for People: Program Summary Datasheet
- TOGAF 9 Certified Datasheet
- The Open Group Certification for People: Certification Policy for Examination-Based Programs
- The Open Group Certification for People: TOGAF Program Configuration
- The Open Group Certification for People: TOGAF Conformance Requirements (Multi-level)
- The Open Group TOGAF 9 Certification website: www.opengroup.org/certifications/togaf9
- The TOGAF information website: www.togaf.info
- TOGAF 9 People Certification Overview presentation: www.togaf.info/sg01

---

3   Additional time is allowed for candidates for whom English is a second language where the examination is not available in the local language. For further information see the advice to candidates sheet on The Open Group TOGAF 9 certification website.

PART 1

TOGAF 9 Architecture Development Method (ADM)

In this Part, we take a tour of the Architecture Development Method (ADM) which forms the core of the TOGAF standard. The descriptions in this Part focus on the detail of the inputs, steps, and outputs of each phase and build upon rather than duplicate the TOGAF 9 Foundation Syllabus.

Recommended reading before commencing this Part of the Study Guide includes:
- TOGAF 9 Foundation Study Guide, Chapter 5, Introduction to the Architecture Development Method
- Introduction to the ADM presentation: www.togaf.info/sg02

Chapter 2
Preliminary Phase

2.1 Key Learning Points

This chapter describes the Preliminary Phase within the TOGAF Architecture Development Method (ADM). This chapter will help you understand how to apply the Preliminary Phase to develop an Enterprise Architecture.

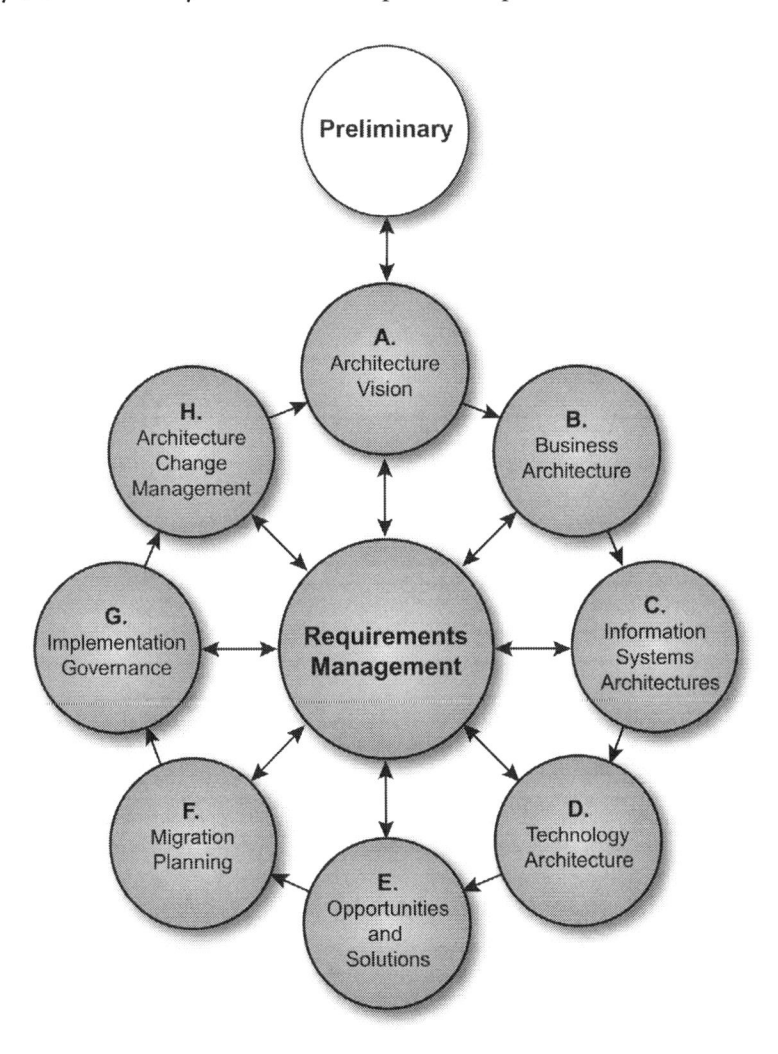

Figure 3: Preliminary Phase

> **Key Points Explained**
>
> Upon completion of this chapter you should be able to:
> 1. Understand the inputs to the phase, and be able to explain the following key elements:
>   - Architecture Frameworks
>   - Business principles, business goals, and business drivers
> 2. Explain the influence of pre-existing architectural inputs on the phase
> 3. Understand the steps, and be able to:
>   - Describe how to establish an Enterprise Architecture team and organization
>   - Identify and establish a set of Architecture Principles for a given scenario
>   - Discuss the appropriate considerations for tailoring the TOGAF framework
> 4. Understand the outputs, and be able to explain the following key elements:
>   - Architecture Principles
>   - Architecture Governance Framework
>   - Request for Architecture Work

2.2 Objectives

The objectives of the Preliminary Phase are to:

- Determine the Architecture Capability desired by the organization:
  - Review the organizational context for conducting Enterprise Architecture
  - Identify and scope the elements of the enterprise organizations affected by the Architecture Capability
  - Identify the established frameworks, methods, and processes that intersect with the Architecture Capability
  - Establish a Capability Maturity target
- Establish the Architecture Capability:
  - Define and establish the Organizational Model for Enterprise Architecture
  - Define and establish the detailed process and resources for Architecture Governance
  - Select and implement tools that support the Architecture Capability
  - Define the Architecture Principles

2.3 Inputs

(Syllabus Reference: Unit 1, Learning Outcome 1: You should understand the inputs to the phase.)

The Preliminary Phase takes as inputs:
- The TOGAF Library
- Other architecture framework(s)
- Board strategies and board business plans, business strategy, IT strategy
- Business principles, business goals, and business drivers
- Major frameworks operating in the business
- Governance and legal frameworks, including Architecture Governance strategy
- Existing Organizational Model for Enterprise Architecture
- Existing architecture framework, if any

2.3.1 Architecture Frameworks

(Syllabus Reference: Unit 1, Learning Outcome 1.1: You should be able to explain the key element: Architecture Frameworks.)

An architecture framework is a tool for assisting in the acceptance, production, use, and maintenance of architectures. The TOGAF standard is an example of an architecture framework. It is based on an iterative process model supported by best practices and a re-usable set of existing architectural assets. Other popular architecture frameworks include Zachman®, Gartner, DoDAF, FEAF, and TEAF.

2.3.2 Business Principles, Business Goals, and Business Drivers

(Syllabus Reference: Unit 1, Learning Outcome 1.2: You should be able to explain the key element: business principles, business goals, and business drivers.)

A statement of the business principles, goals, and drivers usually exists in an enterprise before the architecture activity starts (for example, the annual report). Architecture work is guided by business principles as well as Architecture Principles. The Architecture Principles themselves are also normally based in part on business principles.

See also Section 2.5.5.

2.3.3 Pre-Existing Architectural Inputs

(Syllabus Reference: Unit 1, Learning Outcome 2: You should be able to explain the influence of pre-existing architectural inputs on this phase.)

Pre-existing architectural inputs can influence the approach taken. For example, existing models for operating an Enterprise Architecture Capability can be used as a baseline for the Preliminary Phase.

Typical inputs to consider include:
- The Organizational Model for Enterprise Architecture, including:
  - Scope of organizations impacted
  - Maturity assessment, gaps, and resolution approach
  - Roles and responsibilities for architecture team(s)
  - Budget requirements
  - Governance and support strategy
- Existing architecture framework, if any, including:
  - Architecture method
  - Architecture content
  - Configured and deployed tools
  - Architecture Principles
  - Architecture Repository

2.4 Steps

(Syllabus Reference: Unit 1, Learning Outcome 3: You should understand the steps in this phase.)

The Preliminary Phase consists of the following steps:
1. Scope the enterprise organizations impacted
2. Confirm governance and support frameworks
3. Define and establish the Enterprise Architecture team and organization
4. Identify and establish Architecture Principles
5. Tailor the TOGAF framework and, if any, other selected architecture frameworks
6. Develop a strategy and implementation plan for tools and techniques

The steps are described in more detail in the following subsections.

2.4.1 Scope the Enterprise Organizations Impacted

The TOGAF standard recommends identification of various units of an enterprise scoped by the impact of the Enterprise Architecture activity:

- Identify those who will be the most affected and who stand to get the most value from the work: this is the *core* enterprise or unit(s)
- Identify those who will see change to their capability and work with core units, but are otherwise not directly affected: this is the *soft* enterprise or unit
- Identify those units outside the scoped enterprise who will be affected in their own Enterprise Architecture: this is the *extended* enterprise
- Identify those stakeholders who will be affected and who are in groups: this is known as *communities*
- Finally in this step, we must determine the *governance* involved, including legal frameworks and geographies

2.4.2 Confirm Governance and Support Frameworks

Part of the major output of this phase is a framework for Architecture Governance. Here we must decide how architectural material is brought under governance and the required characteristics for a governance repository.

It is likely that the existing governance and support models of an organization will need to change to support the newly adopted architecture framework. To manage the change required to adopt the new architecture framework, the current enterprise governance and support models will need to be assessed to understand their overall shape and content. Additionally, the sponsors and stakeholders for architecture will need to be consulted on potential impacts that could occur.

Upon completion of this step, the architecture touch-points and likely impacts should be understood and agreed by relevant stakeholders.

> The TOGAF standard provides significant guidance on establishing effective Architecture Governance and coordinating with other governance processes within the organization. Effective governance ensures that problems are identified early and that subsequent changes to the environment occur in a controlled manner.
> *Bill Estrem, "TOGAF to the Rescue"* (www.opengroup.org/downloads)

2.4.3 Define and Establish the Enterprise Architecture Team and Organization

(Syllabus Reference: Unit 1, Learning Outcome 3.1: You should be able to describe how to establish an Enterprise Architecture team and organization.)

The TOGAF standard recommends the following to define and establish the Enterprise Architecture team/organization:
- Determine the existing enterprise and business capability
- Conduct an architecture/business change maturity assessment
- Identify gaps in existing work areas
- Allocate key roles and responsibilities for Enterprise Architecture Capability management and governance
- Write requests for change for existing projects
- Determine constraints on Enterprise Architecture work
- Review and agree with sponsors and board
- Assess budget requirements

2.4.4 Identify and Establish Architecture Principles

(Syllabus Reference: Unit 1, Learning Outcome 3.2: You should be able to identify and establish a set of Architecture Principles for a given scenario.)

Principles are general rules and guidelines that inform the way in which an organization fulfills its mission. Principles are intended to be enduring and seldom amended.

> **Prerequisite Knowledge**
> This Study Guide assumes a prior knowledge equivalent to TOGAF 9 Foundation. This includes understanding the need for principles and where they are used in the TOGAF standard, the standard template for principles, as well as what makes a good principle. [TOGAF 9 Foundation Study Guide, Section 8.3]
> For further information on principles, see Part III, Architecture Principles.

2.4.4.1 Developing Architecture Principles

Architecture Principles are typically developed by the Enterprise Architects, in conjunction with the key stakeholders, and are approved by the Architecture Board.

The following typically influences the development of Architecture Principles:
- **Enterprise mission and plans**: the mission, plans, and organizational infrastructure of the enterprise
- **Enterprise strategic initiatives**: the characteristics of the enterprise – its strengths, weaknesses, opportunities, and threats – and its current enterprise-wide initiatives (such as process improvement and quality management)
- **External constraints**: market factors (e.g., time-to-market imperatives, customer expectations, etc.); existing and potential legislation
- **Current systems and technology**: the set of information resources deployed within the enterprise, including systems documentation, equipment inventories, network configuration diagrams, policies, and procedures
- **Computer industry trends**: predictions about the usage, availability, and cost of computer and communication technologies, taken from credible sources along with associated best practices presently in use

> **Principles and the Content Metamodel**
> Information related to principles can be modeled, if the right information is captured. The metamodel relates principles back to specific drivers, goals, and objectives and defines the principles catalog as an artifact produced in the Preliminary Phase.

2.4.4.2 Applying Architecture Principles

Architecture Principles are used to capture the fundamental truths about how the enterprise will use and deploy IT resources and assets. The principles are used in a number of different ways:
- To provide a framework within which the enterprise can start to make conscious decisions about Enterprise Architecture and projects that implement the target Enterprise Architecture
- As a guide to establishing relevant evaluation criteria, thus exerting strong influence on the selection of products, solutions, or solution architectures in the later stages of managing compliance to the Enterprise Architecture
- As drivers for defining the functional requirements of the architecture
- As an input to assessing both existing implementations and the future strategic portfolio, for compliance with the defined architectures; these

assessments will provide valuable insights into the transition activities needed to implement an architecture, in support of business goals and priorities
- The Rationale statements in the TOGAF template for principles highlight the value of the architecture to the enterprise, and therefore provide a basis for justifying architecture activities
- The Implications statements in the TOGAF template for principles provide an outline of the key tasks, resources, and potential costs to the enterprise of following the principle; they also provide valuable inputs to future transition initiatives and planning activities
- To support the Architecture Governance activities in terms of:
  - Providing support for the standard Architecture Compliance assessments where some interpretation is allowed or required
  - Supporting a decision to initiate a dispensation request where the implications of a particular architecture amendment cannot be resolved within local operating procedures

Principles are inter-related and need to be applied as a set. Principles will sometimes compete; for example, the principles of "accessibility" and "security". Each principle must be considered in the context of "all other things being equal". At times a decision will be required as to which principle will take precedence on a particular issue. The rationale for such decisions should always be documented. The fact that a principle seems self-evident does not mean that the principle is actually observed or accepted in an organization, even when there are verbal acknowledgements of the principle. Although specific penalties are not prescribed in a declaration of principles, violations of principles generally cause operational problems and inhibit the ability of the organization to fulfill its mission.

Principles in Federated Architectures

In large organizations with federated architectures, requirements from a higher-level architecture often appear as "principles" in lower-level ones. This usually takes the form of a principle stating that the lower-level architecture must adhere to the principles of the higher-level architecture. Another example might be a technology principle that has been passed down, such as "all network assets must be IPV6-capable."

Example 1 is a set of principles[4] developed in the Preliminary Phase by The Open Group in one of its own architecture projects.

Example 1: Preliminary Phase Principles

> **An Example Statement of Principles**
>
> Principles guide us in developing the architecture. They should neither undermine each other nor behave as a blockage to the achievement of others. Policies direct execution. We are unlikely to achieve the principles all of the time – but should aspire to get there.
>
> The following set of principles have been approved by the Internal Architecture Board:
>
> **Business Principles**
> 1. Primacy of Principles
> 2. Maximize Benefit to the Enterprise
> 3. Compliance with Law
> 4. Availability at Anytime from Anywhere
> 5. Business Continuity
> 6. Citizenship
> 7. Custodianship
> 8. De-Customization
> 9. Painless User Experience
> 10. Self-Serve
>
> **Architecture Principles**
> 1. De-Skill
> 2. One Source
> 3. Content Management

Each of these principles is then expanded into a statement with rationale and implications, as shown in Example 2 and Example 3.

---

4 A Case Study covering the development of these Architecture Principles is published by The Open Group – see References.

Example 2: Sample Principle 1

Primacy of Principles	
Statement	Principles apply throughout the enterprise and override all other considerations when decisions are made.
Rationale	The only way we can provide a recognized, consistent, and measurable level of operations is if all parts of the enterprise abide by the principles when making decisions.
Implications	Without this principle, short-term considerations, supposedly convenient exceptions, and inconsistencies would rapidly undermine the management of information. Information management initiatives will not be permitted to begin until they are examined for compliance with the principles. A conflict with a principle will be resolved by changing the conflicting initiative, which could delay or prevent the initiative.

Example 3: Sample Principle 2

Self-Serve	
Statement	Customers should be able to serve themselves.
Rationale	Applying this principle will improve customer satisfaction, reduce administrative overhead, and potentially improve revenue.
Implications	There is an implication to improve ease-of-use and minimize training needs; for example, members should be able to update their contact details, etc., and be able to buy additional membership products online.

See also Exercise 2-1.

2.4.5 Tailor the TOGAF Framework and, if any, Other Selected Architecture Frameworks

(Syllabus Reference: Unit 1, Learning Outcome 3.3: You should be able to discuss the appropriate considerations for tailoring the framework.)

To use the TOGAF standard most effectively, it should be tailored for the architecture project in the Preliminary Phase.

Firstly, it is necessary to tailor the TOGAF model for integration into the enterprise. This tailoring should include integration with project and process management frameworks, customization of terminology, development of presentational styles, selection, configuration, and deployment of architecture tools, etc. The formality and detail of any frameworks adopted should also be aligned with other contextual factors for the enterprise, such as culture, stakeholders, commercial models for Enterprise Architecture, and the existing level of Architecture Capability.

> **Why is it necessary to Adapt the ADM?**
> The ADM is a generic method for architecture development, which is designed to deal with most system and organizational requirements. However, it will often be necessary to modify or extend the ADM to suit specific needs. One of the tasks before applying the ADM is to review its components for applicability, and then tailor them as appropriate to the circumstances of the individual enterprise. This activity may well produce an "enterprise-specific" ADM.
> [Source: The TOGAF Standard, Version 9.2 Part II, Introduction to Part II]

Once the framework has been tailored to the enterprise, further tailoring is necessary in order to fit the framework to the specific architecture project. Tailoring at this level will select appropriate deliverables and artifacts to meet project and stakeholder needs.

Considerations for tailoring include the following:
- **Terminology tailoring**: the terminology used should be that which is understood across the enterprise
  Tailoring should produce an agreed terminology set for the description of architectural content. A glossary should be developed, if appropriate.
- **Process tailoring**: the ADM is a generic process
  Process tailoring allows for the removal of tasks that are already carried out elsewhere in the organization, the addition of organization-specific tasks (such as specific checkpoints), and the alignment of the ADM processes to external process frameworks.
- **Content tailoring**: using the Architecture Content Framework and the Enterprise Continuum as a basis, tailoring of the content structure and classification approach allows for adoption of third-party content frameworks and also customization of the framework to support organization-specific requirements

The outcome of this step should be a description of how the TOGAF standard is to be adapted for use in the enterprise.

> **Content Tailoring and the Architecture Content Framework**
> The TOGAF 9 Architecture Content Framework includes the concept of extensions enabling an architecture engagement to select precisely which parts of the TOGAF 9 framework, over and above the lightweight core, are needed.
> See Chapter 16 for more information.

2.4.6 Develop a Strategy and Implementation Plan for Tools and Techniques

As part of the Preliminary Phase, the architect should develop a tools strategy to support the architecture activity. The development of a tools strategy is recommended that reflects the understanding and level of formality required by the enterprise's stakeholders. The strategy should encompass management techniques, decision management, workshop techniques, business modeling, detailed infrastructure modeling, office products, languages, and repository management as well as more formal architecture tools.

The implementation of the tools strategy may be based on common off-the-shelf tools or may be based on a customized deployment of specialist management and architecture tools. Change management of the artifact deliverables is a major consideration and a degree of management control and governance of artifacts needs to be considered.

Issues in tools standardization are described in Part V, Tools for Architecture Development.

2.5 Outputs

(Syllabus Reference: Unit 1, Learning Outcome 4: You should understand the outputs and be able to explain the following key elements: Architecture Principles, Governance Framework, Request for Architecture Work.)

The outputs of this phase are:
- Organizational Model for Enterprise Architecture
- Tailored Architecture Framework, including Architecture Principles

- Initial Architecture Repository
- Restatement of, or reference to, business principles, business goals, and business drivers
- Request for Architecture Work
- Architecture Governance Framework

> **Descriptions of Phase Outputs**
> Where an output of a phase is first introduced in this Study Guide, a description of the contents appears in the Outputs section for the phase. This description is not duplicated in later phases.
> The purpose of each deliverable is covered in Chapter 12 of the TOGAF 9 Foundation Study Guide.

2.5.1 Architecture Principles

(Syllabus Reference: Unit 1, Learning Outcome 4.1: You should be able to explain the key element: Architecture Principles.)

See also Section 2.4.4.

2.5.2 Organizational Model for Enterprise Architecture

An important deliverable produced in the Preliminary Phase is the Organizational Model for Enterprise Architecture.

In order for an architecture framework to be used successfully, it must be supported by the appropriate organization, roles, and responsibilities within the enterprise. Of particular importance is the definition of boundaries between different Enterprise Architecture practitioners and the governance relationships that span across these boundaries.

Typical contents of an Organizational Model for Enterprise Architecture are:
- Scope of organizations impacted
- Maturity assessment, gaps, and resolution approach
- Roles and responsibilities for architecture team(s)
- Constraints on the architecture work
- Budget requirements
- Governance and support strategy

2.5.3 Tailored Architecture Framework

The following contents are typical within a tailored architecture framework:
- Tailored architecture method
- Tailored architecture content (deliverables and artifacts)
- Configured and deployed tools
- Interfaces with governance models and other frameworks; examples of other frameworks include Corporate Business Planning, Enterprise Architecture, Portfolio Management, Program Management, Project Management, System Development/Engineering, and Operations (Services)

2.5.4 Architecture Repository

The Architecture Repository acts as a content management system for all architecture-related projects within the enterprise. The repository allows projects to manage their deliverables, locate re-usable assets, and publish outputs to stakeholders and other interested parties.

The following contents are typical within an Architecture Repository:
- Architecture Framework
- Standards Information Base
- Architecture Landscape
- Reference Architectures
- Governance Log
- Architecture Requirements
- Solutions Landscape

The initial repository content in the Preliminary Phase includes the architecture framework.

See also Chapter 18.

2.5.5 Business Principles, Business Goals, and Business Drivers

A statement of the business principles, goals, and drivers has usually been defined elsewhere in the enterprise prior to the architecture activity. They are restated as an output of the Preliminary Phase and reviewed again as a part of Phase A: Architecture Vision. Part III: ADM Guidelines and Techniques contains an example set of business principles that is a useful starting point.

There is no defined content for this deliverable as its content and structure are likely to vary considerably from one organization to the next.

See also Section 2.3.2.

2.5.6 Architecture Governance Framework

(Syllabus Reference: Unit 1, Learning Outcome 4.2: You should be able to explain the key element: Architecture Governance Framework.)

An Enterprise Architecture is only as good as the decision-making framework that is established around it. This is known as an Architecture Governance Framework. Guidance on establishing Architecture Governance is provided in Part VII: Architecture Capability Framework.

See also Chapter 21.

2.5.7 Request for Architecture Work

(Syllabus Reference: Unit 1, Learning Outcome 4.3: You should be able to explain the key element: Request for Architecture Work.)

This is a document that is sent from the sponsoring organization to the architecture organization to trigger the start of an Architecture Development Cycle. It is produced with the assistance of the architecture organization as an output of the Preliminary Phase. Requests for Architecture Work will also be created as a result of approved architecture Change Requests, or terms of reference for architecture work originating from migration planning. In general, all the information in this document should be at a high level and free of implementation details.

The suggested contents of this document are as follows:
- Organization sponsors
- Organization's mission statement
- Business goals (and changes)
- Strategic plans of the business
- Time limits
- Changes in the business environment
- Organizational constraints
- Budget information, financial constraints

- External constraints, business constraints
- Current business system description
- Current architecture/IT system description
- Description of the organization developing the architecture
- Description of resources available to the organization developing the architecture

2.6 Summary

The objective of the Preliminary Phase is to prepare an organization for successful Enterprise Architecture projects by defining "how this enterprise does architecture". Key activities are as follows:

- Understand the business environment
- Obtain high-level management commitment
- Obtain agreement on scope
- Establish Architecture Principles
- Establishing governance structure
- Tailor the architecture method

The outputs should be an initial set of Architecture Principles, a statement of the tailored architecture method, and a restatement of the business principles, goals, and drivers.

2.7 Exercises

Exercise 2-1
Compare and contrast the TOGAF framework with two other architecture frameworks.

Exercise 2-2
Select seven principles at random from the *Example Set of Architecture Principles* in Part III, Architecture Principles. For each selected principle, state whether it applies to your organization or not, and give your reasons.

Exercise 2-3

Select two business goals from the list below and for each develop an Architecture Principle:
- Minimize time when people are not doing productive, profitable work
- Maximize availability of executives for decision-making
- Maximize competitive advantage by the timely availability of information
- Improve the quality of enterprise information

Exercise 2-4

Identify three or more sources of information within your organization that can be used for creating a statement of the business principles, goals, and drivers.

2.8 Recommended Reading

The following are recommended sources of further information for this chapter:
- The TOGAF Standard, Version 9.2 Part II, Preliminary Phase
- The TOGAF Standard, Version 9.2 Part III, Architecture Principles
- The TOGAF Standard, Version 9.2 Part IV, Architecture Deliverables
- The TOGAF Standard, Version 9.2 Part VI, Establishing an Architecture Capability
- The TOGAF Standard, Version 9.2 Part VI, Architecture Governance
- The TOGAF Standard, Version 9.2 Part VI, Architecture Board
- TOGAF 9 Foundation Study Guide, Section 8.3, Architecture Principles
- TOGAF 9 Foundation Study Guide, Chapter 9, Architecture Governance
- The Open Group Architecture Principles, Case Study

Chapter 3
Phase A: Architecture Vision

3.1 Key Learning Points

This chapter describes Phase A: Architecture Vision of the TOGAF Architecture Development Method (ADM).

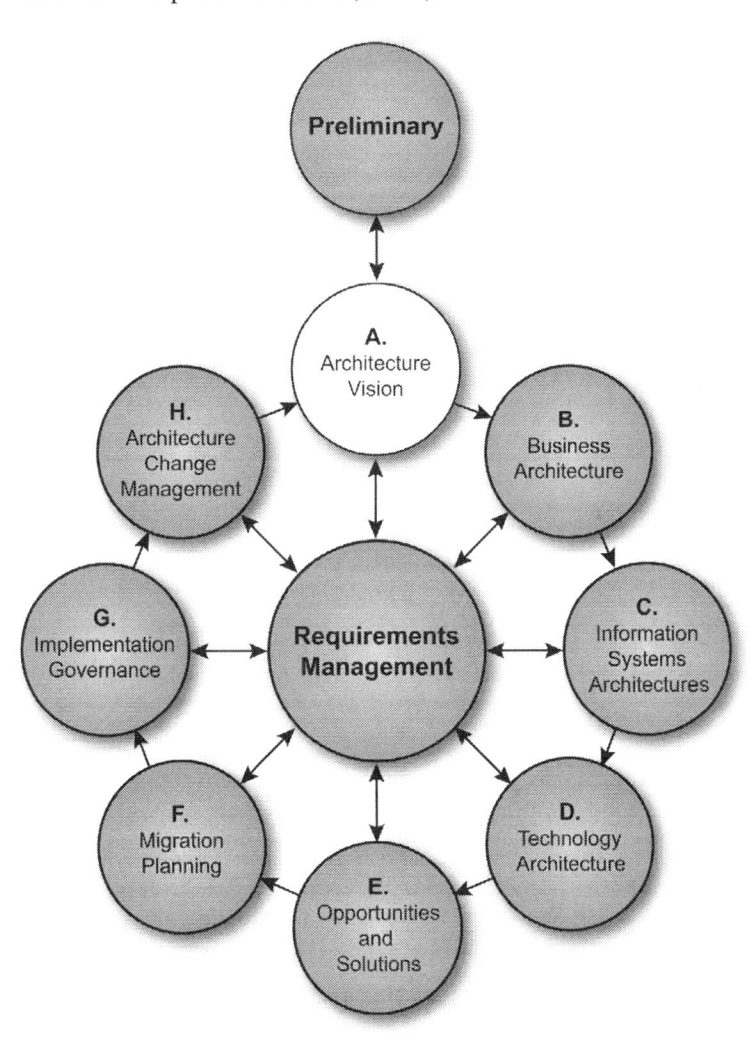

Figure 4: Phase A: Architecture Vision

Key Points Explained

Upon completion of the chapter you should be able to:

1. Understand the inputs to the phase, and be able to:
   - Describe the typical contents of the Architecture Repository at this point
2. Understand the steps, and be able to:
   - Describe how to identify stakeholders, their concerns, and business requirements
   - Explain the purpose of a Business Transformation Readiness Assessment
   - Describe the risk assessment approach taken in this phase
3. Understand the outputs, and be able to explain the following key elements including their purpose:
   - Statement of Architecture Work
   - Capability Assessment
   - Architecture Vision
   - Communications Plan

In addition, you should be able to:

- Describe the steps in developing a Stakeholder Map
- Use a Stakeholder Map to identify stakeholders and their concerns
- Explain the benefits of creating architecture views
- Explain how Capability-Based Planning is applied in an Enterprise Architecture context
- Explain the factors that influence Business Transformation Readiness
- Describe the properties of a good Business Scenario
- Explain how to develop and validate a Business Scenario

3.2 Objectives

The objectives of Phase A: Architecture Vision are to:

- Develop a high-level aspirational vision of the capabilities and business value to be delivered as a result of the proposed Enterprise Architecture
- Obtain approval for a Statement of Architecture Work that defines a program of works to develop and deploy the architecture outlined in the Architecture Vision

3.3 Inputs

(Syllabus Reference: Unit 4, Learning Outcome 1: You should understand the inputs to the phase, and be able to describe the typical contents of the Architecture Repository at this point.)

The inputs to this phase are:
- Request for Architecture Work
- Business principles, business goals, and business drivers
- Organizational Model for Enterprise Architecture
- Tailored Architecture Framework, including Architecture Principles
- Populated Architecture Repository; that is, existing architecture documentation (framework description, architecture descriptions, existing baseline descriptions, etc.)

3.4 Steps

(Syllabus Reference: Unit 4, Learning Outcome 2: You should understand the steps in this phase.)

Phase A consists of the following steps:
1. Establish the architecture project
2. Identify stakeholders, concerns, and business requirements
3. Confirm and elaborate business goals, business drivers, and constraints
4. Evaluate capabilities
5. Assess readiness for business transformation
6. Define scope
7. Confirm and elaborate Architecture Principles, including business principles
8. Develop Architecture Vision
9. Define the Target Architecture value propositions and KPIs
10. Identify the business transformation risks and mitigation activities
11. Develop Statement of Architecture Work; secure approval

The steps are described in more detail in the following subsections.

3.4.1 Establish the Architecture Project

In this step you must conduct the necessary procedures to obtain recognition of the project, endorsement by corporate management, and the support and commitment of line management. Reference must be made to the other management frameworks in use in the enterprise and an explanation provided of how this project relates to those frameworks.

3.4.2 Identify Stakeholders, Concerns, and Business Requirements

(Syllabus Reference: Unit 4, Learning Outcome 2.1: You should understand how to identify stakeholders, their concerns, and business requirements.)

In this step you must identify key stakeholders, their concerns, and define the key business requirements to be addressed in the architecture engagement. The key technique for Stakeholder Management is to generate a Stakeholder Map, which should then be used to support various outputs of the Architecture Vision phase. The concerns and viewpoints that are relevant to this project should be documented in the Architecture Vision. The stakeholders that are involved with the project and their positions should be used to form the starting point for a Communications Plan. The key roles and responsibilities within the project should be included within the Statement of Architecture Work.

3.4.2.1 *Stakeholder Management*

Stakeholder Management is an important discipline that successful architects can use to win support from others. It helps them ensure that their projects succeed where others fail. The technique should be used during Phase A to identify the key players in the engagement, and should also be updated throughout each phase.

The benefits of successful Stakeholder Management are that:
- The most powerful stakeholders can be identified early and their input can then be used to shape the architecture; this ensures their support and improves the quality of the models produced
- Support from the more powerful stakeholders will help the engagement win more resources; thus making the architecture engagement more likely to succeed
- By communicating with stakeholders early and frequently, the architecture team can ensure that they fully understand the architecture process, and the benefits of Enterprise Architecture; this means they can support the architecture team more actively when necessary

- The architecture team can more effectively anticipate likely reactions to the architecture models and reports, and can build into the plan the actions that will be needed to capitalize on positive reaction whilst avoiding or addressing any negative reactions
- The architecture team can identify conflicting or competing objectives among stakeholders early and develop a strategy to resolve the issues arising from them

3.4.2.2 The Stakeholder Management Process
(Syllabus Reference: Unit 6, Learning Outcome 1: You should be able to describe the steps in developing a Stakeholder Map.)

The TOGAF standard defines a process for creation of a Stakeholder Map as follows:

Identify Stakeholders

The first task is to determine who the main Enterprise Architecture stakeholders are. The TOGAF standard provides a sample stakeholder analysis that distinguishes 22 types of stakeholder in five broad categories, as shown in Figure 5. Any particular architecture project may have more, fewer, or different stakeholders; and they may be grouped into more, fewer, or different categories.

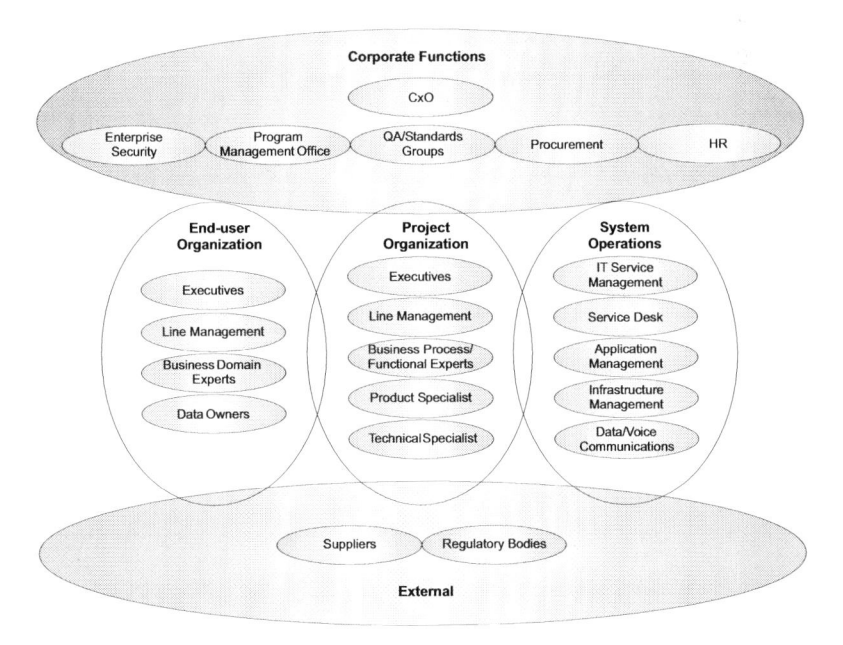

Figure 5: Sample Stakeholders and Categories

Classify Stakeholder Positions

Develop a good understanding of the most important stakeholders and record this analysis (as shown in the example in Table 1) for reference during the project. It may be necessary to refresh the analysis periodically.

Table 1: Example Stakeholder Analysis

Stakeholder Group	Stakeholder	Ability to Disrupt the Change	Current Understanding	Required Understanding	Current Commitment	Required Commitment	Required Support
CIO	Smith	H	M	H	L	M	H
CFO	Brown	M	M	M	L	M	M

Key: H = High, M = Medium, L = Low

Determine Stakeholder Management Approach

This enables the team to easily see which stakeholders are expected to be blockers or critics, and which stakeholders are likely to be advocates and supporters of the initiative.

Work out stakeholder power, influence, and interest, so as to focus the Enterprise Architecture engagement on the key individuals. These can be mapped onto a power *versus* interest matrix, which also indicates the strategy to adopt for engaging with them.

Figure 6 shows an example power *versus* interest matrix.

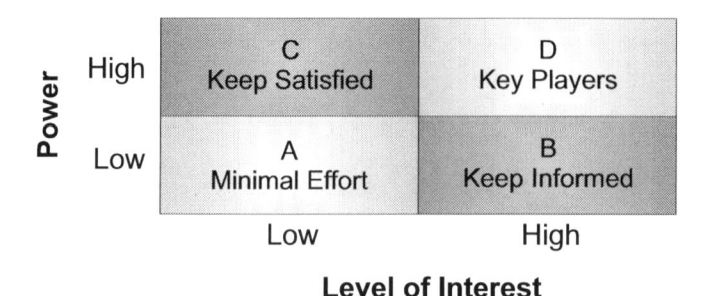

	Low	High
High Power	C Keep Satisfied	D Key Players
Low Power	A Minimal Effort	B Keep Informed

Level of Interest

Figure 6: Power versus Interest Matrix

Tailor Engagement Deliverables

Identify the catalogs, matrices, and diagrams that the architecture engagement needs to produce and validate with each stakeholder group to deliver an effective architecture model. This enables the architecture to be communicated to, and understood by, all the stakeholders, and enables them to verify that the Enterprise Architecture initiative will address their concerns.

> **Architecture View Creation**
>
> *(Syllabus Reference: Unit 6, Learning Outcome 2: You should be able to explain the benefits of creating architecture views.)*
>
> Architecture views are representations of the architecture in terms meaningful to stakeholders that make it simpler to comprehend. They enable stakeholders to verify that the resulting architecture will address their concerns.
>
> It is often possible to create the required views for a particular architecture by referring to and selecting from an existing library of architecture viewpoints (known as a viewpoint library).
>
> This approach brings a number of benefits, such as reduced effort for the architects as the architecture viewpoints have already been defined, improved comprehensibility for stakeholders since the viewpoints are familiar, and greater confidence in the validity of the architecture views since they have been used before.

Example Stakeholder Map

A Stakeholder Map can be used to record the findings of Stakeholder Management. The TOGAF standard provides an example, a summary extract of which is provided in Table 2.

Table 2: Example Stakeholder Map (Summary Extract)

STAKEHOLDER	KEY CONCERNS	CLASS	CATALOGS, MATRICES, AND DIAGRAMS
CxO (Corporate Functions) For example, CEO, CFO, CIO, COO	The high-level drivers, goals, and objectives of the organization, and how these are translated into an effective process and IT architecture to advance the business.	KEEP SATISFIED	Business Footprint Diagram Goal/Objective/Service Diagram Organization Decomposition Diagram Business Capabilities catalog Capability/Organization matrix Strategy/Capability Map
Program Management Office (Corporate Functions) For example, Project Portfolio Managers	Prioritizing, funding, and aligning change activity. An understanding of project content and technical dependencies between projects adds a further dimension of richness to portfolio management decision-making.	KEEP SATISFIED	Requirements Catalog Project Context Diagram Benefits Diagram Business Footprint Diagram Application Communication Diagram Functional Decomposition Diagram
Procurement (Corporate Functions) For example, Acquirers	Understanding what building blocks of the architecture can be bought, and what constraints (or rules) exist that are relevant to the purchase. Acquirers will shop with multiple vendors looking for the best cost solution while adhering to the constraints (or rules) applied by the architecture, such as standards. The key concern is to make purchasing decisions that fit the architecture, and thereby to reduce the risk of added costs arising from non-compliant components.	KEY PLAYERS	Technology Portfolio Catalog Technology Standards Catalog

STAKEHOLDER	KEY CONCERNS	CLASS	CATALOGS, MATRICES, AND DIAGRAMS
IT Service Management (Systems Operations) For example, Service Delivery Manager	Ensuring that IT services provided to the organization meet the service levels required by that organization to succeed in business.	KEEP INFORMED	Technology Standards Catalog Technology Portfolio Catalog Contract/Measure Catalog Process/Application Realization Diagram Enterprise Manageability Diagram

3.4.3 Confirm and Elaborate Business Goals, Business Drivers, and Constraints

Here you must identify business goals and strategic drivers of the organization. If these have already been defined elsewhere, ensure that the existing definitions are current and clarify any areas of ambiguity. Otherwise, go back to the originators of the Statement of Architecture Work, define these items again, and get their endorsement by management.

3.4.4 Evaluate Capabilities

The purpose of this step is to understand the capabilities within the enterprise. This refers to the capability of the enterprise to develop and consume the architecture, and also the baseline and target capability level of the enterprise. The results of this activity are documented in a Capability Assessment (see Section 3.5).

Any gaps identified in the Architecture Capability will require iteration between Architecture Vision and Preliminary Phase to ensure that the Architecture Capability is suitable to address the scope of the architecture project.

3.4.4.1 Capability-Based Planning

(Syllabus Reference: Unit 8, Learning Outcome 4: You should be able to explain how Capability-Based Planning is applied in an Enterprise Architecture context.)

Capability-Based Planning ensures that the corporate strategic plan drives the enterprise from a top-down approach. It focuses on delivery of business outcomes rather than technical deliverables; for example, an Enterprise Architecture project would be provision of electronic service delivery, rather than delivery of a web-based commerce solution.

In an Enterprise Architecture context the capabilities to be developed should be derived from the corporate strategic plan. All architectures should be expressed in terms of the business outcomes and business value they deliver, thereby ensuring IT alignment with the business. In Phase A, the Architecture Vision should be driven by the corporate strategic direction. The focus of the architecture development in Phases B, C, and D will be the specific capabilities. In Phase E work packages and projects are identified to deliver the capabilities.

It is recommended to break a capability into capability increments because a new capability can take an extended period of time to be developed and can involve many projects delivering numerous increments. This has the advantage of potentially providing real business value to stakeholders in the form of discrete, visible, and quantifiable outcomes that can provide focus for Transition Architectures.

The capability increments driving the Transition Architectures in Phase E lead to the identification of project increments, the actual delivery of which is coordinated through the Implementation and Migration Plan completed in Phase F.

3.4.5 Assess Readiness for Business Transformation
(Syllabus Reference: Unit 4, Learning Outcome 2.2: You can explain the purpose of a Business Transformation Readiness Assessment.)

A Business Transformation Readiness Assessment can be used to evaluate and quantify the organization's readiness to undergo a change. This assessment is based upon the determination of a series of readiness factor ratings.

Understanding the readiness of the organization to accept change, identifying the issues, and then dealing with them is a key part of successful architecture transformation. This assessment is recommended to be a joint effort between corporate staff, lines of business, and IT planners.

To do this, the readiness factors that will impact the organization must be determined and presented using maturity models. The risks for each readiness factor should be assessed and improvement actions to mitigate the risk identified. The TOGAF standard recommends creation of a summary table to consolidate factors and provide a management overview. The findings are then documented into the Capability Assessment (see Section 3.5.2), and later incorporated into the Implementation and Migration Plan (see Section 10.5.1).

3.4.5.1 *Transformation Readiness Factors*

(Syllabus Reference: Unit 8, Learning Outcome 2: You should be able to explain the factors that influence Business Transformation Readiness.)

The following is an example list of readiness factors that can impact the business transformation when migrating from Baseline to Target Architectures. These have been drawn from the Canadian Government Business Transformation Enablement Program (BTEP):[5]

- **Vision**: the ability to clearly define and communicate what is to be achieved
- **Desire, Willingness, and Resolve**: the presence of a desire to achieve the results, willingness to accept the impact of doing the work, and the resolve to follow through and complete the endeavor
- **Need**: there is a compelling need to execute the endeavor
- **Business Case Exists**: creates a strong focus for the project, identifying benefits that must be achieved and thereby creating an imperative to succeed
- **Funding**: in the form of a clear source of fiscal resources, funding exists that meets the endeavor's potential expenditures
- **Sponsorship and Leadership:** exists and is broadly shared, but not so broadly as to diffuse accountability
- **Governance:** the ability to engage the involvement and support of all parties with an interest in or responsibility to the endeavor with the objective of ensuring that the corporate interests are served and the objectives achieved
- **Accountability**: the assignment of specific and appropriate responsibility, the recognition of measurable expectations by all concerned parties, and

---

5   See www.tbs-sct.gc.ca/btep-pto/index_e.asp.

the alignment of decision-making between areas of responsibility and where the impact of the decisions will be felt
- **Workable Approach and Execution Model**: an approach that makes sense relative to the task, with a supporting environment modeled after a proven approach
- **IT Capacity to Execute**: the ability to perform all the IT tasks required by the project, including the skills, tools, processes, and management capability
- **Enterprise Capacity to Execute:** the ability of the enterprise to perform all the tasks required by the endeavor, in areas outside of IT, including the ability to make decisions within tight time constraints
- **Enterprise Ability to Implement and Operate:** the transformation elements and their related business processes operationally absorb the changes arising from implementation

3.4.6 Define Scope

Here you must define the scope of the architecture work (see Part II, Scoping the Architecture. In particular, define:
- Breadth of coverage
- Level of detail
- The partitioning characteristics of the architecture
- The specific architecture domains to be covered (Business, Data, Application, Technology)
- Schedule the project milestones, including intermediate milestones (termed by the TOGAF standard as the extent of the time period)
- The architecture assets to be leveraged from the organization's Enterprise Architecture Continuum, including assets created in previous iterations of the ADM cycle, and assets available elsewhere in industry (other frameworks, systems models, vertical industry models, etc.)

3.4.7 Confirm and Elaborate Architecture Principles, including Business Principles

In this step you should review the principles, developed in the Preliminary Phase, under which the architecture is to be developed. Architecture Principles are usually based on the principles developed in the Preliminary Phase. Ensure the existing definitions are current, and clarify any areas of ambiguity. Otherwise, go back to the body responsible and work with them to define these essential items.

3.4.8 Develop Architecture Vision

Based on the stakeholder concerns, business capability requirements, scope, constraints, and principles, create a high-level view of the Baseline and Target Architectures. Business scenarios are an appropriate technique to discover and document business requirements, and to produce an Architecture Vision (see Section 3.5.3).

This step will generate the first, very high-level definitions of the baseline and target environments, from a business, information systems, and technology perspective.

> **Business Scenarios**
>
> The TOGAF standard recommends the use of the business scenarios technique for identifying and articulating the business requirements implied in new business functionality. Business scenarios are documented in the TOGAF® Series Guide: Business Scenarios.
>
> *(Syllabus Reference: Unit 3, Learning Outcome 1: You should be able to describe the properties of a good Business Scenario.)*
>
> A good business scenario is representative of a significant business need or problem, enables vendors to understand the value of a developed solution for a customer, and is "SMART" – Specific (defines what needs to be done in the process), Measurable (has clear metrics for success), Actionable (clearly segments the problem and provides a basis to find the solution), Realistic (defines the bounds of the technology capability and cost constraints), and Time-bound (gives a clear understanding of when a solution expires).
>
> *(Syllabus Reference: Unit 3, Learning Outcome 2: You should be able to explain how to develop and validate a Business Scenario.)*
>
> The generic business scenario process is as follows:
> - Identify, document, and rank the problem that is driving the project
> - Document, as high-level architecture models, the business and technical environments where the problem situation is occurring
> - Identify and document desired objectives; the results of handling the problems successfully
> - Identify human actors and their place in the business model, the human participants, and their roles
> - Identify computer actors and their place in the technology model, the computing elements, and their roles

> - Identify and document roles, responsibilities, and measures of success per actor, the required scripts per actor, and the desired results of handling the situation properly
> - Check for fitness-for-purpose of inspiring subsequent architecture work, and refine only if necessary
>
> See also the exercises in Section 3.7.

3.4.9 Define the Target Architecture Value Propositions and KPIs

This step defines value propositions and Key Performance Indicators (KPIs) for the Target Architecture:

- Develop the business case for the architectures and changes required
- Produce the value proposition for each of the stakeholder groupings
- Assess and define the procurement requirements
- Review and agree on the value propositions with the sponsors and stakeholders concerned
- Define the performance metrics and measures to be built into the Enterprise Architecture to meet the business needs
- Assess the business risk

The outputs from this activity should be incorporated into the Statement of Architecture Work to allow performance to be tracked accordingly.

3.4.10 Identify the Business Transformation Risks and Mitigation Activities

(Syllabus Reference: Unit 4, Learning Outcome 2.3: You can describe the risk assessment approach taken in this phase.)

In this step, identify the risks associated with the Architecture Vision and assess the initial level of risk (e.g., catastrophic, critical, marginal, or negligible) and the potential frequency associated with it. Assign a mitigation strategy for each risk.

There are two levels of risk that should be considered, namely:

- **Initial Level of Risk**: risk categorization prior to determining and implementing mitigating actions
- **Residual Level of Risk**: risk categorization after implementation of mitigating actions (if any)

Risk mitigation activities should be included in the Statement of Architecture Work. The TOGAF standard provides risk identification and mitigation assessment worksheet examples that can be used as governance artifacts.

3.4.10.1 Risk Assessment
(Syllabus Reference: Unit 8, Learning Outcome 3: You can explain how to determine requirements for risk assessments.)

The TOGAF standard provides guidance on techniques for risk management in Part III, Risk Management. This includes a risk classification scheme and sample worksheets for risk assessment. The process for risk management documented by the TOGAF standard is:
- Risk classification
- Risk identification
- Initial risk assessment
- Risk mitigation and residual risk assessment
- Risk monitoring

As well as identifying risks in Phase A, the TOGAF standard states that risk monitoring should occur in Phase G. This may then lead to Change Requests related to risk management being handled in Phase H.

3.4.11 Develop Statement of Architecture Work; Secure Approval
The Statement of Architecture Work should then be produced (see Section 3.5.1), and approval of this document obtained from the governing body (usually the Architecture Board).

3.5 Outputs
(Syllabus Reference: Unit 4, Learning Outcome 3: You should understand the outputs.)

The outputs of this phase are:
- Statement of Architecture Work
- Refined statements of business principles, business goals, and business drivers
- Architecture Principles
- Capability Assessment

- Tailored Architecture Framework
- Architecture Vision, including:
  - Problem description
  - Objective of the Statement of Architecture Work
  - Summary views
  - Business scenario (optional)
  - Refined key high-level stakeholder requirements
- Draft Architecture Definition Document (see Section 4.5.1), including (when in scope):
  - Baseline Business Architecture (high-level)
  - Baseline Data Architecture (high-level)
  - Baseline Application Architecture (high-level)
  - Baseline Technology Architecture (high-level)
  - Target Business Architecture (high-level)
  - Target Data Architecture (high-level)
  - Target Application Architecture (high-level)
  - Target Technology Architecture (high-level)
- Communications Plan
- Additional content populating the Architecture Repository

The outputs may also include the Principles catalog.

3.5.1 Statement of Architecture Work

(Syllabus Reference: Unit 4, Learning Outcome 3.1: You should be able to explain the Statement of Architecture Work.)

The Statement of Architecture Work is created as a deliverable of Phase A and is effectively a contract between the architecting organization and the sponsor of the architecture project. This document is a response to the Request for Architecture Work input document (see Section 2.5.7). It should describe an overall plan to address the request for work and propose how solutions to the problems that have been identified will be addressed through the architecture process. The suggested contents of this document are as follows:

- Title
- Architecture project request and background
- Architecture project description and scope
- Overview of Architecture Vision
- Specific change of scope procedures

- Roles, responsibilities, and deliverables
- Acceptance criteria and procedures
- Architecture project plan and schedule
- Approvals

3.5.2 Capability Assessment

(Syllabus Reference: Unit 4, Learning Outcome 3.2: You should be able to explain the Capability Assessment.)

Before embarking upon a detailed Architecture Definition, it is valuable to understand the baseline and target capability level of the enterprise. This Capability Assessment is first carried out in Phase A, and updated in Phase E. It can be examined on several levels:

- What is the capability level of the enterprise as a whole? Where does the enterprise wish to increase or optimize capability? What are the architectural focus areas that will support the desired development of the enterprise?
- What is the capability or maturity level of the IT function within the enterprise? What are the likely implications of conducting the architecture project in terms of design governance, operational governance, skills, and organization structure? What is an appropriate style, level of formality, and amount of detail for the architecture project to fit with the culture and capability of the IT organization?
- What are the capability and maturity of the architecture function within the enterprise? What architectural assets are currently in existence? Are they maintained and accurate? What standards and reference models need to be considered? Are there likely to be opportunities to create re-usable assets during the architecture project?
- Where capability gaps exist, to what extent is the business ready to transform in order to reach the target capability? What are the cultural barriers, risks to transformation, and other considerations to be addressed beyond the basic capability gap?

The following contents are typical within a Capability Assessment deliverable:
- Business Capability Assessment, including:
  - Capabilities of the business
  - Baseline state assessment of the performance level of each capability
  - Future state aspiration for the performance level of each capability

- Baseline state assessment of how each capability is realized
- Future state aspiration for how each capability should be realized
- Assessment of likely impacts to the business organization resulting from the successful deployment of the Target Architecture
• IT Capability Assessment, including:
    - Baseline and target maturity level of the change process
    - Baseline and target maturity level of operational processes
    - Baseline capability and capacity assessment
    - Assessment of likely impacts to the IT organization resulting from the successful deployment of the Target Architecture
• Architecture Maturity Assessment, including:
    - Architecture Governance processes, organization, roles, and responsibilities
    - Architecture skills assessment
    - Breadth, depth, and quality of landscape definition, standards definition, and reference model definition within the Architecture Repository
    - Assessment of re-use potential
• Business Transformation Readiness Assessment, including:
    - Readiness factors
    - Vision for each readiness factor
    - Current and target readiness ratings
    - Readiness risks

3.5.3 Architecture Vision

(Syllabus Reference: Unit 4, Learning Outcome 3.3: You should be able to explain the Architecture Vision.)

The Architecture Vision is created in Phase A and provides a high-level summary of the changes to the enterprise that will follow from successful deployment of the Target Architecture. The purpose of the vision is to agree at the outset what the desired outcome should be for the architecture, so that architects can then focus on the detail necessary to validate feasibility. Providing an Architecture Vision also supports stakeholder communication by providing a summary version of the full Architecture Definition.

Business scenarios are an appropriate and important technique that can be used as part of the process of developing an Architecture Vision document.

The suggested contents are as follows:
- Problem description, including the stakeholders and their concerns, and the list of issues/scenarios to be addressed
- Objective of the Statement of Architecture Work
- Summary views necessary for the Request for Architecture Work and the high-level Business, Application, Data, and Technology Architectures
- Mapped requirements
- Reference to the Draft Architecture Definition Document

3.5.4 Communications Plan

(Syllabus Reference: Unit 4, Learning Outcome 3.4: You should be able to explain the key element including its purpose: Communications Plan.)

Enterprise Architectures contain large volumes of complex and interdependent information. Effective communication of targeted information to the right stakeholders at the right time is a Critical Success Factor (CSF) for Enterprise Architecture. Development of a Communications Plan in Phase A allows for this communication to be carried out within a planned and managed process.

Typically, a Communications Plan includes the identification of:
- Stakeholders grouped by communication requirements
- The communication needs, key messages in relation to the Architecture Vision, communication risks, and CSFs
- Methods that will be used to communicate with stakeholders and allow access to architecture information, such as meetings, newsletters, repositories, etc.
- A communications timetable, showing which communications will occur with which stakeholder groups at what time and in what location

3.6 Summary

Phase A: Architecture Vision is about project establishment and initiates an iteration of the architecture process. It sets the scope, constraints, and expectations for this iteration of the ADM. It is required at the start of every architecture cycle, in order to validate the business context and create the Statement of Architecture Work.

3.7 Exercises

Exercise 3-1
Write a business scenario describing how you would choose a new car. Include the following in your answer: (a) Problem description; (b) Detailed objectives; (c) Views of environments and processes; (d) Actors, their roles, and responsibilities; (e) Principles and constraints; (f) Requirements; (g) Next steps.

Make the objectives SMART.

Exercise 3-2
Consider the following objective: "The system's security could be improved. This will reduce the loss of revenue when our system is accessed by unauthorized users."

How could this be re-phrased to make it into a SMART objective?

Exercise 3-3
Match the most applicable Roles below to the following Computer actors:
1. Business applications
2. Enterprise computers
3. Information services
4. Network devices
5. User devices

Roles:
A: User access to core technical activities; local application execution; local information store
B: Operated by enterprises and service providers; supplies information to users
C: Information transport; switching and routing of information in transit; security of information in transit; control of access to networks and systems; network quality of service; sessions management; bandwidth management
D: Run on users' devices and/or on servers; information processing and display

E: Operated by enterprises and service providers; central application processing and information store; platform for information services; user identification, authentication, and access control

Exercise 3-4

Consider the Vehicle Licensing Bureau (or equivalent in your country), that handles car registrations, driving licenses, car taxes, and insurance records. Identify the stakeholders (human actors) and their place in the business model, the human participants and their roles. Identify computer actors and their place in the technology model. Also, identify the computing elements, and their roles. For each stakeholder, identify the stakeholder concerns.

Exercise 3-5

Select a business problem from your own organization. Identify the stakeholders and categorize them. Classify the stakeholder positions and determine the Stakeholder Management approach. Identify the engagement deliverables for each stakeholder. Finally, create a Stakeholder Map to summarize your findings.

Exercise 3-6

(Syllabus Reference: Unit 6, Learning Outcome 3)

For the example view from Part IV, Example of Architecture Views and Architecture Viewpoints: (1) describe the stakeholders and their concerns; (2) define a Stakeholder Map.

Exercise 3-7

Select a business problem from your own organization where there is a need for significant change. Rate your organization's readiness for change using the Business Factor Assessment Summary table from Part III, Readiness Factor Rating.

Exercise 3-8

Suppose your role is the Lead Architect for a program rolling out a potentially disruptive upgrade of new equipment to all your customers. How would you manage the risk?

3.8 Recommended Reading

The following are recommended sources of further information for this chapter:

- The TOGAF Standard, Version 9.2 Part II, Introduction to Part II
- The TOGAF Standard, Version 9.2 Part II, Phase A: Architecture Vision
- The TOGAF Standard, Version 9.2 Part III, Architecture Principles
- The TOGAF Standard, Version 9.2 Part III, Stakeholder Management
- TOGAF® Series Guide: Business Scenarios
- The TOGAF Standard, Version 9.2 Part III, Business Transformation Readiness Assessment
- The TOGAF Standard, Version 9.2 Part III, Risk Management
- The TOGAF Standard, Version 9.2 Part III, Capability-Based Planning
- The TOGAF Standard, Version 9.2 Part IV, Architecture Deliverables

Chapter 4
Phase B: Business Architecture

4.1 Key Learning Points

This chapter describes Phase B: Business Architecture of the TOGAF Architecture Development Method (ADM).

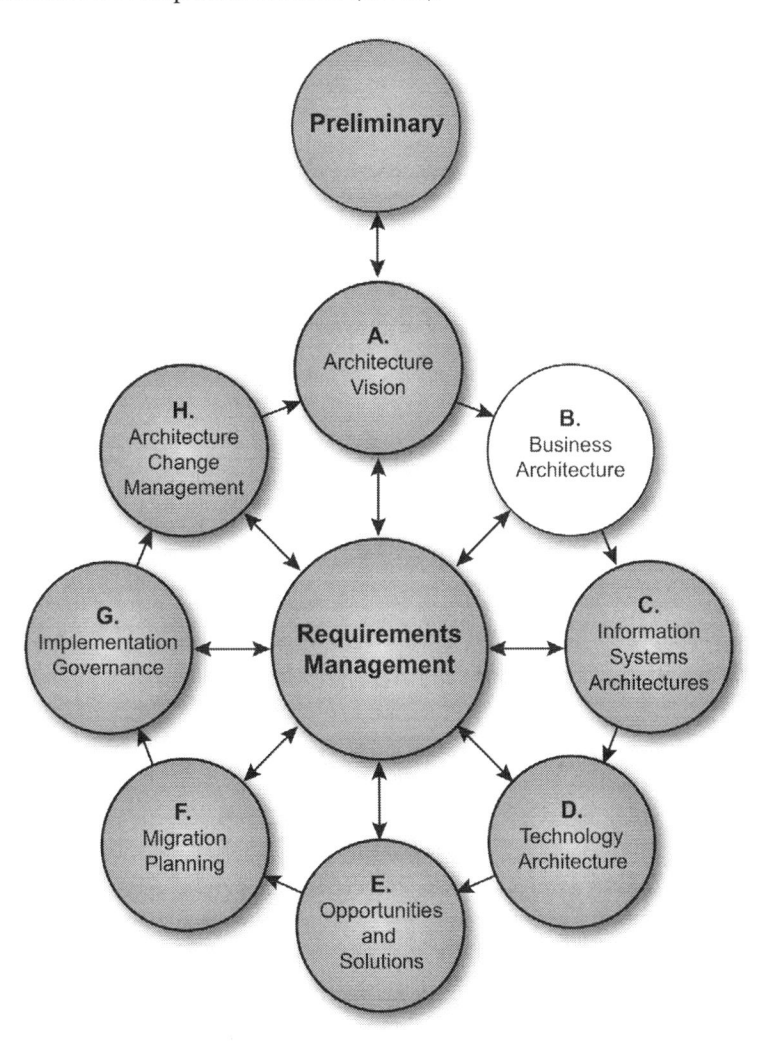

Figure 7: Phase B: Business Architecture

> **Key Points Explained**
>
> Upon completion of this chapter you should be able to:
> 1. Understand the inputs to the phase, and explain the following key elements:
>   - Business principles, business goals, and business drivers
> 2. Understand the steps, and be able to:
>   - Describe techniques for business modeling
>   - Explain the considerations for selecting reference models, viewpoints, and tools
>   - Explain the technique of gap analysis
>   - Explain how building blocks are used in the development of the Business Architecture
> 3. Understand the outputs, and be able to explain the following key elements:
>   - Business Architecture components of the Architecture Definition Document
>   - Business Architecture components of the Architecture Requirements Specification

4.2 Objectives

The objectives of Phase B: Business Architecture are to:

- Develop the Target Business Architecture that describes how the enterprise needs to operate to achieve the business goals, and respond to the strategic drivers set out in the Architecture Vision, in a way that addresses the Statement of Architecture Work and stakeholder concerns
- Identify candidate Architecture Roadmap components based upon gaps between the Baseline and Target Business Architectures

4.3 Inputs

(Syllabus Reference: Unit 9, Learning Outcome 1: You should understand the inputs to the phase, and also be able to explain the key elements: business principles, business goals, and business drivers.)

The inputs to this phase are:
- Request for Architecture Work
- Business principles, business goals, and business drivers (see Section 2.5.5)
- Capability Assessment

- Communications Plan
- Organizational Model for Enterprise Architecture
- Tailored Architecture Framework
- Approved Statement of Architecture Work
- Architecture Principles, including business principles, when pre-existing
- Enterprise Continuum
- Architecture Repository
- Architecture Vision, including:
  - Problem
  - Objective of the Statement of Architecture Work
  - Summary views
  - Business scenario (optional)
  - Refined key high-level stakeholder requirements
- Draft Architecture Definition Document, including (when in scope):
  - Baseline Business Architecture (high-level)
  - Baseline Data Architecture (high-level)
  - Baseline Application Architecture (high-level)
  - Baseline Technology Architecture (high-level)
  - Target Business Architecture (high-level)
  - Target Data Architecture (high-level)
  - Target Application Architecture (high-level)
  - Target Technology Architecture (high-level)

4.3.1 Business Principles

Business principles form part of the overarching set of Architecture Principles, initially developed in the Preliminary Phase. Example business principles drawn from Part III, Architecture Principles are summarized in Table 3.

Table 3: Example Business Principles

Principle	Summary
Primacy of Principles	These principles of information management apply to all organizations within the enterprise.
Maximize Benefit to the Enterprise	Information management decisions are made to provide maximum benefit to the enterprise as a whole.
Information Management is Everybody's Business	All organizations in the enterprise participate in information management decisions needed to accomplish business objectives.

Principle	Summary
Business Continuity	Enterprise operations are maintained in spite of system interruptions.
Common Use Applications	Development of applications used across the enterprise is preferred over the development of similar or duplicate applications which are only provided to a particular organization.
Service Orientation	The architecture is based on a design of services which mirrors real-world business activities comprising the enterprise (or inter-enterprise) business processes.
Compliance with Law	Enterprise information management processes comply with all relevant laws, policies, and regulations.
IT Responsibility	The IT organization is responsible for owning and implementing IT processes and infrastructure that enable solutions to meet user-defined requirements for functionality, service levels, cost, and delivery timing.
Protection of Intellectual Property	The enterprise's Intellectual Property (IP) must be protected. This protection must be reflected in the IT architecture, implementation, and governance processes.

4.4 Steps

(Syllabus Reference: Unit 9, Learning Outcome 2: You understand the steps in this phase.)

Phase B consists of the following steps:
1. Select reference models, viewpoints, and tools
2. Develop Baseline Business Architecture Description
3. Develop Target Business Architecture Description
4. Perform gap analysis
5. Define candidate roadmap components
6. Resolve impacts across the Architecture Landscape
7. Conduct formal stakeholder review
8. Finalize the Business Architecture
9. Create the Architecture Definition Document

> The order of the steps should be adapted to the situation: in particular, you should determine whether it is appropriate to do the Baseline Business Architecture or the Target Business Architecture development first.

The level of detail addressed in Phase B will depend on the scope and goals of the overall architecture effort. New models characterizing the needs of the business will need to be defined in detail during Phase B. Existing business artifacts to be carried over and supported in the target environment may already have been adequately defined in previous architectural work; but, if not, they too will need to be defined in Phase B. The steps are described in more detail in the following sections.

4.4.1 Select Reference Models, Viewpoints, and Tools

(Syllabus Reference: Unit 9, Learning Outcome 2.2: You should be able to explain the considerations for selecting reference models, viewpoints, and tools.)

In this step, select relevant Business Architecture resources (reference models, patterns, etc.) from the Architecture Repository, on the basis of the business drivers, and the stakeholders and their concerns. Also, select relevant Business Architecture viewpoints (e.g., operations, management, financial); that is, those that demonstrate how the stakeholder concerns are being addressed in the Business Architecture. Then, identify appropriate tools and techniques to be used for the capture, modeling, and the analysis of the selected viewpoints.

4.4.1.1 *Determine Overall Modeling Process*

Business modeling and strategy assessments are effective techniques for framing the target state of an organization's Business Architecture. The output from that activity can be used to articulate the business capabilities, organizational structure, and value streams required to close gaps between the current and target state.

For each viewpoint, select the models needed to support the specific view required, using the selected tool or method. Confirm that all stakeholders' concerns are addressed. If they are not, create new models to address concerns not covered, or augment existing models. Business scenarios are a useful technique to discover and document business requirements.

Suggested modeling techniques include:
- Capability Mapping: identifies, categorizes, and decomposes the business capabilities required for the business to have the ability to deliver value to one or more stakeholders
- Organization Mapping: a representation of the organizational structure of the business (including third-party domains), depicting business units, the decomposition of those units into lower-level functions, and organizational relationships (unit-to-unit and mapping to business capabilities, locations, and other attributes)
- Value Stream Mapping: the breakdown of activities that an organization performs to create the value being exchanged with stakeholders
  Value stream maps illustrate how an organization delivers value and are in the context of a specific set of stakeholders, and leverage business capabilities in order to create stakeholder value and align to other aspects of the Target Business Architecture.
- Structured Analysis: identifies the key business functions within the scope of the architecture, and maps those functions onto the organizational units within the business
- Use-Case Analysis: the breakdown of business-level functions across actors and organizations allows the actors in a function to be identified and permits a breakdown into services supporting/delivering that functional capability
- Process Modeling: the breakdown of a function or business service through process modeling allows the elements of the process to be identified, and permits the identification of lower-level business services or functions

4.4.1.2 Identify Required Service Granularity Level, Boundaries, and Contracts

Identify which components of the architecture are functions and which are services. Specify the required service levels. This can lead to the generation of formal Service Level Agreements (SLAs).

4.4.1.3 Identify Required Catalogs, Matrices, and Diagrams

The TOGAF standard provides definitions of catalogs, matrices, and diagrams for use in the development of a Business Architecture. *Catalogs* capture inventories of the core assets of the business. *Matrices* show the core relationships between model entities. *Diagrams* represent the Business Architecture information from a set of different perspectives (viewpoints).

The TOGAF standard recommends that the catalogs, matrices, and diagrams shown in Table 4 be considered in Phase B and provides guidance on their structure in Part IV, Content Metamodel.

Table 4: Phase B Catalogs, Diagrams, and Matrices

Catalogs	Matrices	Diagrams
Value Stream catalog	Value Stream/Capability matrix	Business Model diagram
Business Capabilities catalog	Strategy/Capability matrix	Business Capability Map
Value Stream Stages catalog	Capability/Organization matrix	Value Stream Map
Organization/Actor catalog	Business Interaction matrix	Organization Map
Driver/Goal/Objective catalog	Actor/Role matrix	Business Footprint diagram
Role catalog		Business Service/Information diagram
Business Service/Function catalog		Functional Decomposition diagram
Location catalog		Product Lifecycle diagram
Process/Event/Control/Product catalog		Goal/Objective/Service diagram
Contract/Measure catalog		Use-Case diagram
		Organization Decomposition diagram
		Process Flow diagram
		Event diagram

4.4.1.4 *Identify Types of Requirement to be Collected*

Once the catalogs, matrices, and diagrams have been developed, modeling should be completed by formalizing the business requirements for the Target Architecture. The architect should identify types of requirements to be met by the architecture. These requirements may relate to the business domain, may provide requirements input into the Data, Application, and Technology Architectures, or may provide detailed guidance to be reflected during design and implementation.

4.4.2 **Develop Baseline Business Architecture Description**

Develop a Baseline Description of the existing Business Architecture, to the extent necessary to support the Target Business Architecture. The scope and level of detail to be defined will depend on the extent to which existing business elements are likely to be carried over into the Target Business

Architecture, and on whether Architecture Descriptions exist. Where possible, identify the relevant Business Architecture building blocks, drawing on the Architecture Repository. Where new architecture models need to be developed to satisfy stakeholder concerns, use the models identified within Step 1 as a guideline for creating new architecture content to describe the Baseline Architecture.

4.4.3 Develop Target Business Architecture Description

Develop a Target Description for the Business Architecture, to the extent necessary to support the Architecture Vision. The scope and level of detail to be defined will depend on the relevance of the business elements to attaining the Target Architecture Vision, and on whether architectural descriptions exist. Where possible, identify the relevant Business Architecture building blocks, drawing on the Architecture Repository. Where new architecture models need to be developed to satisfy stakeholder concerns, use the models identified within Step 1 as a guideline for creating new architecture content to describe the Target Architecture.

> **Business Modeling**
>
> *(Syllabus Reference: Unit 9, Learning Outcome 2.1: You should be able to describe techniques for business modeling.)*
>
> A variety of modeling techniques may be employed, if considered appropriate. These include Business Capability maps, Value Stream maps, and Organization maps.
>
> The **Business Capability map** located or developed in the Architecture Vision phase provides a self-contained view of the business that is independent of the current organizational structure, business processes, information systems and applications, and the rest of the product or service portfolio.
>
> **Value Streams** provide valuable stakeholder context into why the organization needs business capabilities, while business capabilities provide what the organization needs for a particular value stage to be successful.
>
> An **Organization Map** shows the key organizational units, partners, and stakeholder groups that make up the enterprise ecosystem.
>
> Additional techniques include:
>
> **Activity Models** (also called Business Process Models) describe the functions associated with the enterprise's business activities, the data and/or information exchanged between activities (internal exchanges), and the data and/or

information exchanged with other activities that are outside the scope of the model (external exchanges). Activity models are hierarchical in nature. They capture the activities performed in a business process, and the ICOMs (inputs, controls, outputs, and mechanisms/resources used) of those activities. Activity models can be annotated with explicit statements of business rules, which represent relationships among the ICOMs. One technique for creating activity models is the IDEF (Integrated Computer Aided Manufacturing (ICAM) DEFinition) modeling technique.

The Object Management Group® (OMG®) has developed the Business Process Modeling Notation™ (BPMN™), a standard for business process modeling that includes a language with which to specify business processes, their tasks/steps, and the documents produced.

Use-Case Models can describe either business processes or systems functions, depending on the focus of the modeling effort. A use-case model describes the business processes of an enterprise in terms of use-cases and actors corresponding to business processes and organizational participants (people, organizations, etc.). The use-case model is described in use-case diagrams and use-case specifications.

Class Models are similar to logical data models. A class model describes static information and relationships between information. A class model also describes informational behaviors. Like many of the other models, it can also be used to model various levels of granularity. Depending on the intent of the model, a class model can represent business domain entities or systems implementation classes. Specifications further elaborate and detail information that cannot be represented in the class diagram.

Gap Analysis

(Syllabus Reference: Unit 9, Learning Outcome 2.3: You should be able to explain the Gap Analysis technique.)

The technique known as gap analysis is widely used in the TOGAF ADM to validate an architecture that is being developed. The technique involves drawing up a matrix to highlight any shortfalls between a Baseline Architecture and a Target Architecture. See Part III: ADM Guidelines and Techniques for full details of the gap analysis technique, including an example.

4.4.4 Perform Gap Analysis

Verify the architecture models for internal consistency and accuracy. Perform trade-off analysis to resolve conflicts (if any) among the different views. Check that the models support the principles, objectives, and constraints. Note changes to the viewpoint(s) represented in the selected models from the Architecture Repository, and document them. Test architecture models for completeness against requirements. Finally, identify gaps between the baseline and target using the gap analysis technique.

4.4.5 Define Candidate Roadmap Components

Following creation of a Baseline Architecture, a Target Architecture, and gap analysis results, a Business Roadmap is required to prioritize activities over the coming phases. This initial Business Architecture Roadmap (see Section 4.5.3) will be used as raw material to support a more detailed definition of a consolidated, cross-discipline roadmap within Phase E: Opportunities & Solutions.

4.4.6 Resolve Impacts across the Architecture Landscape

Once the Business Architecture is finalized, it is necessary to understand any wider impacts or implications. At this stage, other architecture artifacts in the Architecture Landscape should be examined to address the following:

- Does this Business Architecture impact any pre-existing architectures?
- Have recent changes been made that impact the Business Architecture?
- Are there any opportunities to re-use work from this Business Architecture in other areas of the organization?
- Does this Business Architecture impact other projects (those planned, as well as those in progress)?
- Will this Business Architecture be impacted by other projects (those planned, as well as those in progress)?

4.4.7 Conduct Formal Stakeholder Review

Check the original motivation for the architecture project and the Statement of Architecture Work against the proposed Business Architecture, asking if it is fit for the purpose of supporting subsequent work in the other architecture domains. Refine the proposed Business Architecture only if necessary.

4.4.8 Finalize the Business Architecture

Select standards for each of the building blocks, re-using as much as possible from the reference models selected from the Architecture Repository. Fully document each building block, then conduct a final cross-check of overall architecture against business goals; document the rationale for building block decisions in the architecture document. Document the final requirements traceability report. Document the final mapping of the architecture within the Architecture Repository. From the selected building blocks, identify those that might be re-used (working practices, roles, business relationships, job descriptions, etc.) and publish via the Architecture Repository. Finalize all the work products.

4.4.9 Create the Architecture Definition Document

Document the rationale for building block decisions in the Architecture Definition Document. Prepare the business sections of the Architecture Definition Document (see Section 4.5.1.1). Send the document for review by relevant stakeholders, and incorporate any feedback.

> **Building Blocks**
>
> *(Syllabus Reference: Unit 9, Learning Outcome 3: You should be able to explain how building blocks are used in the development of a Business Architecture.)*
>
> Building blocks are used widely within the TOGAF standard for building architectures, where they are known as Architecture Building Blocks (ABBs) and for building solutions, where they are known as Solution Building Blocks (SBBs). The way in which functionality, products, and custom developments are assembled into building blocks varies widely between individual architectures. Every organization must decide for itself what arrangement of building blocks works best for it. A good choice of building blocks can lead to improvements in legacy system integration, interoperability, and flexibility in the creation of new systems and applications.
>
> In Phase B, when creating the Baseline and Target Architecture Descriptions, the architect should identify relevant Business Architecture building blocks, drawing on the Architecture Repository if possible. A number of catalogs are provided to help to model the decomposition of a building block and also decompositions across related building blocks. Once the initial Baseline and Target Architectures are complete, a gap analysis is then used to identify building blocks to carry over

> to the target; eliminated building blocks; and new, required building blocks. When finalizing the Business Architecture, standards are selected for each building block, each building block is documented, and those which look likely to be reusable are published in the Architecture Repository.

4.5 Outputs

(Syllabus Reference: Unit 9, Learning Outcome 4: You should understand the outputs.)

The outputs of this phase are:
- Statement of Architecture Work, updated if necessary
- Validated business principles, business goals, and business drivers
- Refined and updated Business Architecture Principles, if applicable
- Draft Architecture Definition Document (see Section 4.5.1) containing content updates (see Section 4.5.1.1)
- Draft Architecture Requirements Specification (see Section 4.5.2), including content updates (see Section 4.5.2.1)
- Business Architecture components of an Architecture Roadmap (see Section 4.5.3)

The outputs may also include some or all of the catalogs, matrices, and diagrams listed in Table 4.

4.5.1 Architecture Definition Document

(Syllabus Reference: Unit 9, Learning Outcome 4.1: You should be able to explain the key element: Business Architecture components of the Architecture Definition Document.)

The Architecture Definition Document is the deliverable container for the core architectural artifacts created during a project and for important related information. The Architecture Definition Document spans all four architecture domains (Business, Data, Application, and Technology) and also examines all relevant states of the architecture (baseline, transition, and target). It is first created in Phase A, where it is populated with artifacts created to support the Architecture Vision. It is updated in Phase B, with Business Architecture-related material, and subsequently updated with Information Systems Architecture material in Phase C, and then with

Technology Architecture material in Phase D. Where the scope of change to implement the Target Architecture requires an incremental approach, the Architecture Definition Document will be updated to include one or more Transition Architectures in Phase E (see Section 10.5.2).

The Architecture Definition Document is a companion to the Architecture Requirements Specification, with a complementary objective to provide a qualitative view of the solution. The aim is to communicate the intent of the architects. The Architecture Requirements Specification, on the other hand, provides a quantitative view of the solution, stating measurable criteria that must be met during the implementation of the architecture.

The following contents are typically found within an Architecture Definition Document:
- Scope
- Goals, objectives, and constraints
- Architecture Principles
- Baseline Architecture
- Architecture models (for each state to be modeled); such as models for Business Architecture, Data Architecture, Application Architecture, and Technology Architecture
- Rationale and justification for architectural approach
- Mapping to Architecture Repository, including mappings to the Architecture Landscape, the reference models, the standards, as well as a re-use assessment
- Gap analysis
- Impact assessment
- Transition Architecture (see Section 10.5.2)

4.5.1.1 Business Architecture Components

The topics that should be addressed in the Architecture Definition Document related to Business Architecture are as follows:
- Baseline Business Architecture, if appropriate; this is a description of the existing Business Architecture
- Target Business Architecture, including:
  - Organization structure identifying business locations and relating them to organizational units

- Business goals and objectives for the enterprise and each organizational unit
- Business functions identified using a detailed, recursive step involving successive decomposition of major functional areas into sub-functions
- Business services that the enterprise and each enterprise unit provides to its customers, both internally and externally
- Business processes, including measures and deliverables
- Business roles, including development and modification of skills requirements
- Business data model
- A correlation of organization and functions which relate business functions to organizational units in the form of a matrix report

- Views corresponding to the selected viewpoints addressing key stakeholder concerns

4.5.2 Architecture Requirements Specification

(*Syllabus Reference: Unit 9, Learning Outcome 4.2: You should be able to explain the key element: Business Architecture components of the Architecture Requirements Specification.*)

The Architecture Requirements Specification provides a set of quantitative statements that outline what an implementation project must do in order to comply with the architecture. An Architecture Requirements Specification will typically form a major component of an implementation contract or contract for more detailed Architecture Definition. As mentioned in Section 4.5.1, the Architecture Requirements Specification is a companion to the Architecture Definition Document, and provides a quantitative view.

The following contents are typical within an Architecture Requirements Specification:

- Success measures
- Architecture requirements
- Business service contracts
- Application service contracts
- Implementation guidelines
- Implementation specifications
- Implementation standards

- Interoperability requirements
- IT service management requirements
- Constraints
- Assumptions

4.5.2.1 *Business Architecture Requirements*

Business Architecture requirements populating the Architecture Requirements Specification in Phase B include:

- Gap analysis results
- Technical requirements: an initial set of technical requirements should be generated as the output of Phase B: Business Architecture
  These are the drivers for the Technology Architecture work that follows, and should identify, categorize, and prioritize the implications for work in the remaining architecture domains; for example, by a dependency/priority matrix (e.g., guiding trade-offs between speed of transaction processing and security); a list of the specific models that are expected to be produced (e.g., expressed as primitives of the Zachman Framework).
- Updated business requirements, identified by use of the business scenarios technique

4.5.3 Architecture Roadmap

The Architecture Roadmap lists individual work packages that will realize the Target Architecture and lays them out on a timeline to show progression from the Baseline Architecture to the Target Architecture. The Architecture Roadmap highlights individual work packages' business value at each stage. Transition Architectures necessary to effectively realize the Target Architecture are identified as intermediate steps. The Architecture Roadmap is incrementally developed throughout Phases E and F, and informed by the roadmap components developed in Phases B, C, and D.

The following contents are typically found within an Architecture Roadmap:
- Work package portfolio:
  - Work package description (name, description, objectives, deliverables)
  - Functional requirements
  - Dependencies
  - Relationship to opportunity

- Relationship to Architecture Definition Document and Architecture Requirements Specification
  - Business value
- Implementation Factor Assessment and Deduction matrix, including:
  - Risks
  - Issues
  - Assumptions
  - Dependencies
  - Actions
  - Impact
- Consolidated Gaps, Solutions, and Dependencies Matrix, including:
  - Architecture domain
  - Gap
  - Potential solutions
  - Dependencies
- Transition Architectures, if any
- Implementation recommendations:
  - Criteria/measures of effectiveness of projects
  - Risks and issues
  - Solution Building Blocks (SBBs)

4.6 Summary

Phase B is about development of the Business Architecture; a holistic representation of business capabilities, end-to-end value delivery, information, and organizational structure, along with the relationships to strategies, products, policies, initiatives, and stakeholders. It should show how the organization meets its business goals.

4.7 Exercises

Exercise 4-1
Identify five sources of information within your organization that could be used to draw up a Baseline Business Architecture Description.

Exercise 4-2

Which of the Phase B catalogs, matrices, and diagrams would be most suitable for addressing the following concerns?
- Identifying where the enterprise carries out its business operations
- Identifying all agreed service contracts
- Identifying relationships between organizations and business functions in the enterprise

Exercise 4-3

Which of the Phase B catalogs, matrices, and diagrams would be most suitable for addressing the following stakeholders?
- Human Resource Managers
- Chief Financial Officer

4.8 Recommended Reading

The following are recommended sources of further information for this chapter:
- The TOGAF Standard, Version 9.2 Part II, Phase B: Business Architecture
- The TOGAF Standard, Version 9.2 Part IV, Architecture Deliverables
- Sample Catalogs, Matrices, and Diagrams presentation: www.togaf.info/sg03

Chapter 5

Phase C: Information Systems Architectures

5.1 Key Learning Points

This chapter describes Phase C: Information Systems Architectures of the TOGAF Architecture Development Method (ADM).

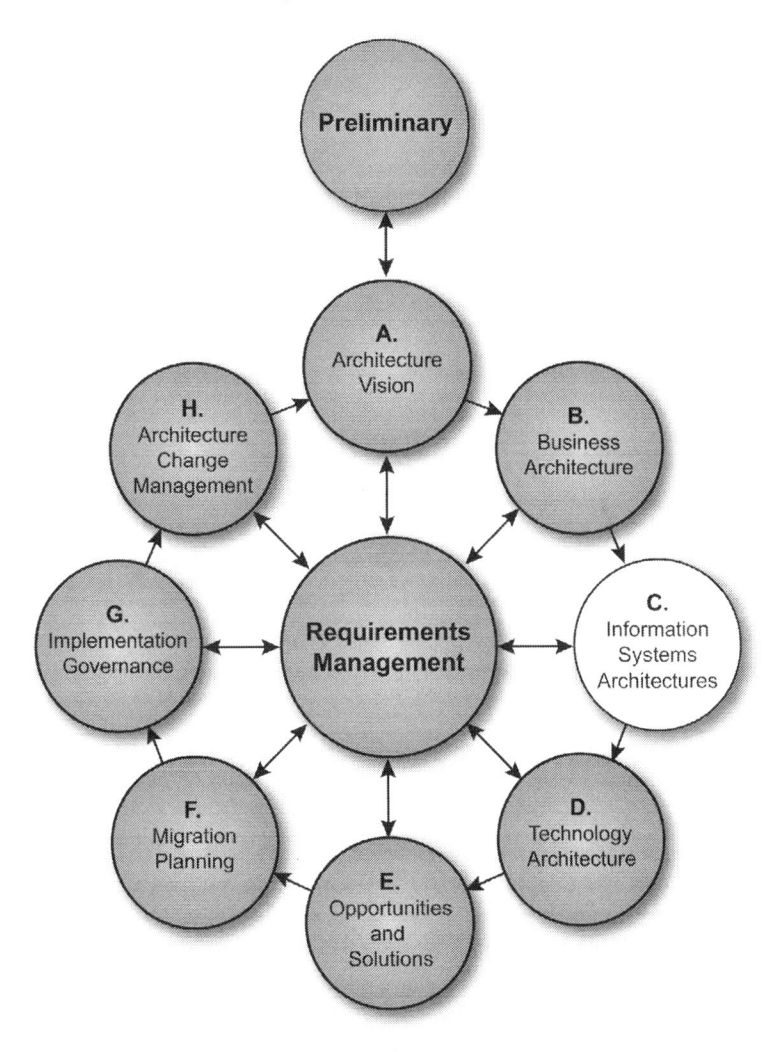

Figure 8: Phase C: Information Systems Architectures

> **Key Points Explained**
>
> Upon completion of this chapter you should be able to:
> 1. Explain the considerations for the implementation order and approach of the Data and Application Architectures

5.2 Objectives

The objectives of Phase C: Information Systems Architectures are to:
- Develop the Target Information Systems (Data and Application) Architectures that enable the Business Architecture and the Architecture Vision, in a way that addresses the Statement of Architecture Work and stakeholder concerns
- Identify candidate Architecture Roadmap components based upon gaps between the Baseline and Target Information Systems (Data and Application) Architectures

5.3 Considerations for the Implementation Order

(Syllabus Reference: Unit 10, Learning Outcome 1: You should be able to explain the considerations for the implementation order of the Data and Application Architectures.)

Phase C involves some combination of Data and Application Architecture. These may be developed in either order, or in parallel. There will need to be some iteration to ensure consistency.

5.4 Inputs

See Chapter 6 and Chapter 7.

5.5 Steps

See Chapter 6 and Chapter 7.

5.6 Outputs

See Chapter 6 and Chapter 7.

5.7 Summary

Phase C: Information Systems Architectures documents the fundamental organization of an organization's IT systems, embodied in the major types of information and the applications that process them, their relationships to each other and the environment, and the principles governing their design and evolution. It involves some combination of Data and Application Architecture, which may be developed either sequentially or concurrently.

5.8 Exercises

See Chapter 6 and Chapter 7.

5.9 Recommended Reading

The following are recommended sources of further information for this chapter:
- The TOGAF Standard, Version 9.2 Part II, Phase C: Information Systems Architectures

Chapter 6

Phase C: Data Architecture

6.1 Key Learning Points

This chapter describes the Data Architecture part of Phase C: Information Systems Architectures of the TOGAF Architecture Development Method (ADM).

> **Key Points Explained**
>
> Upon completion of this chapter you should be able to:
> 1. Understand the inputs to the phase, and explain Data Principles
> 2. Understand the steps, and be able to explain the considerations for selecting reference models, viewpoints, and tools
> 3. Understand the outputs, and be able to explain the following key elements:
>   - Data Architecture components of the Architecture Definition Document
>   - Data Architecture components of the Architecture Requirements Specification

6.2 Objectives

The objectives of the Data Architecture part of Phase C are to:
- Develop the Target Data Architecture that enables the Business Architecture and the Architecture Vision, in a way that addresses the Statement of Architecture Work and stakeholder concerns
- Identify candidate Architecture Roadmap components based upon gaps between the Baseline and Target Data Architectures

6.3 Inputs

(Syllabus Reference: Unit 10, Learning Outcome 2: You should understand the inputs to the phase.)

The inputs to this phase are:
- Request for Architecture Work
- Capability Assessment
- Communications Plan
- Organizational Model for Enterprise Architecture
- Tailored Architecture Framework
- Data principles, if existing
- Statement of Architecture Work
- Architecture Vision
- Architecture Repository
- Draft Architecture Definition Document:
  - Baseline Business Architecture (detailed)
  - Target Business Architecture (detailed)
  - Baseline Data Architecture (high-level)
  - Target Data Architecture (high-level)
  - Baseline Application Architecture (high-level or detailed)
  - Target Application Architecture (high-level or detailed)
  - Baseline Technology Architecture (high-level)
  - Target Technology Architecture (high-level)
- Draft Architecture Requirements Specification:
  - Gap analysis results
  - Relevant technical requirements
- Business Architecture components of an Architecture Roadmap

6.3.1 Data Principles

(Syllabus Reference: Unit 10, Learning Outcome 2.1: You should be able to explain the following key element: Data Principles.)

Data principles should form part of the overarching set of Architecture Principles, initially developed in the Preliminary Phase. Example data principles drawn from Part III, Architecture Principles are summarized in Table 5.

Table 5: Example Data Principles

Principle	Summary
Data is an Asset	Data is an asset that has value to the enterprise and is managed accordingly.
Data is Shared	Users have access to the data necessary to perform their duties; therefore, data is shared across enterprise functions and organizations.
Data is Accessible	Data is accessible for users to perform their functions.
Data Trustee	Each data element has a trustee accountable for data quality.
Common Vocabulary and Data Definitions	Data is defined consistently throughout the enterprise, and the definitions are understandable and available to all users.
Data Security	Data is protected from unauthorized use and disclosure. In addition to the traditional aspects of national security classification, this includes, but is not limited to, protection of pre-decisional, sensitive, source selection-sensitive, and proprietary information.

6.4 Steps

(Syllabus Reference: Unit 10, Learning Outcome 3: You should understand the steps in this phase.)

Phase C: Data Architecture consists of the following steps:
1. Select reference models, viewpoints, and tools
2. Develop Baseline Data Architecture Description
3. Develop Target Data Architecture Description
4. Perform gap analysis
5. Define candidate roadmap components
6. Resolve impacts across the Architecture Landscape
7. Conduct formal stakeholder review
8. Finalize the Data Architecture
9. Create Architecture Definition Document

> The order of the steps should be adapted to the situation. In particular, you should determine whether it is appropriate to do the Baseline Data Architecture or the Target Data Architecture development first.

The steps are described in more detail in the following sections.

6.4.1 Select Reference Models, Viewpoints, and Tools

(Syllabus Reference: Unit 10, Learning Outcome 3.1: You should be able to explain the considerations for selecting reference models, viewpoints, and tools.)

After reviewing and validating the set of data principles, select relevant Data Architecture resources (reference models, patterns, etc.) from the Architecture Repository, on the basis of the business drivers, stakeholders, concerns, and the Business Architecture. Also, select relevant Data Architecture viewpoints; for example, stakeholders of the data (regulatory bodies, users, generators, subjects, auditors, etc.), various time dimensions (real-time, reporting period, event-driven, etc.), locations; business processes; i.e., those that will enable the architect to demonstrate how the stakeholder concerns are being addressed in the Data Architecture. Then, identify appropriate tools and techniques to be used for data capture, modeling, and analysis, in association with the selected viewpoints.

6.4.1.1 *Determine Overall Modeling Process*

For each viewpoint, select the models needed to support the specific view required, using the selected tool or method. Examples of data models include the DoDAF Logical Data Model, the ARTS data model, the Pipeline Open Data Standard (PODS) data model, the Professional Petroleum Data Management (PPDM) Association data model, and the Energistics® Epicenter data model. Confirm that all stakeholder concerns have been addressed. If they are not, create new models to address concerns not covered, or augment the existing models.

The recommended process for developing a Data Architecture is as follows:
- Collect data-related models from existing Business Architecture and Application Architecture materials
- Rationalize data requirements and align with any existing enterprise data catalogs and models; this allows the development of a data inventory and entity relationship model
- Update and develop matrices across the architecture by relating data to business services, business functions, access rights, and applications
- Elaborate Data Architecture views by examining how data is created, distributed, migrated, secured, and archived

6.4.1.2 Identify Required Catalogs, Matrices, and Diagrams

The TOGAF standard provides definitions of catalogs, matrices, and diagrams for use in development of a Data Architecture. Catalogs capture inventories of the core assets of the business. Matrices show the core relationships between model entities. Diagrams represent the Data Architecture information from a set of different perspectives (viewpoints). The TOGAF standard recommends that the catalogs, matrices, and diagrams shown in Table 6 be considered in Phase C: Data Architecture and provides guidance on their structure in Part IV, Content Metamodel.

Table 6:   Phase C: Data Architecture Catalogs, Matrices, and Diagrams

Catalogs	Matrices	Diagrams
Data Entity/Data Component catalog	Data Entity/Business Function matrix Application/Data matrix	Conceptual Data diagram Logical Data diagram Data Dissemination diagram Data Lifecycle diagram Data Security diagram Data Migration diagram

6.4.1.3 Identify Types of Requirement to be Collected

Once the catalogs, matrices, and diagrams have been developed, modeling should be completed by formalizing the data-focused requirements for the Target Architecture. The architect should identify types of requirements to be met by the architecture. These requirements may relate to the data domain, may provide requirements input into the Application and Technology Architectures, or may provide detailed guidance to be reflected during design and implementation.

6.4.2 Develop Baseline Data Architecture Description

Develop a Baseline Description of the existing Data Architecture to the extent necessary to support the Target Data Architecture. The scope and level of detail to be defined will depend on the extent to which existing data elements are likely to be carried over into the Target Data Architecture, and on whether there are any existing architectural descriptions. Where possible, identify the relevant Data Architecture building blocks, drawing on the architecture. Where new architecture models need to be developed to satisfy stakeholder concerns, use the models identified within Step 1 as a guideline for creating new content to describe the Baseline Architecture.

6.4.3 Develop Target Data Architecture Description

Develop a Target Description for the Data Architecture to the extent necessary to support the Architecture Vision and Target Business Architecture. The scope and level of detail to be defined will depend on the relevance of the data elements to the Target Architecture, and on whether architectural descriptions exist. Where possible, identify the relevant Data Architecture building blocks, drawing on the architecture. Where new architecture models need to be developed to satisfy stakeholder concerns, use the models identified within Step 1 as a guideline for creating new content to describe the Target Architecture.

6.4.4 Perform Gap Analysis

Verify the architecture models for internal consistency and accuracy. Document changes to the viewpoint(s) represented in the selected models from the Architecture Repository. Test the architecture models for completeness against requirements. Finally, identify gaps between the baseline and target using gap analysis.

6.4.5 Define Candidate Roadmap Components

Following creation of a Baseline Architecture, Target Architecture, and gap analysis, a Data Architecture Roadmap is required to prioritize activities over the coming phases. This initial Data Architecture Roadmap will be used to support more detailed definition of a consolidated, cross-discipline roadmap within Phase E: Opportunities & Solutions.

6.4.6 Resolve Impacts Across the Architecture Landscape

Once the Data Architecture is finalized, it is necessary to understand any wider impacts or implications. At this stage, other architecture artifacts in the Architecture Landscape should be examined to determine the following:
- Does this Data Architecture impact any pre-existing architectures?
- Have recent changes been made that impact the Data Architecture?
- Are there any opportunities to re-use work from this Data Architecture in other areas of the organization?
- Does this Data Architecture impact other projects (planned or in progress)?

- Will this Data Architecture be impacted by other projects (planned or in progress)?

6.4.7 Conduct Formal Stakeholder Review

Check the original motivation for the architecture project and the Statement of Architecture Work against the proposed Data Architecture. Conduct an impact analysis to identify any areas where the Business and Application Architectures (e.g., business practices) may need to change in light of changes in the Data Architecture (for example, changes to forms or procedures, applications, or database systems). If the impact is significant, this may warrant the Business and Application Architectures being revisited.

Identify any areas where the Application Architecture (if it exists at this point) may need to change in light of changes in the Data Architecture or to identify constraints on the Application Architecture about to be designed. If the impact is significant, it may be appropriate to do a short iteration of the Application Architecture.

Identify any constraints on the Technology Architecture about to be designed, refining the proposed Data Architecture only if necessary.

6.4.8 Finalize the Data Architecture

Select standards for each of the building blocks, re-using as much as possible from the reference models selected from the Architecture Repository. Fully document each building block, then conduct a final cross-check of the overall architecture against business requirements; document rationale for building block decisions in the architecture document. Document the final requirements traceability report. Document the final mapping of the architecture within the Architecture Repository. From the selected building blocks, identify those that might be re-used, and publish them in the Architecture Repository. Finalize all the work products.

6.4.9 Create Architecture Definition Document

Document the rationale for building block decisions in the Architecture Definition Document. Prepare the Data Architecture sections of the Architecture Definition Document (see Section 6.5.1). Send the document for review by relevant stakeholders, and incorporate feedback.

6.5 Outputs

(Syllabus Reference: Unit 10, Learning Outcome 4: You should understand the outputs of this phase.)

The outputs of this phase are:
- Statement of Architecture Work, updated if necessary
- Validated data principles, or new data principles
- Draft Architecture Definition Document, containing content updates (see Section 6.5.1)
- Draft Architecture Requirements Specification, including content updates (see Section 6.5.2)
- Data Architecture components of an Architecture Roadmap

The outputs may also include some or all of the catalogs, matrices, and diagrams listed in Table 6.

6.5.1 Components of the Architecture Definition Document

(Syllabus Reference: Unit 10, Learning Outcome 4.1: You should be able to explain the following key element: Data Architecture Components of the Architecture Definition Document.)

The topics that should be addressed in the Architecture Definition Document that are related to the Data Architecture are as follows:
- Baseline Data Architecture, if appropriate
  - Target Data Architecture, including models for business data, logical data and the data management process, as well as a Data Entity/Business Function matrix
- Data Architecture views corresponding to the selected viewpoints addressing key stakeholder concerns

6.5.2 Components of the Architecture Requirements Specification

(Syllabus Reference: Unit 10, Learning Outcome 4.2: You should be able to explain the following key element: Data Architecture Components of the Architecture Requirements Specification.)

Data Architecture requirements populating the Architecture Requirements Specification in Phase C include:

- Gap analysis results
- Data interoperability requirements (e.g., XML schema, security policies)
- Areas where the Business Architecture may need to change in order to comply with changes in the Data Architecture
- Constraints on the Technology Architecture about to be designed
- Updated business requirements, if appropriate
- Updated application requirements, if appropriate

6.6 Summary

The Data Architecture part of Phase C defines the types and sources of data needed to support the business, and does so in a way that can be understood by stakeholders. The architecture team should consider existing relevant data models, such as the ARTS and POSC models.

6.7 Exercises

Exercise 6-1
Identify five sources of information within your organization that could be used to draw up a Baseline Data Architecture Description.

Exercise 6-2
Which of the Phase C: Data Architecture catalogs, matrices, and diagrams would be most suitable to address the following concerns:
- Enabling development of data governance programs across the enterprise
- Identifying systems that access and update data
- Depicting critical relationships between data entities within the enterprise
- Determining who or what has access to enterprise data

6.8 Recommended Reading

The following are recommended sources of further information for this chapter:
- The TOGAF Standard, Version 9.2 Part II, Phase C: Information Systems Architectures – Data Architecture

- The TOGAF Standard, Version 9.2 Part IV, Architecture Deliverables
- Sample Catalogs, Matrices, and Diagrams presentation: www.togaf.info/sg03

Chapter 7

Phase C: Application Architecture

7.1 Key Learning Points

This chapter describes the Application Architecture part of Phase C: Information Systems Architectures of the TOGAF Architecture Development Method (ADM).

> **Key Points Explained**
>
> Upon completion of this chapter you should be able to:
> 1. Understand the inputs to the phase, and explain Application Principles
> 2. Understand the steps, and be able to explain the considerations for selecting reference models, viewpoints, and tools
> 3. Understand the outputs, and be able to explain the following key elements:
>   - Application Architecture components of the Architecture Definition Document
>   - Application Architecture components of the Architecture Requirements Specification

7.2 Objectives

The objectives of the Application Architecture part of Phase C are to:
- Develop the Target Application Architecture that enables the Business Architecture and the Architecture Vision, in a way that addresses the Statement of Architecture Work and stakeholder concerns
- Identify candidate Architecture Roadmap components based upon gaps between the Baseline and Target Application Architectures

7.3 Inputs

(Syllabus Reference: Unit 11, Learning Outcome 1: You should understand the inputs to the phase.)

The inputs to this phase are:
- Request for Architecture Work
- Capability Assessment
- Communications Plan
- Organizational Model for Enterprise Architecture
- Tailored Architecture Framework
- Application principles, if existing
- Statement of Architecture Work
- Architecture Vision
- Architecture Repository
- Draft Architecture Definition Document:
  - Baseline Business Architecture (detailed)
  - Target Business Architecture (detailed)
  - Baseline Data Architecture (high-level or detailed)
  - Target Data Architecture (high-level or detailed)
  - Baseline Application Architecture (high-level)
  - Target Application Architecture (high-level)
  - Baseline Technology Architecture (high-level)
  - Target Technology Architecture (high-level)
- Draft Architecture Requirements Specification:
  - Gap analysis results
  - Relevant technical requirements
- Business and Data Architecture components of an Architecture Roadmap, if available

7.3.1 Application Principles

(Syllabus Reference: Unit 11, Learning Outcome 1.1: You should be able to explain the following key element: Application Principles.)

Application principles form part of the overarching set of Architecture Principles, initially developed in the Preliminary Phase. Example application principles drawn from Part III, Architecture Principles are summarized in Table 7.

Table 7: Example Application Principles

Principle	Summary
Technology Independence	Applications are independent of specific technology choices and therefore can operate on a variety of technology platforms.
Ease-of-Use	Applications are easy to use. The underlying technology is transparent to users, so they can concentrate on tasks at hand.

7.4 Steps

(Syllabus Reference: Unit 11, Learning Outcome 2: You should understand the steps for this phase.)

Phase C: Application Architecture consists of the following steps:
1. Select reference models, viewpoints, and tools
2. Develop Baseline Application Architecture Description
3. Develop Target Application Architecture Description
4. Perform gap analysis
5. Define candidate roadmap components
6. Resolve impacts across the Architecture Landscape
7. Conduct formal stakeholder review
8. Finalize the Application Architecture
9. Create Architecture Definition Document

> The order of the steps should be adapted to the situation: in particular, you should determine whether it is appropriate to do the Baseline Application Architecture or the Target Application Architecture development first.

The steps are described in more detail in the following sections.

7.4.1 Select Reference Models, Viewpoints, and Tools

(Syllabus Reference: Unit 11, Learning Outcome 2.1: You should be able to explain the considerations for selecting reference models, viewpoints, and tools.)

Review and validate the set of application principles. Then, select relevant Application Architecture resources (reference models, patterns, etc.) from the Architecture Repository, on the basis of the business drivers, the stakeholders, and their concerns. Next, select relevant Application Architecture viewpoints (for example, stakeholders of the applications, viewpoints relevant to functional and individual users of applications, etc.), those that will enable the architect to demonstrate how the stakeholder concerns are being addressed in the Application Architecture. Then, identify appropriate tools and techniques to be used for the capture, modeling, and analysis of the Application Architecture, in association with the selected viewpoints.

7.4.1.1 Determine Overall Modeling Process

For each viewpoint, select the models needed to support the specific view required, using the selected tool or method. Examples of applications models include those from the TM Forum and the Object Management Group (OMG). Confirm that all stakeholder concerns have been addressed. If they are not, create new models to address concerns not covered, or augment existing models (see above).

The recommended process for developing an Application Architecture is as follows:
- Understand the list of applications or application components that are required, based on the baseline Application Portfolio, what the requirements are, and the Business Architecture scope
- Simplify complicated applications by decomposing them into two or more applications
- Ensure that the set of application definitions is internally consistent, by removing duplicate functionality as far as possible, and combining similar applications into one
- Identify logical applications and the most appropriate physical applications
- Develop matrices across the architecture by relating applications to business services, business functions, data, processes, etc.
- Elaborate a set of Application Architecture views by examining how the applications will function, capturing integration, migration, development, and operational concerns

7.4.1.2 Identify Required Catalogs, Matrices, and Diagrams

The TOGAF standard provides definitions of catalogs, matrices, and diagrams for use in development of an Application Architecture. The TOGAF standard recommends that the catalogs, matrices, and diagrams shown in Table 8 be considered in Phase C: Application Architecture and provides guidance on their structure in Part IV, Content Metamodel.

Table 8: Phase C: Application Architecture Catalogs, Matrices, and Diagrams

Catalogs	Matrices	Diagrams
Application Portfolio catalog	Application/ Organization matrix	Application Communication diagram
Interface catalog	Role/Application matrix	Application and User Location diagram
	Application/Function matrix	Application Use-Case diagram
	Application Interaction matrix	Enterprise Manageability diagram
		Process/Application Realization diagram
		Software Engineering diagram
		Application Migration diagram
		Software Distribution diagram

7.4.1.3 Identify Types of Requirement to be Collected

Once the catalogs, matrices, and diagrams have been developed, modeling should be completed by formalizing the application-focused requirements for the Target Architecture. The architect should identify the types of requirements to be met by the architecture. These requirements may relate to the application domain, may provide requirements input into the Data and Technology Architectures, or may provide detailed guidance to be reflected during design and implementation.

7.4.2 Develop Baseline Application Architecture Description

Develop a Baseline Description of the existing Application Architecture to the extent necessary to support the Target Application Architecture. The scope and level of detail to be defined will depend on the extent to which existing applications are likely to be carried over into the Target Application Architecture, and on whether Architecture Descriptions exist. Where possible, identify the relevant Application Architecture building blocks, drawing on the Architecture Repository. If not already existing within the Architecture Repository, define each application in line with the Application Portfolio catalog. Where new architecture models need to be developed to satisfy stakeholder concerns, use the models identified within Step 1 as a guideline for creating new architecture content to describe the Baseline Architecture.

7.4.3 Develop Target Application Architecture Description

Develop a Target Description for the Application Architecture to the extent necessary to support the Architecture Vision, Target Business Architecture, and Target Data Architecture. The scope and level of detail to be defined will depend on the relevance of the application elements to attaining the Target Architecture Vision, and on whether architectural descriptions exist. Where possible, identify the relevant Application Architecture building blocks, drawing on the Architecture Repository. Where new architecture models need to be developed to satisfy stakeholder concerns, use the models identified within Step 1 as a guideline for creating new architecture content to describe the Target Architecture.

7.4.4 Perform Gap Analysis

First, check the architecture models for internal consistency and accuracy. Note changes to the viewpoint represented in the selected models from the Architecture Repository, and document the changes. Then, test the architecture models for completeness against requirements. Finally, identify gaps between the baseline and target using the gap analysis technique.

7.4.5 Define Candidate Roadmap Components

Following creation of a Baseline Architecture, Target Architecture, and gap analysis, an Application Roadmap is required to prioritize activities over the coming phases. This initial Application Architecture Roadmap will be used as raw material to support the more detailed definition of a consolidated, cross-discipline roadmap within Phase E: Opportunities & Solutions.

7.4.6 Resolve Impacts Across the Architecture Landscape

Once the Application Architecture is finalized, it is necessary to understand any wider impacts or implications. At this stage, other architecture artifacts in the Architecture Landscape should be examined to determine the following:
- Does this Application Architecture impact any pre-existing architectures?
- Have recent changes been made that impact the Application Architecture?
- Are there any opportunities to re-use work from this Application Architecture in other areas of the organization?

- Does this Application Architecture impact other projects (planned or in progress)?
- Will this Application Architecture be impacted by other projects (planned or in progress)?

7.4.7 Conduct Formal Stakeholder Review

Check the original motivation for the architecture project and the Statement of Architecture Work against the proposed Application Architecture. Conduct an impact analysis to identify any areas where the Business and Data Architectures (e.g., business practices) may need to change in light of changes in the Application Architecture (for example, changes to forms or procedures, applications, or database systems). If the impact is significant, this may warrant the Business and Data Architectures being revisited. Finally, identify any constraints on the Technology Architecture (especially the infrastructure) about to be designed.

7.4.8 Finalize the Application Architecture

Select standards for each of the building blocks, re-using as much as possible from the reference models selected from the Architecture Repository. Fully document each building block, and then conduct a final cross-check of overall architecture against business requirements. Document the rationale for building block decisions in the architecture document. Document the final requirements traceability report. Also document the final mapping of the architecture within the Architecture Repository. From the selected building blocks, identify those that might be re-used, and publish them in the Architecture Repository. Finalize all the work products.

7.4.9 Create Architecture Definition Document

Document the rationale for building block decisions in the Architecture Definition Document. Prepare the Application Architecture sections of the Architecture Definition Document (see Section 7.5.1). Send the document for review by relevant stakeholders, and incorporate feedback.

7.5 Outputs

(Syllabus Reference: Unit 11, Learning Outcome 3: You should understand the outputs of the phase.)

The outputs of this phase are:
- Statement of Architecture Work, updated if necessary
- Validated application principles, or new application principles
- Draft Architecture Definition Document, containing content updates (see Section 7.5.1).
- Draft Architecture Requirements Specification, including content updates (see Section 7.5.2)
- Application Architecture components of an Architecture Roadmap

The outputs may also include some or all of the catalogs, matrices, and diagrams listed in Table 8.

7.5.1 Components of the Architecture Definition Document

(Syllabus Reference: Unit 10, Learning Outcome 3.1: You should be able to explain the following key element: Application Architecture Components of the Architecture Definition Document.)

The topics that should be addressed in the Architecture Definition Document related to the Application Architecture are as follows:
- Baseline Application Architecture, if appropriate
- Target Application Architecture:
  - Process systems model
  - Place systems model
  - Time systems model
  - People systems model
- Application Architecture views corresponding to the selected viewpoints, addressing key stakeholder concerns

7.5.2 Components of the Architecture Requirements Specification

(Syllabus Reference: Unit 11, Learning Outcome 3.2: You should be able to explain the following key element: Application Architecture Components of the Architecture Requirements Specification.)

Application Architecture requirements populating the Architecture Requirements Specification in Phase C include:
- Gap analysis results
- Applications interoperability requirements

- Relevant technical requirements that will apply to this evolution of the Architecture Development Cycle
- Constraints on the Technology Architecture about to be designed
- Updated business requirements, if appropriate
- Updated data requirements, if appropriate

7.6 Summary

This phase defines the *kinds* of applications necessary to process the data and support the business. The goal is to define the kinds of applications that are relevant and what those applications need to do. The applications are not described as computer systems but as logical groups of capabilities that manage data and support business functions. Thus, the applications and their capabilities should be defined without reference to particular technologies. This is because the applications should be stable, whereas the technology used to implement them may not be.

7.7 Exercises

Exercise 7-1
Identify five sources of information within your organization that could be used to draw up a Baseline Application Architecture Description.

Exercise 7-2
Which of the Phase C: Application Architecture catalogs, matrices, and diagrams would be most suitable for addressing the following concerns:
- Identifying which business functions use which applications within the enterprise
- Identifying all applications in the enterprise
- Identifying where the users of applications are located

Exercise 7-3
Which of the Phase C: Application Architecture catalogs, matrices, and diagrams would be most suitable for addressing the following stakeholders:
- External suppliers who need to exchange information

7.8 Recommended Reading

The following are recommended sources of further information for this chapter:

- The TOGAF Standard, Version 9.2 Part II, Phase C: Information Systems Architectures – Application Architecture
- The TOGAF Standard, Version 9.2 Part IV, Architecture Deliverables
- Sample Catalogs, Matrices, and Diagrams presentation: www.togaf.info/sg03

Chapter 8
Phase D: Technology Architecture

8.1 Key Learning Points

This chapter describes Phase D: Technology Architecture of the TOGAF Architecture Development Method (ADM).

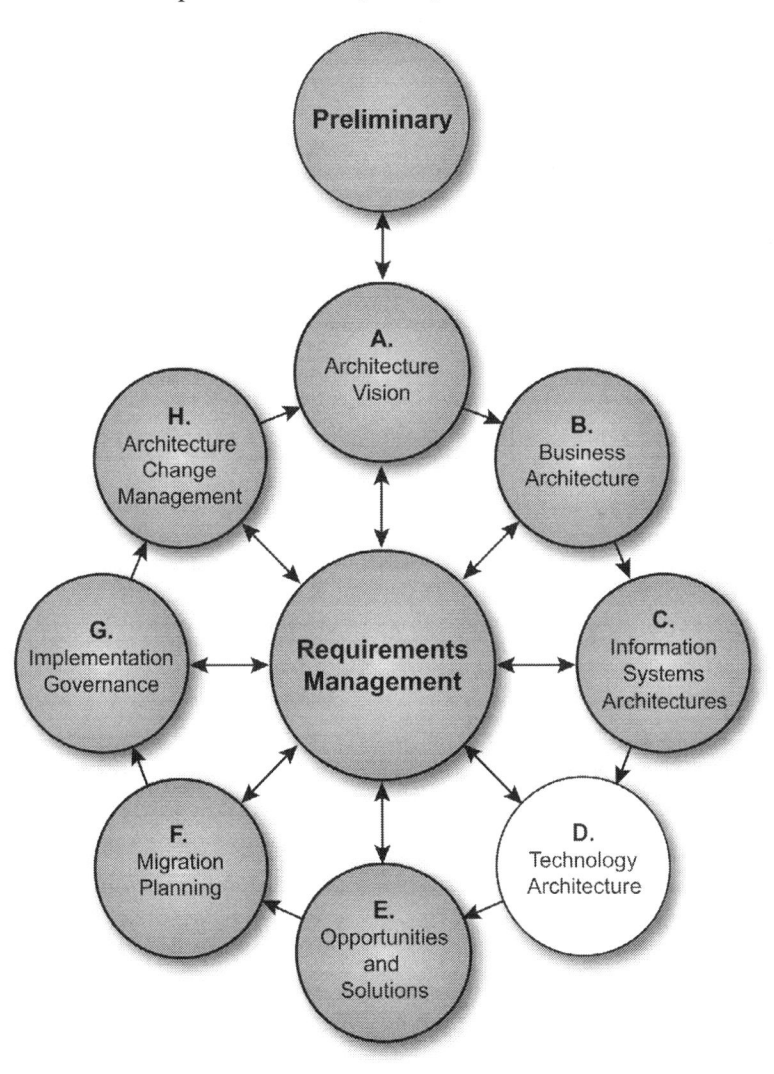

Figure 9: Phase D: Technology Architecture

> **Key Points Explained**
>
> Upon completion of this chapter you should be able to:
> 1. Understand the inputs to the phase, and explain Technology Principles
> 2. Understand the steps, and be able to explain:
>   - How a taxonomy of technology services and technology components can be used when developing a Technology Architecture
>   - The role of Architecture Building Blocks (ABBs)
> 3. Understand the outputs and be able to explain the following key elements:
>   - Technology Architecture components of the Architecture Definition Document
>   - Technology Architecture components of the Architecture Requirements Specification

8.2 Objectives

The objectives of Phase D: Technology Architecture are to:
- Develop the Target Technology Architecture that enables the Architecture Vision, target business, data, and application building blocks to be delivered through technology components and technology services, in a way that addresses the Statement of Architecture Work and stakeholder concerns
- Identify candidate Architecture Roadmap components based upon gaps between the Baseline and Target Technology Architectures

8.3 Inputs

(Syllabus Reference: Unit 14, Learning Outcome 1: You should understand the inputs to the phase.)

The inputs to this phase are:
- Request for Architecture Work
- Capability Assessment
- Communications Plan
- Organizational Model for Enterprise Architecture
- Tailored Architecture Framework
- Technology principles, if existing
- Statement of Architecture Work
- Architecture Vision

- Architecture Repository
- Draft Architecture Definition Document:
    - Baseline Business Architecture (detailed)
    - Target Business Architecture (detailed)
    - Baseline Data Architecture (detailed)
    - Target Data Architecture (detailed)
    - Baseline Application Architecture (detailed)
    - Target Application Architecture (detailed)
    - Baseline Technology Architecture (high-level)
    - Target Technology Architecture (high-level)
- Draft Architecture Requirements Specification:
    - Gap analysis results
    - Relevant technical requirements
- Business, Data, and Application Architecture components of an Architecture Roadmap

8.3.1 Technology Principles

(Syllabus Reference: Unit 14, Learning Outcome 1.1: You should be able to explain the following key element: Technology Principles.)

Technology principles form part of the overarching set of Architecture Principles, initially developed in the Preliminary Phase. Example technology principles drawn from Part III, Architecture Principles are summarized in Table 9.

Table 9: Example Technology Principles

Principle	Summary
Requirements-based Change	Changes to applications and technology are made only in response to business needs.
Responsive Change Management	Changes to the enterprise information environment are implemented in a timely manner.
Control Technical Diversity	Technological diversity is controlled to minimize the non-trivial cost of maintaining expertise in and connectivity between multiple processing environments.
Interoperability	Software and hardware should conform to defined standards that promote interoperability for data, applications, and technology.

8.4 Steps

(Syllabus Reference: Unit 14, Learning Outcome 2: You should understand the steps in the phase.)

Phase D consists of the following steps:
1. Select reference models, viewpoints, and tools
2. Develop Baseline Technology Architecture Description
3. Develop Target Technology Architecture Description
4. Perform gap analysis
5. Define candidate roadmap components
6. Resolve impacts across the Architecture Landscape
7. Conduct formal stakeholder review
8. Finalize the Technology Architecture
9. Create Architecture Definition Document

> The order of the steps should be adapted to the situation. In particular, you should determine whether it is appropriate to do the Baseline Technology Architecture or the Target Technology Architecture development first.

The steps are described in more detail in the following sections.

8.4.1 Select Reference Models, Viewpoints, and Tools

Review and validate the set of technology principles. Select relevant Technology Architecture resources (reference models, patterns, etc.) from the Architecture Repository on the basis of the business drivers, stakeholders, and their concerns. Select relevant Technology Architecture viewpoints that will enable the architect to demonstrate how the stakeholder concerns are being addressed in the Technology Architecture. Identify appropriate tools and techniques to be used for the capture, modeling, and analysis, in association with the selected viewpoints.

8.4.1.1 Determine the Overall Modeling Process

For each viewpoint, select the models needed to support the specific view required, using the selected tool or method. Ensure that all stakeholder concerns have been addressed. If they are not, create new models to address them, or augment existing models.

8.4.1.2 Identify Required Catalogs, Matrices, and Diagrams

Catalogs are inventories of the core assets of the business. They are hierarchical in nature and capture the decomposition of a metamodel entity and also decompositions across related model entities (e.g., platform service to logical technology component to physical technology component). The Technology Architecture should create technology catalogs as follows:

- Based on existing technology catalogs and the analysis of applications carried out in the Application Architecture phase, collect a list of products in use
- If the requirements identified in the Application Architecture are not met by existing products, extend the product list by examining products that provide the required functionality and meet the required standards
- Classify products against the selected taxonomy if appropriate, extending the model as necessary to fit the classification of technology products in use
- If technology standards are currently in place, apply these to the technology component catalog to gain a baseline view of compliance with technology standards

Diagrams present the Technology Architecture from a set of different perspectives (viewpoints) according to the requirements of the stakeholders. This activity provides a link between platform requirements and hosting requirements, as a single application may need to be physically located in several environments to support local access, development lifecycles, and hosting requirements.

For major baseline applications or application platforms, produce a stack diagram showing how hardware, operating system, software infrastructure, and packaged applications combine. If appropriate, extend the Application Architecture diagrams of software distribution to show how applications map onto the technology platform. For each environment produce a logical diagram of hardware and software infrastructure showing the contents of the environment and logical communications between components. Where available, collect capacity information on the deployed infrastructure. For each environment, produce a physical diagram of the communications infrastructure, such as routers, switches, firewalls, and network links. Where available, collect capacity information on the communications infrastructure.

The TOGAF standard recommends that the catalogs, matrices, and diagrams shown in Table 10 be considered in Phase D and provides guidance on their structure in Part IV, Content Metamodel.

Table 10: Phase D: Technology Architecture Catalogs, Matrices, and Diagrams

Catalogs	Matrices	Diagrams
Technology Standards catalog Technology Portfolio catalog	Application/ Technology matrix	Environments and Locations diagram Platform Decomposition diagram Processing diagram Networked Computing/Hardware diagram Communications Engineering diagram

8.4.1.3 Identify Types of Requirements to be Collected

Once the Technology Architecture catalogs, matrices, and diagrams have been developed, modeling should be completed by formalizing the business requirements for the Target Architecture. The architect should identify types of requirements to be met by the architecture. These requirements may relate to the technology domain, or may provide detailed guidance to be reflected during design and implementation.

8.4.1.4 Select Services

The services portfolios are combinations of basic services from the service categories in the defined taxonomy that do not conflict. The combinations of services are again tested to ensure support for the applications. This is a prerequisite to the later step of fully defining the architecture.

For each building block, build up a service description portfolio as a set of non-conflicting services. The set of services should be checked to ensure that the functionality provided meets application requirements.

8.4.2 Develop Baseline Technology Architecture Description

Develop a Baseline Description of the existing Technology Architecture to support the Target Technology Architecture. The scope and level of detail to be defined will depend on the extent to which existing technology components are likely to be carried over into the Target Technology Architecture, and on whether architectural descriptions exist. Identify the relevant Technology Architecture building blocks, drawing on any artifacts held in the Architecture Repository. If nothing exists within the Architecture Repository, define each application in line with the Technology Portfolio catalog; see Part IV, Content Metamodel.

(Syllabus Reference: Unit 14, Learning Outcome 2.1: You should be able to explain how a taxonomy of technology services and technology components can be used when developing a Technology Architecture.)

Begin by converting the description of the existing environment into the terms of the organization's Foundation Architecture (e.g., the TOGAF Technical Reference Model). This will allow the team developing the architecture to gain experience and understanding of the taxonomy. The team may be able to take advantage of a previous architectural definition, but it is assumed that some adaptation may be required to match the architectural definition techniques described as part of this process. Another important task is to set down a list of key questions which can be used later in the development process to measure the effectiveness of the new architecture.

Where new architecture models need to be developed to satisfy stakeholder concerns, use the models identified within Step 1 as a guideline for creating new architecture content to describe the Baseline Architecture.

8.4.3 Develop Target Technology Architecture Description

Develop a Target Description for the Technology Architecture to the extent necessary to support the Architecture Vision, Target Business Architecture, and Target Information Systems Architecture. The scope and level of detail to be defined will depend on the relevance of the technology elements to the Target Architecture, and on whether architectural descriptions exist. As far as possible, identify the relevant Technology Architecture building blocks from the Architecture Repository.

(Syllabus Reference: Unit 14, Learning Outcome 2.2: You should be able to explain the role of ABBs when developing a Technology Architecture.)

A key process in the creation of a broad architectural model of the target system is the conceptualization of building blocks. Architecture Building Blocks (ABBs) describe the required functionality and how it may be implemented without the detail introduced by configuration or detailed design. The method of defining building blocks, along with some general guidelines for their use in creating an architectural model, is described in Part IV, Building Blocks and the ADM.

Where new architecture models need to be developed to satisfy stakeholder concerns, use the models identified within Step 1 as a guideline for creating new architecture content to describe the Target Architecture.

8.4.4 Perform Gap Analysis

Verify the architecture models for internal consistency and accuracy. Document any changes to the viewpoints represented in the selected models from the Architecture Repository. Test architecture models for completeness against requirements. Identify gaps between the baseline and target using gap analysis.

8.4.5 Define Candidate Roadmap Components

Following creation of a Baseline Architecture, Target Architecture, and gap analysis, a Technology Architecture Roadmap is required to prioritize activities over the coming phases. This initial Technology Architecture Roadmap will be used as raw material to support more detailed definition of a consolidated, cross-discipline roadmap within Phase E: Opportunities & Solutions.

8.4.6 Resolve Impacts Across the Architecture Landscape

Once the Technology Architecture is finalized, it is necessary to understand any wider impacts or implications. At this stage, other architecture artifacts in the Architecture Landscape should be examined to determine the following:
- Does this Technology Architecture impact any pre-existing architectures?
- Have recent changes been made that impact the Technology Architecture?
- Are there any opportunities to re-use work from this Technology Architecture in other areas of the organization?
- Does this Technology Architecture impact other projects (planned or those in progress)?
- Will this Technology Architecture be impacted by other projects (planned or those in progress)?

8.4.7 Conduct Formal Stakeholder Review

Check the original motivation for the architecture project and the Statement of Architecture Work against the proposed Technology Architecture, asking if it is fit for the purpose of supporting subsequent work in the other architecture domains. Refine the proposed Technology Architecture only if necessary.

8.4.8 Finalize the Technology Architecture

Select standards for each of the building blocks, re-using as much as possible from the reference models selected from the Architecture Repository. Fully document each building block, then conduct a final cross-check of the overall architecture against business goals; document rationale for building block decisions in the architecture document. Document the final requirements traceability report. Document the final mapping of the architecture within the Architecture Repository. From the selected building blocks, identify those that might be re-used (working practices, roles, business relationships, job descriptions, etc.), and publish them in the Architecture Repository. Finalize all the work products.

8.4.9 Create Architecture Definition Document

Document the rationale for building block decisions in the Architecture Definition Document. Prepare the Technology Architecture sections of the Architecture Definition Document (see Section 8.5.1). Send the document for review by relevant stakeholders, and incorporate any feedback.

8.5 Outputs

(Syllabus Reference: Unit 14, Learning Outcome 3: You should understand the outputs of this phase.)

The outputs of this phase are:
- Statement of Architecture Work, updated if necessary
- Validated technology principles or new technology principles (if generated here)
- Draft Architecture Definition Document (see Section 4.5.1), containing content updates (see Section 8.5.1)
- Draft Architecture Requirements Specification (see Section 4.5.2), including content updates (see Section 8.5.2)
- Technology Architecture components of an Architecture Roadmap

The outputs may also include some or all of the catalogs, matrices, and diagrams listed in Table 10.

8.5.1 Components of the Architecture Definition Document

(Syllabus Reference: Unit 14, Learning Outcome 3.1: You should be able to explain the following key element: Technology Architecture Components of the Architecture Definition Document.)

The topics that should be addressed in the Architecture Definition Document related to Technology Architecture are as follows:
- Baseline Technology Architecture, if appropriate
- Target Technology Architecture, including:
  - Technology components and their relationships to information systems
  - Technology platforms and their decomposition, showing the combinations of technology required to realize a particular technology "stack"
  - Environments and locations with a grouping of the required technology into computing environments (e.g., development, production)
  - Expected processing load and distribution of load across technology components
  - Physical (network) communications
  - Hardware and network specifications
- Views corresponding to the selected viewpoints addressing key stakeholder concerns

8.5.2 Components of the Architecture Requirements Specification

(Syllabus Reference: Unit 14, Learning Outcome 3.2: You should be able to explain the following key element: Technology Architecture Components of the Architecture Requirements Specification.)

Technology Architecture requirements added to the Architecture Requirements Specification in Phase D include:
- Gap analysis results
- Updated technology requirements

8.6 Summary

This phase documents the Technology Architecture that will form the basis of subsequent implementation and migration work, in terms of hardware, software, and communications technology, their relationships to each other and the environment, and the principles governing its design and evolution.

8.7 Exercises

Exercise 8-1
Identify five sources of information within your organization that could be used to draw up a Baseline Technology Architecture Description.

Exercise 8-2
Which of the Phase D: Technology Architecture catalogs, matrices, and diagrams would be most suitable for addressing the following concerns:
- Identifying the types of all hardware platforms in the enterprise
- Identifying which business applications execute on which systems in the enterprise
- Identifying which locations host which applications

Exercise 8-3
Which of the Phase D: Technology Architecture catalogs, matrices, and diagrams would be most suitable for addressing the following stakeholders:
- Network Managers
- Project Managers

8.8 Recommended Reading

The following are recommended sources of further information for this chapter:
- The TOGAF Standard, Version 9.2 Part II, Phase D: Technology Architecture
- The TOGAF Standard, Version 9.2 Part IV, Architecture Deliverables
- Sample Catalogs, Matrices, and Diagrams presentation: www.togaf.info/sg03

Chapter 9

Phase E: Opportunities & Solutions

9.1 Key Learning Points

This chapter describes Phase E: Opportunities & Solutions of the TOGAF Architecture Development Method (ADM).

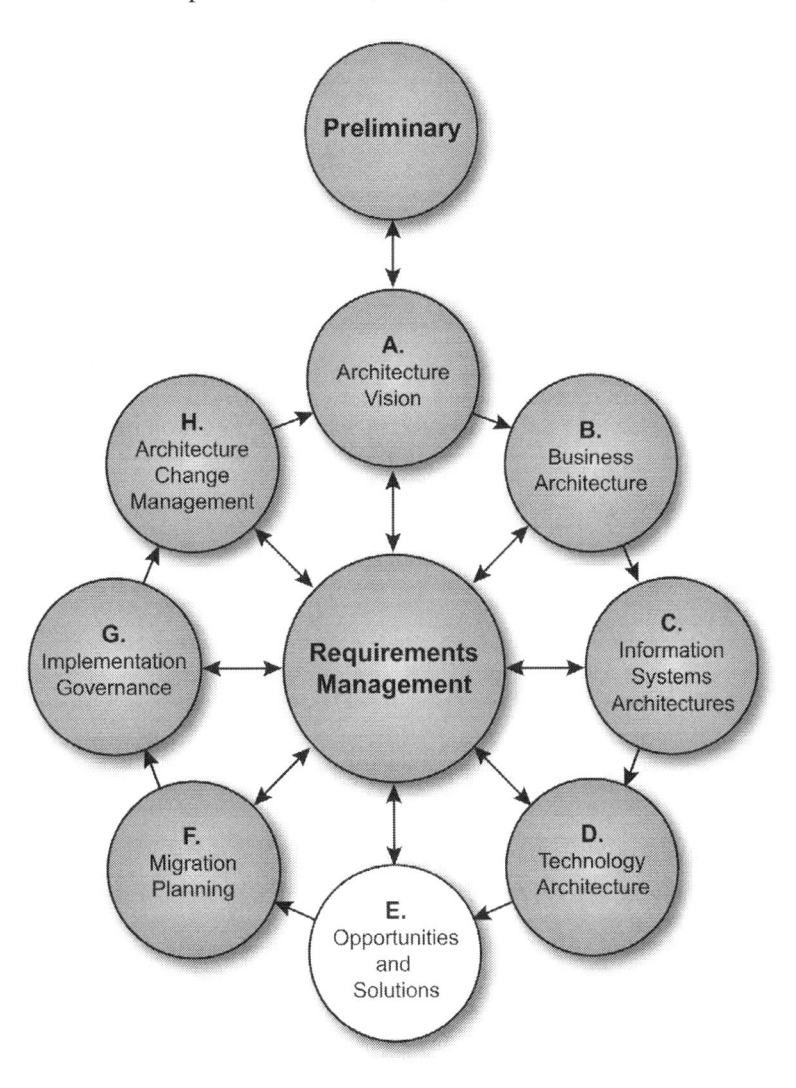

Figure 10:   Phase E: Opportunities & Solutions

> **Key Points Explained**
>
> Upon completion of this chapter you should be able to:
> 1. Describe the key stakeholders involved in this phase
> 2. Explain how migration planning techniques are used in this phase to review and consolidate the gap analysis results from earlier phases
> 3. Describe the steps to create the initial Implementation and Migration Strategy
> 4. Describe three basic approaches to implementation
> 5. Explain how to identify and group work packages
> 6. Explain how Transition Architectures are created and documented
>
> In addition you should be able to:
> - Describe how the Implementation Factor Assessment and Deduction matrix can be used to document factors impacting the Architecture Implementation and Migration Plan
> - Explain the purpose of the Consolidated Gaps, Solutions, and Dependencies matrix

9.2 Objectives

The objectives of Phase E: Opportunities and Solutions are to:

- Generate the initial complete version of the Architecture Roadmap, based upon the Gap Analysis and candidate Architecture Roadmap components from Phases B, C, and D
- Determine whether an incremental approach is required, and if so identify Transition Architectures that will deliver continuous business value
- Define the overall Solution Building Blocks (SBBs) to finalize the Target Architecture based on the Architecture Building Blocks (ABBs)

> **Stakeholders**
>
> *(Syllabus Reference: Unit 16, Learning Outcome 1: You should be able to describe the key stakeholders in this phase.)*
>
> Phase E is a collaborative effort with stakeholders required from both the business and IT sides. It should include both those that implement and those that operate the infrastructure. It should also include those responsible for strategic planning, especially for creating the Transition Architectures, if required.

9.3 Inputs

The inputs to this phase are:
- Product information
- Request for Architecture Work
- Capability Assessment
- Communications Plan
- Planning Methodologies
- Organizational Model for Enterprise Architecture
- Governance Models and Frameworks
- Tailored Architecture Framework
- Statement of Architecture Work
- Architecture Vision
- Architecture Repository
- Draft Architecture Definition Document
- Draft Architecture Requirements Specification
- Change Requests for existing programs and projects
- Candidate Architecture Roadmap components from Phases B, C, and D

9.4 Steps

Phase E consists of the following steps:
1. Determine/confirm key corporate change attributes
2. Determine business constraints for implementation
3. Review and consolidate gap analysis results from Phases B to D
4. Review consolidated requirements across related business functions
5. Consolidate and reconcile interoperability requirements
6. Refine and validate dependencies
7. Confirm readiness and risk for business transformation
8. Formulate Implementation and Migration Strategy
9. Identify and group major work packages
10. Identify Transition Architectures
11. Create the Architecture Roadmap & Implementation and Migration Plan

The steps are described in more detail in the following sections.

9.4.1 Determine/Confirm Key Corporate Change Attributes

This step determines how the Enterprise Architecture can be best implemented to take advantage of the organization's business culture. This should include the creation of an Implementation Factor Assessment and

Deduction matrix to serve as a repository for architecture implementation and migration decisions. The step also includes assessments of the transition capabilities of the organizations involved (including culture and abilities), and assessments of the enterprise (including culture and skill sets). The resulting factors from the assessments should be documented in the Implementation Factor Assessment and Deduction matrix. For organizations where Enterprise Architecture is well established, this step can be simple, but the matrix has to be established so that it can be used as an archive and record of decisions taken.

9.4.1.1 Implementation Factor Assessment and Deduction Matrix

(Syllabus Reference: Unit 15, Learning Outcome 1: You should be able to describe how the Implementation Factor Assessment and Deduction matrix can be used to document factors impacting the Architecture Implementation and Migration Plan.)

The Implementation Factor Assessment and Deduction matrix documents the factors that impact the Implementation and Migration Plan. The matrix should include a list of the factors, their descriptions with rationale, and the deductions (conclusions) that indicate the actions or constraints that have to be taken into consideration when formulating the plan. Production and use of this artifact can be considered as a Risk Management activity. An example matrix is shown in Table 11.

Table 11: Example Implementation Factor Assessment and Deduction Matrix

Implementation Factor Assessment and Deduction Matrix		
Factor	**Description**	**Deduction**
<Name of the Factor>	<Description of the Factor>	<Impact on the Migration Plan>
Change in Technology	Replace the message centers with an email service, saving 700 personnel	Need for personnel training, re-assignment. The switch to email has major personnel savings and should be given priority.
Consolidation of Services	...	...
Introduction of New Customer Service	...	...

9.4.2 Determine Business Constraints for Implementation

Identify any business drivers that would constrain the sequence of implementation. This should include a review of the business and strategic plans, at both a corporate and line-of-business level, and a review of the Enterprise Architecture Maturity Assessment.

9.4.3 Review and Consolidate Gap Analysis Results from Phases B to D

(Syllabus Reference: Unit 16, Learning Outcome 2: You should be able to explain how migration planning techniques are used in this phase to review and consolidate the Gap Analysis results from earlier phases.)

Consolidate and integrate the gap analysis results from the Business, Information Systems, and Technology Architectures (created in Phases B to D) and assess their implications with respect to potential solutions and inter-dependencies. This should be done by creating a Consolidated Gaps, Solutions, and Dependencies matrix, as shown in Section 9.4.3.1, which will enable the identification of Solution Building Blocks (SBBs) that could potentially address one or more gaps and their associated Architecture Building Blocks (ABBs).

Review the Phase B, C, and D gap analysis results and consolidate them in a single list. The gaps should be consolidated along with potential solutions to the gaps and dependencies. A recommended technique for determining the dependencies is to use sets of views such as the Business Interaction matrix, the Data Entity/Business Function matrix, and the Application/Function matrix to completely relate elements from different architectural domains.

Rationalize the Consolidated Gaps, Solutions, and Dependencies matrix. Once all of the gaps have been documented, re-organize the gap list and place similar items together. When grouping the gaps, refer to the Implementation Factor Assessment and Deduction matrix and review the implementation factors. Any additional factors should be added to the Implementation Factor Assessment and Deduction matrix.

9.4.3.1 Consolidated Gaps, Solutions, and Dependencies Matrix

(Syllabus Reference: Unit 15, Learning Outcome 2: You should be able to explain the purpose of the Consolidated Gaps, Solutions, and Dependencies matrix.)

The technique of creating a Consolidated Gaps, Solutions, and Dependencies matrix allows the architect to group the gaps identified in the domain architecture gap analysis results and assess potential solutions and dependencies to one or more gaps. An example is shown in Table 12. This matrix can be used as a planning tool when creating work packages. The identified dependencies drive the creation of projects and migration planning in Phases E and F.

Table 12: Consolidated Gaps, Solutions, and Dependencies Matrix

Consolidated Gaps, Solutions, and Dependencies Matrix				
#	**Architecture**	**Gap**	**Potential Solutions**	**Dependencies**
1	Business	New Order Processing Process	Use COTS software tool process Implement custom solution	Drives Application #2
2	Application	New Order Processing Application	COTS software tool Acme Develop in-house	
3	Data	Consolidated Customer Information Base	Use COTS customer base Develop customer data mart	

9.4.4 Review Consolidated Requirements Across Related Business Functions

Assess the requirements, gaps, solutions, and factors to identify a minimal set of requirements whose integration into work packages would lead to a more efficient and effective implementation of the Target Architecture across the business functions that are participating in the architecture. This functional perspective leads to the satisfaction of multiple requirements through the provision of shared solutions and services. The implications of this consolidation of requirements with respect to architectural components can be significant with respect to the provision of resources. For example, several requirements raised by several lines of business can be resolved through the provision of a shared set of Business Services and Information System Services within a work package or project.

9.4.5 Consolidate and Reconcile Interoperability Requirements

This step consolidates the interoperability requirements identified in previous phases. The Architecture Vision and Target Architectures, as well as the Implementation Factor Assessment and Deduction matrix and Consolidated Gaps, Solutions, and Dependencies matrix, should be consolidated and reviewed to identify any constraints on interoperability required by the potential set of solutions. A key outcome is to minimize interoperability conflicts. Re-used Solution Building Blocks, Commercial Off-The-Shelf (COTS) products, and third-party service providers typically impose interoperability requirements that conflict. Any such conflicts must be addressed in the architecture.

> **Interoperability Requirements and Solutions**
>
> *(Syllabus Reference: Unit 8, Learning Outcome 1: You should be able to explain how to reconcile Interoperability Requirements with potential solutions.)*
>
> The most significant issue to be addressed is business interoperability. Most SBBs or COTS will have their own embedded business processes. Changing the embedded business processes will often require so much work, that the advantages of re-using solutions will be lost with updates being costly and possibly requiring a complete rework. Furthermore, there may be a workflow aspect between multiple systems that has to be taken into account. The acquisition of COTS software has to be seen as a business decision that may require rework of the domain architectures. The Enterprise Architect will have to ensure that any change to the business interoperability requirements is signed off by the business architects and architecture sponsors in a revised Statement of Architecture Work.

9.4.6 Refine and Validate Dependencies

Refine the initial dependencies, ensuring that any constraints on the Implementation and Migration Plans are identified. There are several key dependencies that should be taken into account, such as dependencies on existing implementations of Business Services and Information Systems Services or changes to them. Dependencies should be used for determining the sequence of implementation and identifying the coordination required. A study of the dependencies should group activities together, creating a basis for projects to be established. Examine the relevant projects and see whether logical increments of deliverables can be identified. The dependencies will also help to identify when the identified increment can be delivered. Once finished, these dependencies should be documented as part of the Architecture Roadmap and any necessary Transition Architectures. Adding dependencies serves as the basis for most migration planning.

> **Capability-Based Planning and the ADM**
>
> Specific capabilities targeted for completion will be the focus of the Architecture Definition (Phases B, C, and D) and, based upon the identified work packages Phase E, projects will be conceived. The capability increments will be the drivers for the Transition Architectures (Phase E) that will structure the project increments. The actual delivery will be coordinated through the Implementation and Migration Plans (Phase F).
>
> [Source: The TOGAF Standard, Version 9.2 Part III, Capability-Based Planning]

9.4.7 Confirm Readiness and Risk for Business Transformation

The architects should review the findings of the Business Transformation Readiness Assessment previously conducted in Phase A and determine their impact on the Architecture Roadmap and the Implementation and Migration Strategy. It is important to identify, classify, and mitigate risks associated with the transformation effort. Risks should be documented in the Consolidated Gaps, Solutions, and Dependencies matrix.

9.4.8 Formulate Implementation and Migration Strategy

(Syllabus Reference: Unit 16, Learning Outcome 3: You should be able to describe the steps to create the Implementation and Migration Strategy.)

(Syllabus Reference: Unit 16, Learning Outcome 4: You should be able to describe three basic approaches to implementation.)

Create an overall Implementation and Migration Strategy that will guide the implementation of the Target Architecture and structure any Transition Architectures. The first activity is to determine an overall strategic approach to implementing the solutions and/or exploiting opportunities. There are three basic approaches as follows:
- Greenfield: a completely new implementation
- Revolutionary: a radical change (i.e., switch on, switch off)

- Evolutionary: a strategy of convergence, such as parallel running or a phased approach to introduce new capabilities

Next, determine an approach for the overall strategic direction that will address and mitigate the risks identified in the Consolidated Gaps, Solutions, and Dependencies matrix. The most common implementation methodologies are:
- Quick win (snapshots)
- Achievable targets
- Value chain method (e.g., NASCIO[6] methodology)

These approaches and the identified dependencies should become the basis for the creation of the work packages. This activity terminates with agreement on the Implementation and Migration Strategy for the enterprise.

9.4.9 Identify and Group Major Work Packages

(Syllabus Reference: Unit 16, Learning Outcome 5: You should be able to explain how to identify and group work packages.)

Key stakeholders, planners, and the Enterprise Architect(s) should assess the missing business capabilities identified in the Architecture Vision and Target Architecture.

Using the Consolidated Gaps, Solutions, and Dependencies matrix together with the Implementation Factor Assessment and Deduction matrix, logically group the various activities into work packages (where a work package is an inter-dependent set of activities and deliverables that deliver a discrete enterprise outcome).

Fill in the "Solution" column in the Consolidated Gaps, Solutions, and Dependencies matrix that recommends the proposed solution mechanisms. Indicate for every gap/activity whether the solution should be oriented towards a new development or based upon an existing product and/or use a solution that can be purchased. An existing system may resolve the requirement with minor enhancements. For new development this is a good time to determine whether the work should be conducted in-house or through a contract.

---

[6] NASCIO is the National Association of State Chief Information Officers; see www.nascio.org.

Classify every current system as:
- Mainstream: part of the future information system
- Contain: expected to be replaced or modified in the planning horizon (next three years)
- Replace: to be replaced in the planning horizon

Supporting top-level work packages should then in turn be decomposed into increments to deliver the capability increments. Analyze and refine these work packages, or increments, with respect to their business transformation issues and the strategic implementation approach. Finally, group the work packages into portfolios and then projects within the portfolios taking into consideration the dependencies and the strategic implementation approach.

9.4.10 Identify Transition Architectures
(Syllabus Reference: Unit 16, Learning Outcome 6: You should be able to explain how Transition Architectures are created and documented.)

Where the scope of change to implement the Target Architecture (see Section 10.5.2) requires an incremental approach, then one or more Transition Architectures may be necessary. These provide an ability to identify clear targets along the roadmap to realizing the Target Architecture. The Transition Architectures should provide measurable business value. The time-span between successive Transition Architectures does not have to be of uniform duration.

Development of Transition Architectures must be based upon the preferred implementation approach, the Consolidated Gaps, Solutions, and Dependencies matrix, the listing of projects and portfolios, as well as the enterprise's capacity for creating and absorbing change.

Determine where the difficult activities are, and unless there are compelling reasons, implement them after other activities that most easily deliver missing capability.

9.4.11 Create the Architecture Roadmap & Implementation and Migration Plan
Consolidate the work packages and Transition Architectures into the Architecture Roadmap, Version 0.1, which describes a timeline of the progression from the Baseline Architecture to the Target Architecture. The

timeline informs the Implementation and Migration Plan. The Architecture Roadmap frames the migration planning in Phase F. Identified Transition Architectures and work packages should have a clear set of outcomes. The Architecture Roadmap must demonstrate how the selection and timeline of Transition Architectures and work packages realizes the Target Architecture.

The detail of the Architecture Roadmap, Version 0.1 should be expressed at a similar level of detail to the Architecture Definition Document developed in Phases B, C, and D. Where significant additional detail is required before implementation the architecture is likely transitioning to a different level. See Part III of the TOGAF standard for techniques to manage iteration and different levels of detail.

The Implementation and Migration Plan must demonstrate the activity necessary to realize the Architecture Roadmap. The Implementation and Migration Plan forms the basis of the migration planning in Phase F. The detail of the Implementation and Migration Plan, Version 0.1 must be aligned to the detail of the Architecture Roadmap and be sufficient to identify the necessary projects and resource requirements to realize the roadmap.

When creating the Implementation and Migration Plan there are many approaches to consider, such as a data-driven sequence, where application systems that create data are implemented first, then applications that process the data. A clear understanding of the dependencies and lifecycle of in-place SBBs is required for an effective Implementation and Migration Plan.

Finally, update the Architecture Vision, Architecture Definition Document, and Architecture Requirements Specification with any additional relevant outcomes from this phase.

9.5 Outputs

The outputs of this phase are:
- Statement of Architecture Work, updated if necessary
- Architecture Vision, updated if necessary
- Draft Architecture Definition Document, updated if necessary, including:
  - Transition Architectures (see Section 10.5.2), if any

- Draft Architecture Requirements Specification, including:
  - Consolidated Gaps, Solutions, and Dependencies Assessment
- Capability Assessment (see Section 3.5.2), including:
  - Business Capability Assessment
  - IT Capability Assessment
- Architecture Roadmap, including:
  - Work package portfolio
  - Identification of Transition Architectures, if any
  - Implementation recommendations
- Implementation and Migration Plan (outline) (see Section 10.5.1)

The outputs may also include the following diagrams: a Project Context diagram and a Benefits diagram.

9.6 Summary

Phase E is the first phase which is directly concerned with implementation. It identifies the parameters of change, the work packages, and the necessary projects. The outputs include an outline Implementation and Migration Plan, the Architecture Roadmap, and Transition Architectures, if any.

9.7 Exercises

Exercise 9-1

Describe three or more migration options for phasing in a new business system while maintaining business continuity. You should describe the impact on services, users, and platforms in each option.

9.8 Recommended Reading

The following are recommended sources of further information for this chapter:
- The TOGAF Standard, Version 9.2 Part II, Phase E: Opportunities & Solutions
- The TOGAF Standard, Version 9.2 Part III, Migration Planning Techniques
- The TOGAF Standard, Version 9.2 Part III, Interoperability Requirements
- The TOGAF Standard, Version 9.2 Part IV, Architecture Deliverables

Chapter 10
Phase F: Migration Planning

10.1 Key Learning Points

This chapter describes Phase F: Migration Planning of the TOGAF Architecture Development Method (ADM).

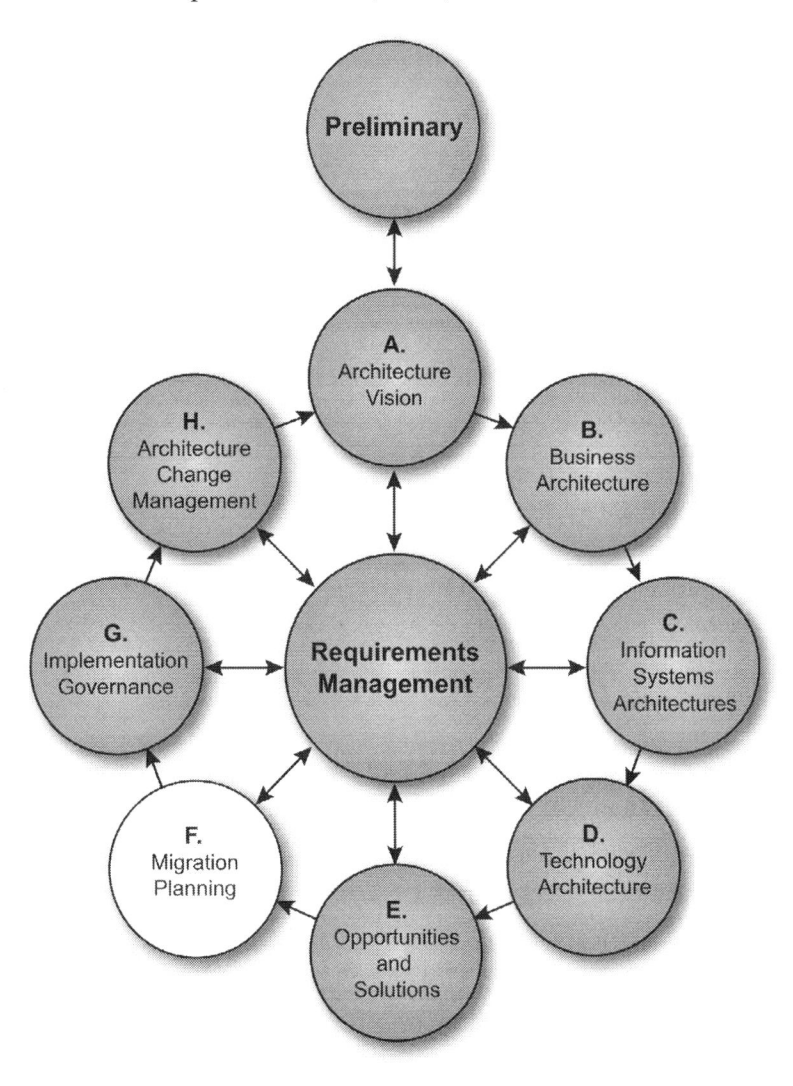

Figure 11: Phase F: Migration Planning

> **Key Points Explained**
>
> Upon completion of this chapter you should be able to:
> 1. Describe the management frameworks that have to be coordinated within this phase
> 2. Explain how business value is assigned to each work package
> 3. Describe the steps to prioritize the migration projects
> 4. Describe the steps to confirm the Architecture Roadmap
> 5. Explain key outputs of this phase, specifically:
>   - mplementation and Migration Plan
>   - Transition Architecture
>   - Architecture Definition Document
>
> In addition you should be able to:
> - Explain how the Business Value Assessment technique can be used in architecture development
> - Explain how the Transition Architecture State Evolution Table can be used in conjunction with a defined taxonomy such as the TOGAF TRM

10.2 Objectives

The objectives of Phase F: Migration Planning are to:
- Finalize the Architecture Roadmap and the supporting Implementation and Migration Plan
- Ensure that the Implementation and Migration Plan is coordinated with the enterprise's approach to managing and implementing change in the enterprise's overall change portfolio
- Ensure that the business value and cost of work packages and Transition Architectures is understood by key stakeholders

10.3 Inputs

The inputs to this phase are:
- Request for Architecture Work
- Communications Plan
- Organizational Model for Enterprise Architecture
- Governance Models and Frameworks
- Tailored Architecture Framework
- Statement of Architecture Work

- Architecture Vision
- Architecture Repository
- Draft Architecture Definition Document, including:
  - Transition Architectures, if any
- Draft Architecture Requirements Specification
- Change Requests for existing programs and projects
- Architecture Roadmap, including:
  - Identification of work packages
  - Identification of Transition Architectures
  - Implementation Factor Assessment and Deduction Matrix
- Capability Assessment
- Implementation and Migration Plan (outline)

10.4 Steps

Phase F consists of the following steps:

1. Confirm management framework interactions for the Implementation and Migration Plan
2. Assign a business value to each work package
3. Estimate resource requirements, project timings, and availability/delivery vehicle
4. Prioritize the migration projects through the conduct of a cost/benefit assessment and risk validation
5. Confirm Architecture Roadmap and update Architecture Definition Document
6. Complete the Implementation and Migration Plan
7. Complete the Architecture Development Cycle and document lessons learned

The steps are described in more detail in the following sections.

10.4.1 Confirm Management Framework Interactions for the Implementation and Migration Plan

(Syllabus Reference: Unit 17, Learning Outcome 1: You should be able to describe the management frameworks that have to be coordinated within this phase.)

This step is about coordinating the Implementation and Migration Plan with the management frameworks within the organization. There are typically four management frameworks that have to work closely together for the Implementation and Migration Plan to succeed:
- Business Planning that conceives, directs, and provides the resources for all of the activities required to achieve concrete business objectives/outcomes
- Enterprise Architecture that structures and gives context to all enterprise activities delivering concrete business outcomes primarily but not exclusively in the IT domain
- Portfolio/Project Management that co-ordinates, designs, and builds the business systems that deliver the concrete business outcomes
- Operations Management that integrates, operates, and maintains the deliverables that deliver the concrete business outcomes

The Implementation and Migration Plan will impact each one of these frameworks and consequently has to be reflected in them. In the course of this step, understand the frameworks within the organization and ensure that these plans are coordinated and inserted (in a summary format) within the plans of each one of these frameworks. The outcome of this step may well be that the Implementation and Migration Plan could be part of a different plan produced by another one of the frameworks with Enterprise Architecture participation.

10.4.2 Assign a Business Value to Each Work Package

(Syllabus Reference: Unit 17, Learning Outcome 2: You should be able to explain how business value is assigned to each work package.)

Establish and assign business values to each of the work packages. The intent is to first establish what constitutes business value within the organization, how value can be measured, and then apply this to each one of the projects and project increments.

If Capability-Based Planning has been used, then the business values associated with the capabilities and associated capability increments should be used to assign the business values for deliverables.

There are several issues to address in this activity:
- Performance Evaluation Criteria are used by portfolio and capability managers to approve and monitor the progress of the architecture transformation
- Return-on-Investment Criteria have to be detailed and signed off by the various executive stakeholders
- Business Value has to be defined as well as techniques, such as the value chain (e.g., NASCIO), which are to be used to illustrate the role in achieving tangible business outcomes

  Business value will be used by portfolio and capability managers to allocate resources and, in cases where there are cutbacks, business value in conjunction with return-on-investment can be used to determine whether an endeavor proceeds, is delayed, or is canceled.

- Critical Success Factors (CSFs) should be established to define success for a project and/or project increment; these will provide managers and implementers with a gauge as to what constitutes a successful implementation
- Measures of Effectiveness (MOE) are often performance criteria and many corporations include them in the CSFs; where they are treated discretely, it should be clear as to how these criteria are to be grouped
- Strategic Fit based upon the overall Enterprise Architecture (all tiers) will be the critical factor for allowing the approval of any new project or initiative and for determining the value of any deliverable

Use the work packages as a basis of identifying projects that will be in the Implementation and Migration Plan. The identified projects will be fully developed in other steps in Phase F. The projects, and project increments, may require adjustment of the Architecture Roadmap and Architecture Definition Document.

Risks should then be assigned to the projects and project increments by aggregating risks identified in the Consolidated Gaps, Solutions, and Dependencies Matrix (from Phase E).

Estimate the business value for each project using the Business Value Assessment Technique.

10.4.2.1 Business Value Assessment Technique

(Syllabus Reference: Unit 15, Learning Outcome 5: You should be able to explain how the Business Value Assessment Technique can be used in architecture development.)

A technique to assess business value is to draw up a matrix based on a value index dimension and a risk index dimension. An example is shown in Figure 12. The value index should include criteria such as compliance to principles, financial contribution, strategic alignment, and competitive position. The risk index should include criteria such as size and complexity, technology, organizational capacity, and impact of a failure. Each criterion should be assigned an individual weight. The index and its criteria and weighting should be developed and approved by senior management. It is important to establish the decision-making criteria before the options are known.

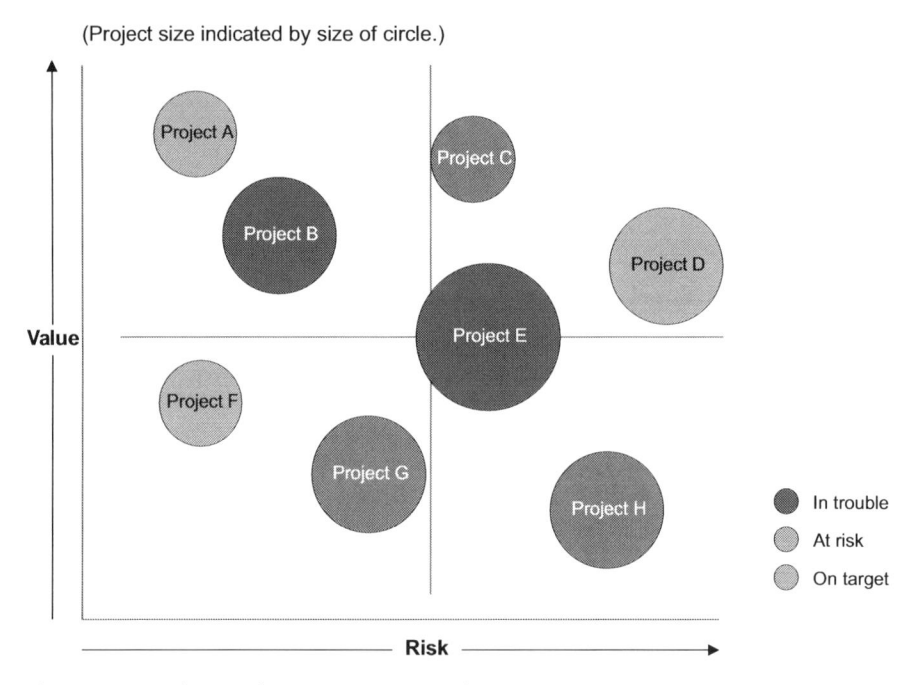

Figure 12: Business Value Assessment Matrix

10.4.3 Estimate Resource Requirements, Project Timings, and Availability/Delivery Vehicle

This step determines the required resources and times for each project and their increments and provides the initial cost estimates. The costs should be broken down into capital (to create the capability) and operations and maintenance (to run and sustain the capability). Opportunities should be identified where the costs associated with delivering new and/or better capability can be offset by decommissioning existing systems. Assign required resources to each activity and aggregate them at the project increment and project level.

10.4.4 Prioritize the Migration Projects through the Conduct of a Cost/Benefit Assessment and Risk Validation

(Syllabus Reference: Unit 17, Learning Outcome 3: You should be able to describe the steps to prioritize the migration projects.)

Prioritize the projects by ascertaining their business value against the cost of delivering them. The approach is to first determine, as clearly as possible, the net benefit of all of the SBBs delivered by the projects, and then verify that the risks have been effectively mitigated and factored in. Afterwards, the intent is to gain the requisite consensus to create a prioritized list of projects that will provide the basis for resource allocation.

It is important to discover all costs, and to ensure that decision-makers understand the net benefit over time.

Review the risks to ensure that the risks for the project deliverables have been mitigated as much as possible. The project list is then updated with risk-related comments.

Have the stakeholders agree upon a prioritization of the projects. Prioritization criteria will use elements identified in creation of the draft Architecture Roadmap in Phase E as well as those relating to individual stakeholders' agendas.

Formally review the risk assessment and revise it as necessary ensuring that there is a full understanding of the residual risk associated with the prioritization and the projected funding line.

10.4.5 Confirm Architecture Roadmap and Update Architecture Definition Document

(Syllabus Reference: Unit 17, Learning Outcome 4: You should be able to describe the steps to confirm the Architecture Roadmap.)

Update the Architecture Roadmap including any Transition Architectures. Review the work to date to assess what the time-spans between Transition Architectures should be, taking into consideration the increments in business value and capability and other factors, such as risk. Once the capability increments have been determined, consolidate the deliverables by project increment for each Transition Architecture. This will result in a revised Architecture Roadmap.

This is needed in order to co-ordinate the development of several concurrent instances of the various architectures. A Transition Architecture State Evolution Table (see Section 10.4.6.1) can be used to show the proposed state of the Domain Architectures at various levels of detail.

If the implementation approach has shifted as a result of confirming the implementation increments, update the Architecture Definition Document. This may include assigning project objectives and aligning projects and their deliverables with the Transition Architectures to create an Architecture Definition Increments Table.

10.4.5.1 Architecture Definition Increments Table

(Syllabus Reference: Unit 15, Learning Outcome 3: You should be able to describe the purpose of an Architecture Definition Increments Table.)

The technique of creating an Architecture Definition Increments Table allows the architect to plan a series of Transition Architectures outlining the status of the Enterprise Architecture at specified times. A table should be drawn up, as shown in Table 13, listing the projects and then assigning their incremental deliverables across the Transition Architectures.

Table 13: Example Architecture Definition Increments Table

Architecture Definition: Project Objectives by Increment				
	Stage 1: April 2019/2020	Stage 2: April 2020/2021	Stage 3: April 2021/2022	
Project	Transition Architecture 1: Preparation	Transition Architecture 2: Initial Operational Capability	Transition Architecture 3: Benefits	Comments
Enterprise e-Services Capability	Training and Business Process	e-Licensing Capability	e-Employment Benefits	
IT e-Forms	Design and Build			
IT e-Information Environment	Design and Build Information Environment	Client Common Data Web Content Design and Build	Enterprise Common Data Document Management Design and Build	
...	...	...	...	...

10.4.6 Complete the Implementation and Migration Plan

This step generates the completed Implementation and Migration Plan. Much of the detail for the plan has already been gathered and this step brings it all together using accepted planning and management techniques.

This should include integrating all of the projects, project increments, and activities as well as dependencies into a project plan. Any Transition Architectures will act as portfolio milestones.

All external dependencies should be captured and included, and the overall availability of resources assessed. The project plans may be included with the Implementation and Migration Plan.

10.4.6.1 Transition Architecture State Evolution Table
(Syllabus Reference: Unit 15, Learning Outcome 4: You should be able to explain how the Transition Architecture State Evolution Table can be used in conjunction with a defined taxonomy such as the TOGAF TRM.)

The technique of creating the Transition Architecture State Evolution Table allows the architect to show the proposed state of the architectures at various levels using the defined taxonomy (e.g., the TOGAF TRM). A table should be created listing the services from the taxonomy used in the enterprise, the Transition Architectures, and proposed transformations, as shown in Table 14.

All Solution Building Blocks (SBBs) should be described with respect to their delivery and impact on these services. They should also be marked to show the progression of the Enterprise Architecture. In the example, where target capability has been reached, this is shown as "new" or "retain"; where capability is transitioned to a new solution, this is marked as "transition"; and where a capability is to be replaced, this is marked as "replace".

Table 14: Example Transition Architecture State Evolution Table

Architectural State Using the Technical Reference Model				
Sub-Domain	Service	Transition Architecture 1	Transition Architecture 2	Transition Architecture 3
Infrastructure Applications	Information Exchange Services	Solution System A (replace)	Solution System B-1 (transition)	Solution System B-2 (new)
	Data Management Services	Solution System D (retain)	Solution System D (retain)	Solution System D (retain)
...	...			

10.4.7 Complete the Architecture Development Cycle and Document Lessons Learned

This step transitions governance from the development of the architecture to the realization of the architecture. If the maturity of the Architecture Capability warrants, an Implementation Governance Model may be produced (see Section 10.5.3). Lessons learned should also be documented and captured by the appropriate governance process in Phase H as inputs to managing the Architecture Capability.

The detail of the Architecture Roadmap and the Implementation and Migration Plan should be expressed at a similar level of detail to the Architecture Definition Document developed in Phases B, C, and D. Where significant additional detail is required by the next phase the architecture is likely transitioning to a different level. Depending upon the level of the Target Architecture and Implementation and Migration Plan it may be necessary to iterate another ADM cycle at a lower level of detail.

10.5 Outputs

(Syllabus Reference: Unit 17, Learning Outcome 5: You should be able to describe the key outputs of this phase.)

The outputs of this phase are:
- Implementation and Migration Plan (detailed)
- Finalized Architecture Definition Document, including:
    - Finalized Transition Architectures, if any
- Finalized Architecture Requirements Specification
- Finalized Architecture Roadmap
- Re-Usable Architecture Building Blocks (ABBs)
- Requests for Architecture Work for a new iteration of the ADM cycle (if any)
- Implementation Governance Model
- Change Requests for the Architecture Capability arising from lessons learned

10.5.1 Implementation and Migration Plan

(Syllabus Reference: Unit 16, Learning Outcome 5.1: You should be able to describe the Implementation and Migration Plan.)

The Implementation and Migration Plan is developed in Phases E and F, and provides a schedule of the projects for implementation of the Target Architecture. The Implementation and Migration Plan includes executable projects grouped into managed portfolios and programs. The Implementation and Migration Strategy identifying the approach to change is a key element of the Implementation and Migration Plan.

Typical contents are as follows:
- Implementation and Migration Strategy:
  - Strategic implementation direction
  - Implementation sequencing approach
- Project and portfolio breakdown of implementation:
  - Allocation of work packages to project and portfolio
  - Capabilities delivered by projects
  - Milestones and timing
  - Work breakdown structure

It may contain:
- Project charters:
  - Included work packages
  - Business value
  - Risk, issues, assumptions, dependencies
  - Resource requirements and costs
  - Benefits of migration, determined (including mapping to business requirements)
  - Estimated costs of migration options

10.5.2 Architecture Definition Document, including Transition Architecture

(Syllabus Reference: Unit 16, Learning Outcome 5.2: You should be able to describe the Architecture Definition Document, including Transition Architectures (if any).)

The Architecture Definition Document is finalized in this phase. For a detailed description see Section 4.5.1.

Where the scope of change to implement the Target Architecture requires an incremental approach, one or more Transition Architectures are defined within the Architecture Definition Document output from Phase E. A Transition Architecture shows the enterprise at an architecturally significant state between the Baseline and Target Architectures. Transition Architectures are used to describe transitional Target Architectures necessary for effective realization of the Target Architecture. These provide an ability to identify clear targets along the roadmap to realizing the Target Architecture.

The following contents are typical within a Transition Architecture:
- Transition Architecture:
    - Definition of transition states
    - Business Architecture for each transition state
    - Data Architecture for each transition state
    - Application Architecture for each transition state
    - Technology Architecture for each transition state

10.5.3 Implementation Governance Model

Once an architecture has been defined, it is necessary to plan how the Transition Architecture that implements the architecture will be governed through implementation. Within organizations that have established architecture functions, there is likely to be a governance framework already in place, but specific processes, organizations, roles, responsibilities, and measures may need to be defined on a project-by-project basis.

The Implementation Governance Model produced as an output of Phase F ensures that a project transitioning into implementation also smoothly transitions into appropriate Architecture Governance (for Phase G).

Typical contents of an Implementation Governance Model are:
- Governance processes
- Governance organization structure
- Governance roles and responsibilities
- Governance checkpoints and success/failure criteria

10.6 Summary

Phase F addresses migration planning; that is, how to move from the Baseline to the Target Architectures. It includes creating the finalized Architecture Definition Document, Architecture Roadmap, and the detailed Implementation and Migration Plan. After completion of this phase the preparation for implementation has been completed.

10.7 Exercises

Exercise 10-1

A project has completed Phase E with delivery of the outline Implementation and Migration Plan. Your role is to lead the Migration Planning phase. Describe your approach to creating the detailed Implementation and Migration Plan, including who you would involve, the steps, and what you would deliver.

10.8 Recommended Reading

The following are recommended sources of further information for this chapter:

- The TOGAF Standard, Version 9.2 Part II, Phase F: Migration Planning
- The TOGAF Standard, Version 9.2 Part III, Migration Planning Techniques
- The TOGAF Standard, Version 9.2 Part IV, Architecture Deliverables

Chapter 11
Phase G: Implementation Governance

11.1 Key Learning Points

This chapter describes Phase G: Implementation Governance of the TOGAF Architecture Development Method (ADM).

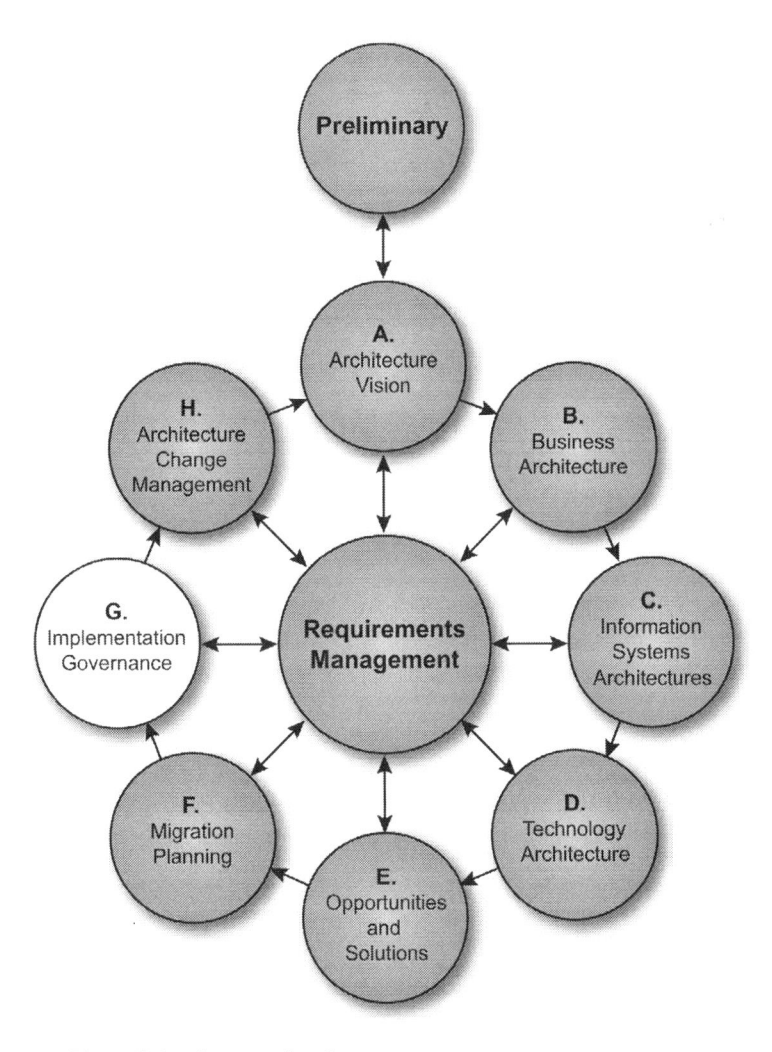

Figure 13: Phase G: Implementation Governance

> **Key Points Explained**
>
> Upon completion of this chapter you should be able to:
> 1. Understand the inputs to the phase
> 2. Understand the steps, and be able to describe the following:
>   - Explain how to tailor and conduct an Architecture Compliance Review
> 3. Understand the outputs, and be able to explain the following key elements:
>   - The contents of Architecture Contracts
>   - Their relationship to Architecture Governance
> 4. Demonstrate the role that risk monitoring plays in this phase

11.2 Objectives

The objectives of Phase G: Implementation Governance are to:
- Ensure conformance with the Target Architecture by implementation projects
- Perform appropriate Architecture Governance functions for the solution and any implementation-driven architecture Change Requests

> **Architecture Governance**
>
> The Architecture Contract produced in this phase features prominently in the area of Architecture Governance (see Chapter 21). It is often used as the means to driving change. In order to ensure that the Architecture Contract is effective and efficient, the following aspects of the governance framework should be introduced in this phase:
> - Simple process
> - People-centered authority
> - Strong communication
> - Timely responses and effective escalation process
> - Supporting organization structures

11.3 Inputs

(Syllabus Reference: Unit 18, Learning Outcome 1: You should understand the inputs to the phase.)

The inputs to this phase are:
- Request for Architecture Work
- Capability Assessment
- Organizational Model for Enterprise Architecture
- Tailored Architecture Framework
- Statement of Architecture Work
- Architecture Vision
- Architecture Repository
- Architecture Definition Document
- Architecture Requirements Specification
- Architecture Roadmap
- Implementation Governance Model
- Architecture Contract
- Request for Architecture Work identified in Phases E and F
- Implementation and Migration Plan

11.4 Steps

(Syllabus Reference: Unit 18, Learning Outcome 2: You should understand the steps for this phase.)

Phase G consists of the following steps:
- Confirm scope and priorities for deployment with development management
- Identify deployment resources and skills
- Guide development of solutions deployment
- Perform enterprise Architecture Compliance Reviews
- Implement business and IT operations
- Perform post-implementation review and close the implementation

The steps are described in more detail in the following sections.

11.4.1 Confirm Scope and Priorities for Deployment with Development Management

This step takes the migration planning outputs and produces recommendations for deployment. This includes identifying priorities for the development teams, identifying issues for the deployment together with recommendations, and identifying building blocks for replacement and update. A gap analysis should be performed between the Enterprise

Architecture and the solutions framework to identify specific Solution Building Blocks (SBBs). The solutions architects should consider whether some SBBs can be used across more than one project.

11.4.2 Identify Deployment Resources and Skills

The deployment resources will need to be educated in the overall Enterprise Architecture deliverables and expectations for the specific development and implementation projects. Considerations addressed in this step should include the identification of the system development methods required for the solutions development, ensuring that they include feedback on the designs to the architecture team.

11.4.3 Guide Development of Solutions Deployment

Project recommendations are created for each separate implementation and deployment project by documenting the scope of the individual project, the strategic requirements (from the architectural perspective), any Change Requests (such as support for a standard interface), rules for conformance, and timeline requirements from the roadmap.

The Architecture Contract (see Section 11.5.1) is documented and signatures are obtained from all developing organizations and the sponsoring organization. The Enterprise Continuum and Architecture Repository should then be populated with the solutions. The Architecture Contract is then used to guide the development of the business and IT operating models for the identified services. This guidance is based upon the business and IT operational requirements derived from the Enterprise Architecture by undertaking a gap analysis between the Solution Architecture and current operations in order to identify missing elements. This can then be used to develop an Implementation Plan.

11.4.4 Perform Enterprise Architecture Compliance Reviews

(Syllabus Reference: Unit 18, Learning Outcome 2.1: You should be able to explain how to tailor and conduct an Architecture Compliance Review.)

> **Prerequisite Knowledge: Architecture Compliance Review Process Steps**
> The TOGAF standard defines a 12-step process for conducting Compliance Reviews. This is omitted here as it is included in the TOGAF 9 Foundation Study Guide. [See Section 9.7.4 of the TOGAF 9 Foundation Study Guide]

Once an architecture has been defined, it is necessary to govern that architecture through implementation to ensure that the original Architecture Vision is realized and that any implementation lessons are fed back into the architecture process. Periodic compliance reviews of implementation projects in Phase G provide a mechanism to review project progress and ensure that the design and implementation are proceeding according to the strategic and architectural objectives.

11.4.4.1 Timing of Compliance Reviews

Compliance reviews should be held at appropriate project milestones or checkpoints in a project's lifecycle. Specific checkpoints should be included:
- Development of the architecture itself (ADM compliance)
- Implementation of the architecture(s) (Architecture Compliance)

Architecture project timings for assessments should include project initiation, initial design, major design changes, and any *ad hoc* assessments needed.

An Architecture Compliance Review is typically targeted at a point in time when the business requirements and the Enterprise Architecture are reasonably firm, and the project architecture is taking shape well before its completion. The aim is to hold the review as soon as practical, at a stage when there is still time to correct any major errors or shortcomings.

11.4.4.2 Review Scenarios

In all cases, the Architecture Compliance Review process needs the backing of senior management, and should be mandated as part of corporate Architecture Governance policies. Normally the enterprise CIO or enterprise Architecture Board will mandate architecture reviews for all major projects, including subsequent annual reviews. The TOGAF standard provides the following guidance for possible review scenarios:
- For smaller-scale projects, the review process could simply take the form of a series of questions that the project architects or project leaders pose to themselves, using the checklists provided to create a project report for management
- Where the project under review has not involved a practicing or full-time architect to date (for example, in an application-level project), the purpose of the review is typically to bring in architectural expertise

In such a case, the Enterprise Architecture function would be organizing, leading, and conducting the review, with the involvement of business domain experts. In such a scenario, the review is not a substitute for the involvement of architects in a project, but it can be a supplement or a guide to their involvement.

- In most scenarios, particularly in larger-scale projects, the architecture function will have been deeply involved in, and perhaps leading, the development project under review

In such a scenario, the review will be coordinated by the lead Enterprise Architect, who will assemble a team of business and technical domain experts for the review, and compile the answers to the questions posed during the review into some form of report. The questions will typically be posed by the business and technical domain experts. Alternatively, the review might be led by a representative of an Architecture Board or some similar body with enterprise-wide responsibilities.

11.4.4.3 Risk Monitoring

(Syllabus Reference: Unit 18, Learning Outcome 5: You should be able to demonstrate the role that risk monitoring plays in Phase G.)

Risk is pervasive in any Enterprise Architecture activity and is present in all phases within the ADM. Risks will have initially been identified in Phase A as part of the Business Transformation Readiness Assessment. The risk identification and mitigation assessment worksheets created at that stage will have become governance artifacts, and part of the compliance review process should include risk monitoring to ensure that any residual risks accepted are being mitigated to an acceptable level. For critical risks that are not being mitigated, a Change Request should be generated that might require another full or partial ADM cycle.

11.4.5 Implement Business and IT Operations

Carry out the deployment projects including IT services delivery implementation, business services delivery implementation, skills development and training implementation, and communications documentation publication. Publish new Baseline Architectures to the Architecture Repository and update other impacted repositories, such as operational configuration management stores.

11.4.6 Perform Post-Implementation Review and Close the Implementation

This step consists of conducting post-implementation reviews, publishing reviews, and closing implementation projects. Closure of Phase G occurs once the solutions are fully deployed.

11.5 Outputs

(Syllabus Reference: Unit 18, Learning Outcome 3: You should understand the outputs of this phase.)

The outputs of this phase are:
- Architecture Contract (signed) (see Section 11.5.1)
- Compliance Assessments
- Change Requests
- Impact Analysis – Implementation Recommendations
- Architecture-compliant solutions deployed, including:
  - The architecture-compliant implemented system
  - Populated Architecture Repository
  - Architecture Compliance recommendations and dispensations
  - Recommendations on service delivery requirements
  - Recommendations on performance metrics
  - Service Level Agreements (SLAs)
  - Architecture Vision, updated post-implementation
  - Architecture Definition Document, updated post-implementation
  - Transition Architecture, updated post-implementation
  - Business and IT operating models for the implemented solution

11.5.1 Architecture Contracts

(Syllabus Reference: Unit 18, Learning Outcome 3.2: You should be able to explain the relationship of Architecture Contracts to Architecture Governance.)

The Architecture Contracts produced in Phase G are the joint agreements between development partners and sponsors on the deliverables, quality, and fitness-for-purpose of an architecture. Successful implementation of these agreements will be delivered through effective architecture. By implementing a governed approach to the management of contracts, the following can be ensured:

- A system of continuous monitoring to check integrity, changes, decision-making, and audit of all architecture-related activities within the organization
- Adherence to the principles, standards, and requirements of the existing or developing architectures
- Identification of risks in all aspects of the development and implementation of the architecture(s) covering the internal development against accepted standards, policies, technologies, and products as well as the operational aspects of the architectures such that the organization can continue its business within a resilient environment
- A set of processes and practices that ensure accountability, responsibility, and discipline with regard to the development and usage of all architectural artifacts
- A formal understanding of the governance organization responsible for the contract, their level of authority, and scope of the architecture under the governance of this body

The TOGAF standard identifies two example contracts: the Architecture Design and Development Contract and the Business Users' Architecture Contract.

(Syllabus Reference: Unit 18, Learning Outcome 3.1: You should be able to explain the contents of Architecture Contracts.)

Typical contents of an Architecture Design and Development Contract are:
- Introduction and background
- The nature of the agreement
- Scope of the architecture
- Architecture and strategic principles and requirements
- Conformance requirements
- Architecture development and management process and roles
- Target Architecture measures
- Defined phases of deliverables
- Prioritized joint work plan
- Time window(s)
- Architecture delivery and business metrics

Typical contents of a Business Users' Architecture Contract are:
- Introduction and background
- The nature of the agreement
- Scope
- Strategic requirements
- Conformance requirements
- Architecture adopters
- Time window
- Architecture business metrics
- Service architecture (includes SLA)
    - This contract is also used to manage changes to the Enterprise Architecture in Phase H.

11.5.2 Compliance Assessments

Typical contents of a Compliance Assessment are:
- Overview of project progress and status
- Overview of project architecture/design
- Completed architecture checklists:
    - Hardware and operating system checklist
    - Software services and middleware checklist
    - Applications checklists
    - Information management checklists
    - Security checklists
    - System management checklists
    - System engineering checklists
    - Methods and tools checklists

11.6 Summary

Phase G: Implementation Governance defines architecture constraints on the implementation projects and obtains signatures on an Architecture Contract. The contract, along with all the documentation, is then delivered to the implementation team. This phase includes governing the architecture through implementation by conducting compliance reviews, and by risk monitoring as well as post-implementation reviews.

11.7 Exercises

Exercise 11-1

The CIO has asked you to organize a compliance review for an Enterprise Architecture project that is migrating the organization's customer information systems to a new platform (both hardware and software platform). She is concerned that the systems meet all applicable regulations for managing personal information. Summarize five key questions for the compliance checklist.

11.8 Recommended Reading

The following are recommended sources of further information for this chapter:
- The TOGAF Standard, Version 9.2 Part II, Phase G: Implementation Governance
- The TOGAF Standard, Version 9.2 Part IV, Architecture Deliverables
- The TOGAF Standard, Version 9.2 Part VI, Architecture Contracts
- The TOGAF Standard, Version 9.2 Part VI, Architecture Governance

Chapter 12
Phase H: Architecture Change Management

12.1 Key Learning Points

This chapter describes Phase H: Architecture Change Management of the TOGAF Architecture Development Method (ADM).

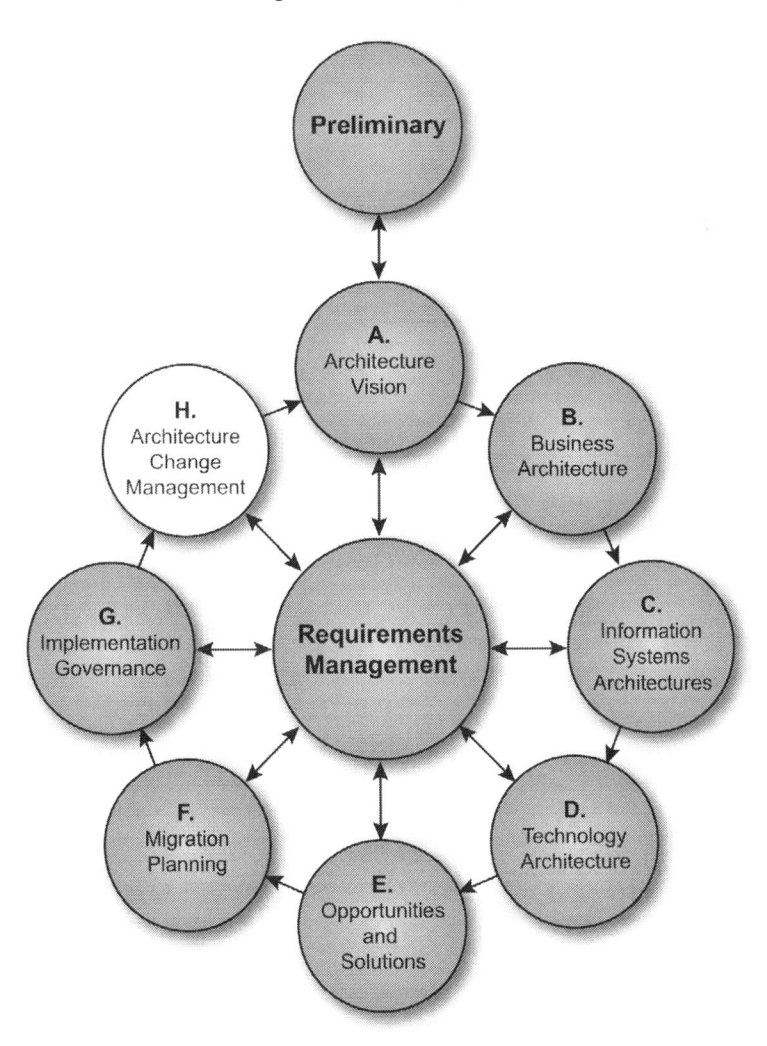

Figure 14: Phase H: Architecture Change Management

> **Key Points Explained**
>
> Upon completion of this chapter you should be able to:
> 1. Understand the inputs to the phase, and be able to explain the following:
>   - Change Requests
> 2. Understand the steps, and be able to describe the following:
>   - Architecture Board meetings
> 3. Understand the outputs, and be able to explain when the following can occur:
>   - Updated Architecture Contracts
>   - A new Request for Architecture Work

12.2 Objectives

The objectives of Phase H: Architecture Change Management are to:
- Ensure that the architecture lifecycle is maintained
- Ensure that the Architecture Governance Framework is executed
- Ensure that the enterprise Architecture Capability meets current requirements

12.3 Inputs

(Syllabus Reference: Unit 19, Learning Outcome 1: You should understand the inputs to the phase.)

The inputs to this phase are:
- Request for Architecture Work identified in Phases E and F
- Organizational Model for Enterprise Architecture
- Tailored Architecture Framework
- Statement of Architecture Work
- Architecture Vision
- Architecture Repository
- Architecture Definition Document
- Architecture Requirements Specification
- Architecture Roadmap
- Change Requests due to technology changes
- Change Requests due to business changes
- Change Requests from lessons learned
- Implementation Governance Model
- Architecture Contract (signed)

- Compliance Assessments
- Implementation and Migration Plan

12.3.1 Change Requests

(Syllabus Reference: Unit 19, Learning Outcome 1.1: You should be able to explain Change Requests.)

Requests for Architecture Change are considered in this phase. During implementation of an architecture, as more facts become known, it is possible that the original Architecture Definition and requirements are not suitable or are not sufficient to complete the implementation of a solution. In these circumstances, it is necessary for implementation projects to either deviate from the suggested architectural approach or to request scope extensions. Additionally, external factors, such as market factors, changes in business strategy, and new technology opportunities, may open up opportunities to extend and refine the architecture. In these circumstances, a Change Request can be submitted in order to initiate a further cycle of architecture work.

Typical contents of a Change Request are:
- Description of the proposed change
- Rationale for the proposed change
- Impact assessment of the proposed change, including:
  - Reference to specific requirements
  - Stakeholder priority of the requirements to date
  - Phases to be revisited
  - Phase to lead on requirements prioritization
  - Results of phase investigations and revised priorities
  - Recommendations on management of requirements
- Repository reference number

12.4 Steps

(Syllabus Reference: Unit 19, Learning Outcome 2: You understand the steps in this phase.)

Phase H consists of the following steps:
1. Establish value realization process
2. Deploy monitoring tools

3. Manage risks
4. Provide analysis for architecture change management
5. Develop change requirements to meet performance targets
6. Manage governance process
7. Activate the process to implement change

The steps are described in more detail in the following sections.

12.4.1 Establish Value Realization Process

This step should establish a process to ensure that business projects realize value from the Enterprise Architecture. The value can be measured in terms of quantifiable measures (reduced costs, reduced time-to-market length) and indirect measures (such as new skills and capabilities).

12.4.2 Deploy Monitoring Tools

Here we deploy and apply tools to enable the following:
- Monitor technology changes which could impact the Baseline Architecture
- Monitor business changes which could impact the Baseline Architecture
- Track business value (e.g., investment appraisal method to determine value metrics for the business objectives)
- Monitor Enterprise Architecture Capability maturity
- Track and assess asset management programs
- Track the QoS performances and usage
- Determine and track business continuity requirements

12.4.3 Manage Risks

In this step the Enterprise Architecture risks should be assessed and recommendations made for risk mitigation.

12.4.4 Provide Analysis for Architecture Change Management

Provide analysis for architecture change management:
- Analyze performance
- Conduct Enterprise Architecture performance reviews with service management
- Assess Change Requests and reporting to ensure that the expected value realization and Service Level Agreement (SLA) expectations of the customers are met

- Undertake a gap analysis of the performance of the Enterprise Architecture
- Ensure change management requests adhere to the enterprise Architecture Governance and framework

12.4.5 Develop Change Requirements to Meet Performance Targets
Make recommendations concerning change requirements to meet performance targets and development of position to act.

12.4.6 Manage Governance Process
(Syllabus Reference: Unit 19, Learning Outcome 2.1: You are able to describe Architecture Board meetings.)

Manage the governance process and framework for the architecture. This includes scheduling and holding meetings of the Architecture Board. The purpose of these meetings is to decide how to handle Change Requests (technology and business) as well as dispensation requests. See also Section 21.4 and Section 21.5.

12.4.7 Activate the Process to Implement Change
Activate the architecture process to implement change by producing a new Request for Architecture Work and request for investment. Ensure any changes implemented in this phase are captured and documented in the Architecture Repository.

12.5 Outputs
(Syllabus Reference: Unit 19, Learning Outcome 3: You understand the outputs of this phase.)

The outputs of this phase are:
- Architecture updates (for maintenance changes)
- Changes to Architecture Framework and principles (for maintenance changes)
- New Request for Architecture Work, to initiate another cycle of the ADM (for major changes)
- Statement of Architecture Work, updated if necessary
- Architecture Contract, updated if necessary
- Compliance Assessments, updated if necessary

(Syllabus Reference: Unit 19, Learning Outcome 3.1: You should be able to explain when Architecture Contracts might be updated.)

The impact of a Change Request may require Architecture Contracts to be updated to reflect the changes agreed.

(Syllabus Reference: Unit 19, Learning Outcome 3.2: You should be able to explain when a new Request for Architecture Work might occur.)

A new Request for Architecture Work should be produced for Change Requests that require a major change. These are called "Re-architecting Changes" and require putting the whole architecture through the ADM cycle.

12.6 Summary

Phase H ensures that changes to the architecture are managed in a cohesive and controlled manner in line with the Architecture Governance processes. It also establishes and supports the Enterprise Architecture to provide flexibility to evolve the architecture rapidly in response to changes in the technology or business environment.

12.7 Exercises

Exercise 12-1

There are three main categories of architecture change:
1. Simplification: this can be handled via change management techniques
2. Incremental: this may be handled via change management techniques, or it may require partial re-architecting
3. Re-architecting: this requires putting the whole architecture through the Architecture Development Cycle again

Explain why each of these changes might occur.

Exercise 12-2

Describe the change impact of the following scenarios:
1. The required change is part of the business strategy and is substantial.
2. A new technology or standard emerges.

3. The change is at an infrastructure level; for example, ten systems are reduced to one system.
4. The Foundation Architecture needs to be re-aligned with the business strategy.
5. Substantial change is required to components and guidelines for use in deployment of the architecture.

12.8 Recommended Reading

The following are recommended sources of further information for this chapter:
- The TOGAF Standard, Version 9.2 Part II, Phase H: Change Management
- The TOGAF Standard, Version 9.2 Part IV, Architecture Deliverables
- The TOGAF Standard, Version 9.2 Part VI, Architecture Board
- The TOGAF Standard, Version 9.2 Part VI, Architecture Governance

Chapter 13

ADM Architecture Requirements Management

13.1 Key Learning Points

This chapter describes ADM Architecture Requirements Management. The process of managing architecture requirements applies to all phases of the ADM cycle, as shown in Figure 15.

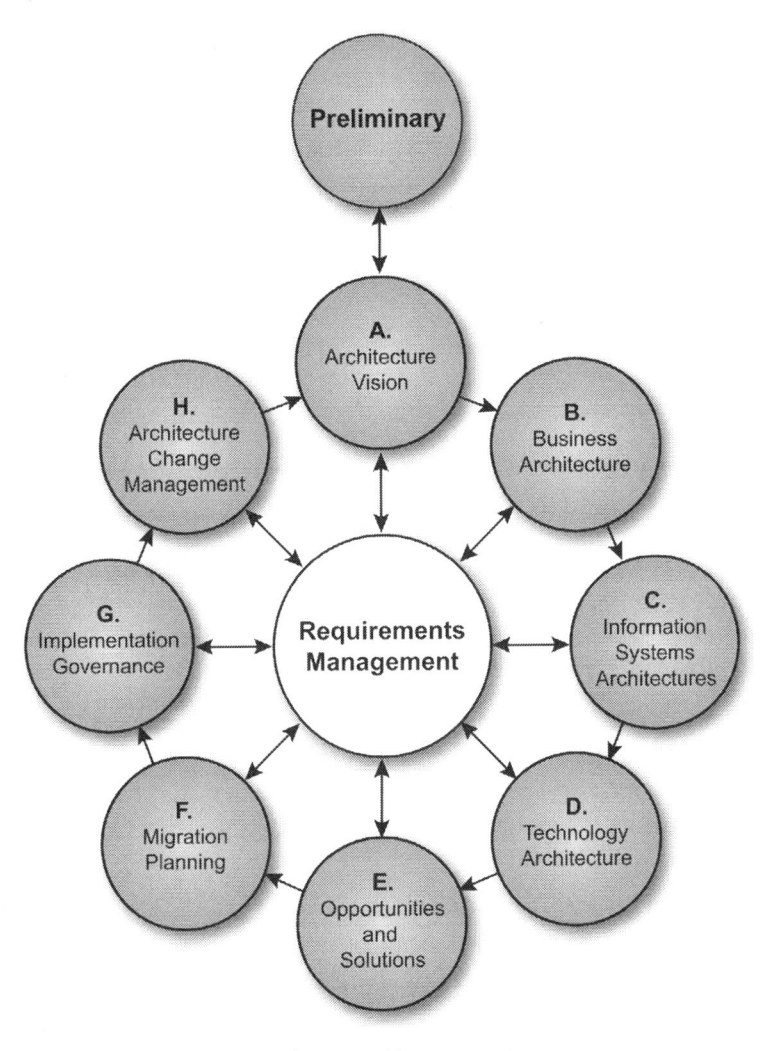

Figure 15:   ADM Architecture Requirements Management

> **Key Points Explained**
>
> Upon completion of this chapter you should be able to:
> 1. Understand the inputs to the Requirements Management process
> 2. Understand the steps and their correspondence to phases
> 3. Explain how the Requirements Management steps correspond to ADM phases
> 4. Explain the purpose of the outputs of Requirements Management

13.2 Objectives

The objectives of the Requirements Management phase are to:
- Ensure that the Requirements Management process is sustained and operates for all relevant ADM phases
- Manage architecture requirements identified during any execution of the ADM cycle or a phase
- Ensure that relevant architecture requirements are available for use by each phase as the phase is executed

13.3 Inputs

(Syllabus Reference: Unit 20, Learning Outcome 1: You should understand the inputs to the Requirements Management process.)

The inputs to the Requirements Management process are the requirements-related outputs from each ADM phase. The first high-level requirements are produced as part of the Architecture Vision. Each architecture domain then generates detailed requirements. Deliverables in later ADM phases contain mappings to new types of requirements (e.g., conformance requirements).

13.4 Steps

(Syllabus Reference: Unit 20, Learning Outcome 2: You should understand the steps and their correspondence to ADM phases.)

(Syllabus Reference: Unit 20, Learning Outcome 3: You should be able to explain how the Requirements Management steps correspond to ADM phases.)

Table 15 lists the correspondence between Requirements Management process steps and ADM phase steps.

Table 15: Correspondence between Requirements Managements and the ADM Phases

Step	Requirements Management Steps	ADM Phase Steps
1		Identify/document requirements – use business scenarios or an analogous technique
2	Baseline requirements: 1. Determine priorities arising from current phase of ADM 2. Confirm stakeholder buy-in to resultant priorities 3. Record requirements priorities and place in Requirements Repository	
3	Monitor baseline requirements	
4		Identify changed requirement: 1. Remove or re-assess priorities 2. Add requirements and re-assess priorities 3. Modify existing requirements
5	Identify changed requirements and record priorities: 1. Identify changed requirements; ensure the requirements are prioritized by the architect(s) responsible for the current phases and by the relevant stakeholders 2. Record new priorities 3. Ensure that any conflicts are identified and managed throughout the phases 4. Generate Requirements Impact Statement for steering the architecture team **Notes:** 1. Changed requirements can come in through any route. To ensure that the requirements are properly assessed and prioritized, this process needs to direct the ADM phases and record the decisions related to the requirements. 2. The Requirements Management phase needs to determine stakeholder satisfaction with the decisions. Where there is dissatisfaction, the phase remains accountable to ensure the resolution of the issues and determine the next steps.	

Step	Requirements Management Steps	ADM Phase Steps
6		1. Assess impact of changed requirements on current (active) phase
2. Assess impact of changed requirements on previous phases
3. Determine whether to implement change, or defer to a later ADM cycle; if the decision is to implement, assess the timescale for change management implementation
4. Issue Requirements Impact Statement, Version n+1
7		Implement requirements arising from Phase H
The architecture can be changed through its lifecycle by the Architecture Change Management phase (Phase H). The Requirements Management process ensures that new or changing requirements that are derived from Phase H are managed accordingly.
8	Update the Architecture Requirements Repository with information relating to the changes requested, including stakeholder views affected.	
9		Implement the change in the current phase
10		Assess and revise gap analysis for past phases
The gap analysis in the ADM Phases B through D identifies the gaps between Baseline and Target Architectures; certain types of gap can give rise to gap requirements.
The ADM describes two kinds of gap:
1. Something that is present in the baseline, but not in the target (i.e., eliminated – by accident or design)
2. Something not in the baseline, but present in the target (i.e., new)
A "gap requirement" is anything that has been eliminated by accident, and therefore requires a change to the Target Architecture.
If the gap analysis generates gap requirements, then this step will ensure that they are addressed, documented, and recorded in the Requirements Repository, and that the Target Architecture is revised accordingly.

13.5 Outputs

(Syllabus Reference: Unit 20, Learning Outcome 4: You should be able to explain the purpose of the outputs of Requirements Management.)

The outputs of the Requirements Management process are:
- Updated Architecture Requirements Specification (see Section 4.5.2)
- Requirements Impact Assessment

The Requirements Repository will be updated as part of the Requirements Management phase |and should contain all requirements information.

13.5.1 Requirements Impact Assessment

Throughout the ADM, new information is collected relating to an architecture. As this information is gathered, new facts may come to light that invalidate existing aspects of the architecture; for example, new requirements arising or existing requirements changing. A Requirements Impact Assessment assesses the current architecture requirements and specification to identify changes that should be made and the implications of those changes. It documents an assessment of the changes and the recommendations for change to the architecture. The statement goes through various iterations until the final version, which includes the full implications of the requirements (e.g., costs, timescales, business metrics) on the architecture development. The recommended contents are as follows:
- Reference to specific requirements
- Stakeholder priority of the requirements to date
- Phases to be revisited
- Phase to lead on requirements prioritization
- Results of phase investigations and revised priorities
- Recommendations on management of requirements
- Repository reference number

These are often produced as a response to a Change Request.

13.6 Summary

Requirements Management is an ongoing activity of the ADM. The Architecture Requirements Repository contains the current requirements for the Target Architecture. When new requirements arise, or existing ones are changed, a Requirements Impact Statement is generated, which identifies the phases of the ADM that need to be revisited to address the changes.

13.7 Exercises

Exercise 13-1

You have been asked to recommend candidate tools for Requirements Management. Identify three or more suitable tools, together with a rationale for why they would suitable for use. (Hint: The Volere website has a useful list of tools.[7])

13.8 Recommended Reading

The following are recommended sources of further information for this chapter:

- The TOGAF Standard, Version 9.2 Part II, ADM Architecture Requirements Management
- The TOGAF Standard, Version 9.2 Part IV, Architecture Deliverables

---

7 Refer to www.volere.co.uk/tools.htm.

PART 2
Guidelines for Adapting the ADM

In this Part, we examine two guidelines for adapting the Architecture Development Method:
- Chapter 14 describes how to apply iteration to the ADM, and how to apply the ADM at different enterprise levels
- Chapter 15 describes security considerations during the application of the ADM

Chapter 14

Iteration and Levels

14.1 Key Learning Points

This chapter describes the guidelines for adapting the ADM using iteration and different levels of architecture engagement. This chapter will help you to apply these guidelines during application of the ADM.

> **Key Points Explained**
>
> Upon completion of this chapter you should be able to:
> 1. Describe the concept of iteration and how it applies to the TOGAF ADM
> 2. Describe the factors influencing the use of iteration
> 3. Describe some suggested iteration cycles
> 4. Describe how the ADM supports different types of engagements within the organization
> 5. Explain how to apply iteration cycles to the ADM phases
> 6. Explain how the concepts of levels and the Enterprise Continuum are used to organize the Architecture Landscape
> 7. Identify the different levels of architecture that exist in an organization

14.2 The Concept of Iteration

(Syllabus Reference: Unit 23, Learning Outcome 1: You should be able to describe the concept of iteration and how it applies to the TOGAF ADM.)

The ADM supports a number of concepts that can be characterized as iteration. First, iteration describes the process of both describing a comprehensive Architecture Landscape through multiple ADM cycles based upon individual initiatives bound to the scope of the Request for Architecture Work. Second, iteration describes the integrated process of developing an architecture where the activities described in different ADM phases interact to produce an integrated architecture. In order to concisely describe the activity and outputs, this latter iteration is described in sequential terms. Third, iteration describes the process of managing change to the organization's Architecture Capability. These are described further below.

14.2.1 Iteration to Develop a Comprehensive Architecture Landscape

Projects will exercise through the entire ADM cycle, commencing with Phase A. Each cycle of the ADM will be bound by a Request for Architecture Work. The architecture output will populate the Architecture Landscape, either extending the landscape described, or changing the landscape where required.

Separate projects may operate their own ADM cycles concurrently, with relationships between the different projects.

One project may trigger the initiation of another project. Typically, this is used when higher-level architecture initiatives identify opportunities or solutions that require more detailed architecture, or when a project identifies landscape impacts outside the scope of its Request for Architecture Work.

14.2.2 Iteration within an ADM Cycle (Architecture Development Iteration)

Projects may operate multiple ADM phases concurrently. Typically, this is used to manage the inter-relationship between Business Architecture, Information Systems Architecture, and Technology Architecture.

Projects may cycle between ADM phases, in planned cycles covering multiple phases. Typically, this is used to converge on a detailed Target Architecture when higher-level architecture does not exist to provide context and constraint.

Projects may return to previous phases in order to circle back and update work products with new information. Typically, this is used to converge on an executable Architecture Roadmap or Implementation and Migration Plan, when the implementation details and scope of change trigger a change or re-prioritization of stakeholder requirements.

14.2.3 Iteration to Manage the Architecture Capability (Architecture Capability Iterations)

Projects may require a new iteration of the Preliminary Phase to (re-) establish aspects of the Architecture Capability identified in Phase A to address a Request for Architecture Work.

Projects may require a new iteration of the Preliminary Phase to adjust the organization's Architecture Capability as a result of identifying new or changed requirements for Architecture Capability as a result of a Change Request in Phase H.

14.3 Factors Influencing the Use of Iteration

(Syllabus Reference: Unit 23, Learning Outcome 2: You should be able to describe the factors influencing the use of iteration.)

Factors influencing the use of iteration include:

- **The formality and nature of established process checkpoints within the organization**
  Does the organization mandate that certain groups of activities are carried out between checkpoints? Does the organization mandate that certain activities must be finalized before other activities can be carried out?
- **The level of stakeholder involvement expected within the process**
  Are stakeholders expecting to be closely involved within the development of a solution, or are they expecting to see a complete set of deliverables for review and approval?
- **The number of teams involved and the relationships between different teams**
  Is the entire architecture being developed by a specific team, or is there a hierarchy of teams with governance relationships between them?
- **The maturity of the solution area and the expected amount of re-work and refinement required to arrive at an acceptable solution**
  Can the solution be achieved in a single pass, or does it require extensive proof-of-concept and prototyping work to evolve a suitable outcome?
- **Attitude to risk**
  Does the organizational culture react negatively to partially complete work products being circulated? Does the organizational culture require solutions to be proved in a trial environment before they can be implemented for mainstream application?
- **The class of engagement**
  What is the context for development of the Enterprise Architecture?

14.4 Iteration Cycles

(Syllabus Reference: Unit 23, Learning Outcome 3: You should be able to describe some suggested iteration cycles.)

The suggested iteration cycles for the TOGAF ADM are shown in Figure 16 and can be used to effectively group related architectural activities to achieve a specific purpose.

Architecture Capability iterations support the creation and evolution of the required Architecture Capability. This includes the initial mobilization of architecture activity for a given purpose or architecture engagement type by establishing or adjusting the architecture approach, principles, scope, vision, and governance.

Architecture Development iterations allow for the creation of architecture content by cycling through, or integrating, Business, Information Systems and Technology Architecture phases. These iterations ensure that the architecture is considered as a whole. In this type of iteration stakeholder reviews are typically broader. As the iterations converge on a target, extensions into the Opportunities and Solutions and Migration Planning phases ensure that the viability of the architecture's implementation is considered as the architecture is finalized.

Transition Planning iterations support the creation of formal change roadmaps for a defined architecture.

Architecture Governance iterations support governance of change activity progressing towards a defined Target Architecture.

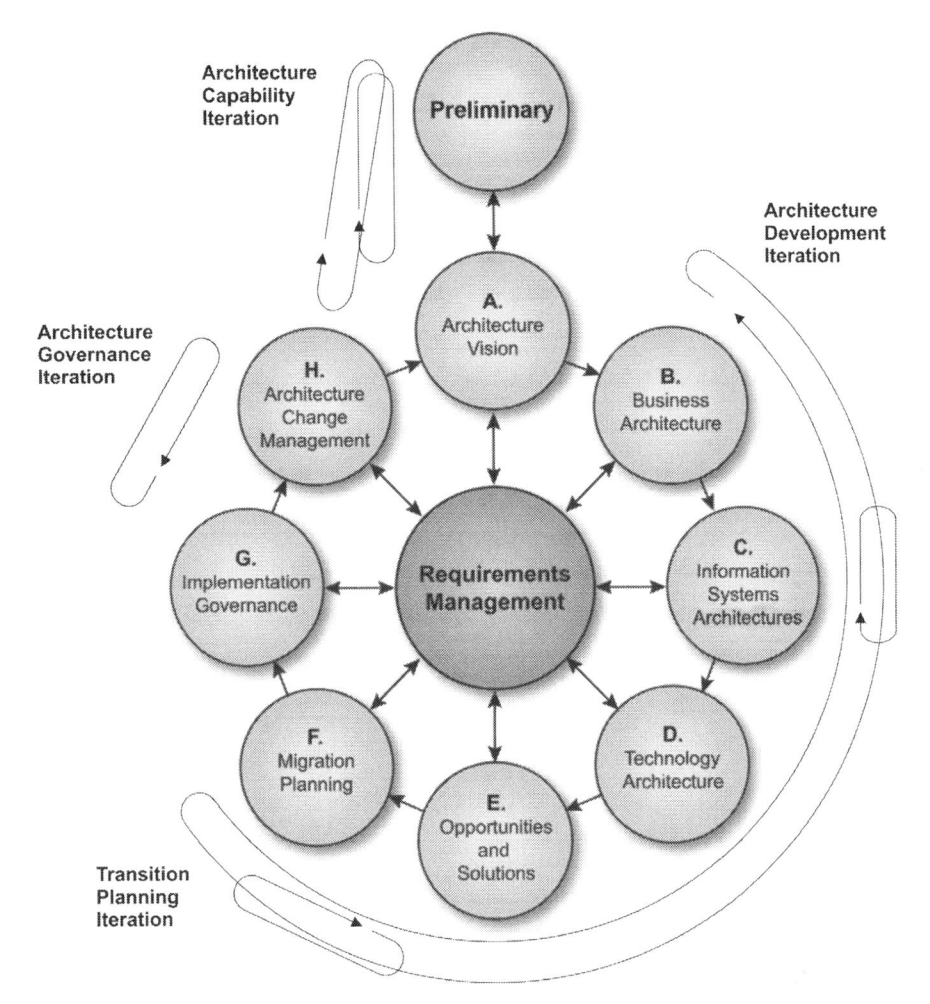

Figure 16: Iteration Cycles

> **Styles of Architecture Definition**
>
> The TOGAF standard suggests two process styles when defining architectures:
>
> **Baseline First**
>
> An assessment of the current state (baseline) is used to identify problem areas and opportunities for improvement. This is a suitable approach when the baseline is complex, not clearly understood or agreed upon.
>
> **Target First**
>
> The target solution is elaborated in detail and then mapped back to the baseline. This is a suitable approach if the target state is agreed at a high level and where the enterprise wishes to effectively transition to the target model.

14.5 Classes of Architecture Engagement

(Syllabus Reference: Unit 23, Learning Outcome 4: You should be able to describe how the ADM supports different types of engagement within an organization.)

An architecture function or services organization may be called on to assist in the development of an enterprise in a number of different contexts, as architectures range from summary to detail, broad to narrow coverage, and current state to future state. In these contexts the concept of iteration should be used in developing the architecture.

The TOGAF standard defines three typical areas of engagement for architects which are classified as *Identification, Definition,* or *Implementation* of the required change. Each of the classifications has its own scenarios or engagement types; for example, supporting a business strategy, architecture portfolio management of the Architecture Landscape, foundational change initiative, etc. These are shown in Figure 17 and described in the following sections.

14.5.1 Identification of Required Change

Outside the context of any change initiative, Enterprise Architecture can be used as a technique to provide visibility of the IT capability to support strategic decision-making and alignment of execution.

14.5.2 Definition of Change

Where a need to change has been identified in an enterprise, Enterprise Architecture can be used as a technique to define the nature and extent of change in a structured fashion. Within large-scale change initiatives, architectures can be developed to provide detailed architecture initiatives that are bounded by the scope of a program or portfolio.

14.5.3 Implementation of Change

Architecture at all levels of the enterprise can be used as a technique to provide design governance to change initiatives by providing overall visibility, and structural constraints, and defining criteria by which to evaluate technical decisions.

CH. 14 ITERATION AND LEVELS

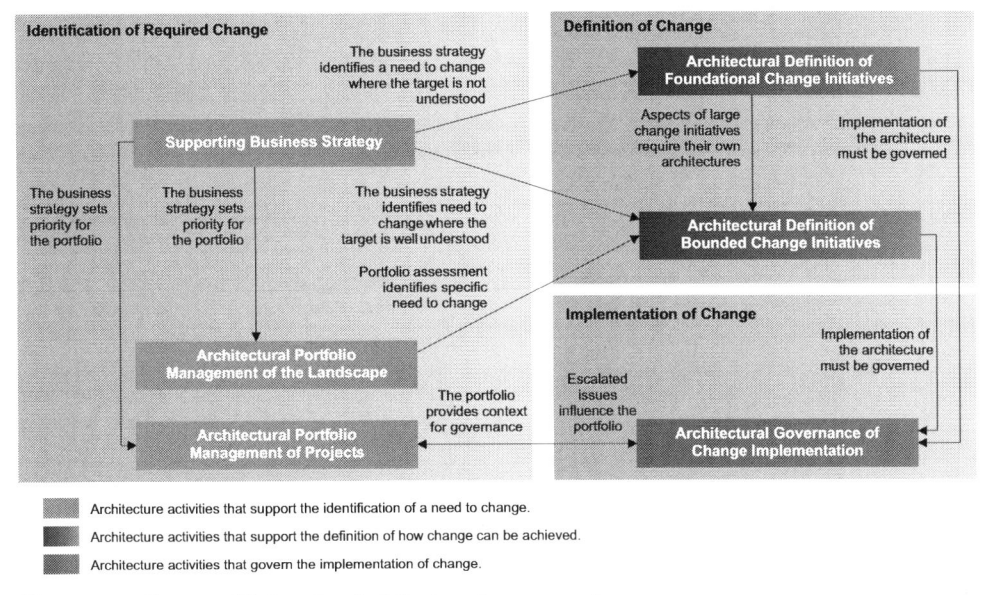

Figure 17: Classes of Enterprise Architecture Engagement

Within the three areas of engagement, the TOGAF standard defines a number of classes of engagement, which are summarized in Table 16.

Table 16: Areas and Classes of Enterprise Architecture Engagement

Area of Engagement	Class of Engagement/ Iteration Focus	Description
Identification of Required Change	Supporting Business Strategy Architecture Capability and Architecture Development (Baseline First) Iterations	This type of engagement is suitable for mergers and acquisitions. As the business strategies, objectives, goals, and drivers change, it is necessary for IT to change in order to maintain alignment. The creation of new business strategies can be supported by the Enterprise Architecture by: • Providing visibility of change opportunities • Providing elaboration on the practical impacts of a particular strategic choice • Providing tests on the feasibility or viability of a particular strategic direction In this engagement type, as business strategies change or new business strategies are created that might impact the whole enterprise, then the focus is to look at the baseline first, with broad shallow consideration given to the Architecture Landscape in order to address a specific strategic question. It should define terms for more detailed efforts to realize the strategy.

Area of Engagement	Class of Engagement/ Iteration Focus	Description
	Architectural Portfolio Management of the Landscape Architecture Capability and Architecture Development (Baseline First) Iterations	This type of engagement is typical for service providers and management to manage a complex IT landscape. It is common practice across large organizations for a Service Management organization to provide operational reporting and management of the IT portfolio. Enterprise Architecture can add a further dimension to Service Management reporting by supporting a linkage between operational performance and the strategic need for IT. Using the traceability between IT and business inherent in Enterprise Architecture, it is possible to evaluate the IT portfolio against operational performance data and business needs (e.g., cost, functionality, availability, responsiveness) to determine areas where misalignment is occurring and change needs to take place. In this type of engagement the focus is to look at the baseline first and to focus on the physical assessment of the current applications and technology infrastructure to identify opportunities for improvement.
	Architectural Portfolio Management of Projects Transition Planning and Architecture Governance Iterations	It is common practice across large organizations for a Program Management organization to provide operational reporting and management of the change portfolio. Enterprise Architecture can add a further dimension to project portfolio management reporting by supporting a link between project scope, architectural impact, and business value. Architectural factors can be added to other quantitative project factors to support strategic decision-making on project priority and funding levels. This type of engagement is focused on projects and their dependencies, aligning the project sequence to optimize the architecture.
Definition of Change	Architectural Definition of Foundational Change Initiatives Architecture Capability, Architecture Development (Baseline First), and Transition Planning	Foundational change initiatives are change efforts that have a known objective, but are not strictly scoped or bounded by a shared vision or requirements. The initial priority is to understand the nature of the problem and to bring structure to the definition of the problem. Once the problem is more effectively understood, it is possible to define appropriate solutions and to align stakeholders around a common vision and purpose. The focus should be to look at the baseline first and to identify what needs to change to transition to the target.

Area of Engagement	Class of Engagement/ Iteration Focus	Description
	Iterations Architectural Definition of Bounded Change Initiatives Architecture Development (Target First) and Transition Planning Iterations	Bounded change initiatives are change efforts that typically arise as the outcome of a prior architectural strategy, evaluation, or vision. Here, the desired outcome is already understood and agreed. The focus of the architecture is to effectively elaborate a future state solution that addresses the identified issues, drivers, and constraints. The focus should be to look at the target first and then to do transition planning. Focus on elaborating the target to meet a previously defined and agreed vision, scope, or set of constraints. Use the target as a basis for analysis to avoid perpetuation of current, sub-optimal architectures.
Implementation of Change	Architectural Governance of Change Implementation Architecture Governance Iteration	Once an architectural solution model has been defined, it provides a basis for solution architecture, design, and implementation. In order to ensure that the objectives and value of the defined Enterprise Architecture are appropriately realized, it is necessary for continuing enterprise Architecture Governance of the implementation process to support design review, architecture refinement, and issue escalation. Use the Architecture Vision, constraints, principles, requirements, Target Architecture definition, and transition roadmap to ensure that projects realize their intended benefit, are aligned with each other, and are aligned with wider business need.

14.6 Mapping TOGAF Phases to Iteration Cycles

(Syllabus Reference: Unit 23, Learning Outcome 5: You should be able to explain how to apply iteration cycles to the ADM phases.)

14.6.1 Iteration between ADM Cycles

In this approach each iteration completes an ADM cycle at a single level of Architecture Description with Phase F (Migration Planning) being used to initiate new more detailed architecture development projects. This type of iteration highlights the need for a higher-level architecture to guide and constrain more detailed architecture(s) and is a method to develop the complete Architecture Landscape for a project in multiple iterations. This approach is shown in Figure 18.

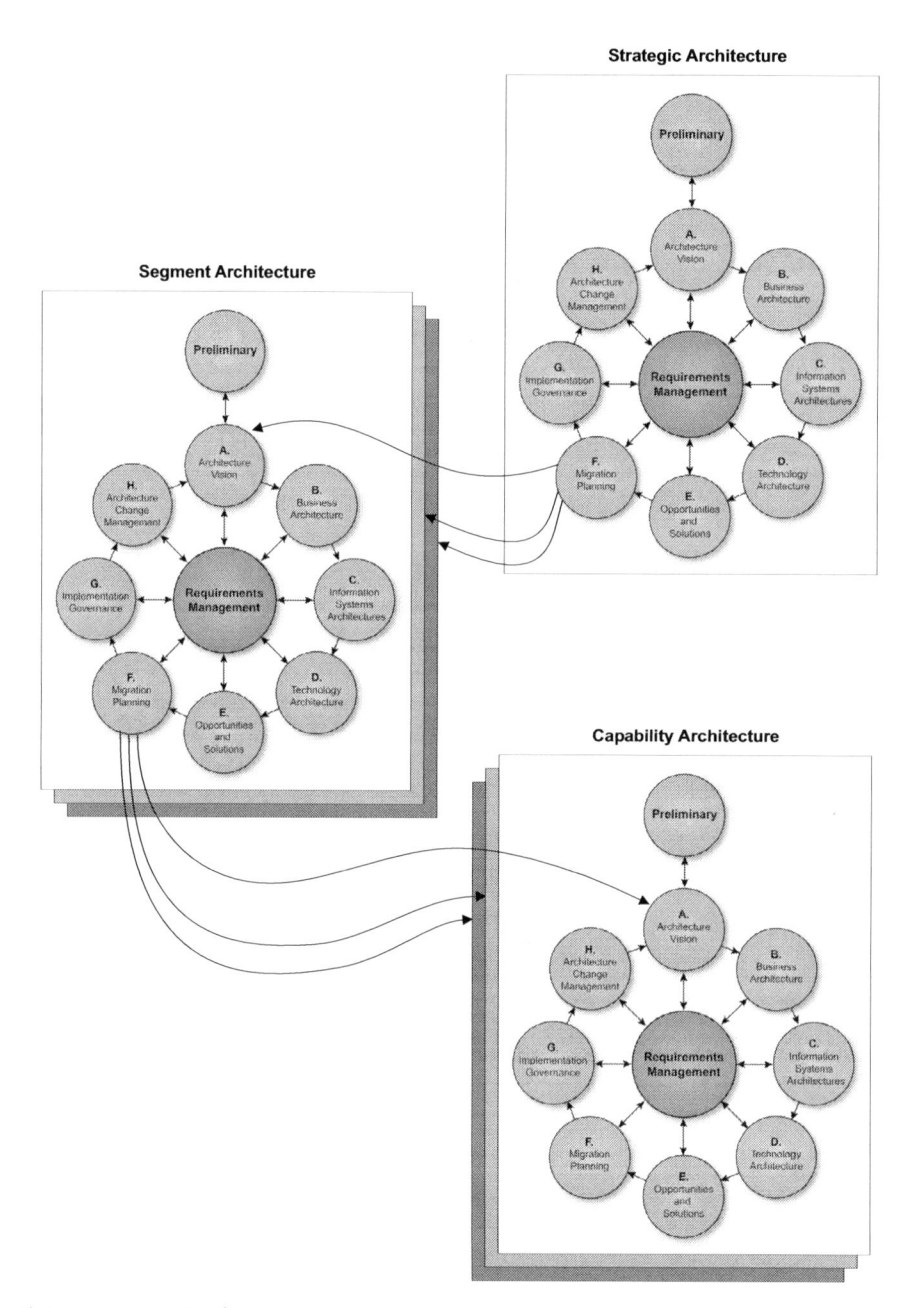

Figure 18: A Hierarchy of ADM Processes Example

14.6.2 Iteration within an ADM Cycle

The TOGAF standard includes suggested iteration cycles for both baseline first and target first Architecture Definitions. The example for target first is shown in Figure 19.

TOGAF Phase		Architecture Development			Transition Planning		Architecture Governance	
		Iteration 1	Iteration 2	Iteration n	Iteration 1	Iteration n	Iteration 1	Iteration n
Preliminary		Informal	Informal	Informal				Light
Architecture Vision		Informal	Informal	Informal	Informal	Informal		Light
Business Architecture	Baseline	Informal	Core	Core	Informal	Informal		Light
	Target	Core	Light	Core	Informal	Informal		Light
Application Architecture	Baseline	Informal	Core	Core	Informal	Informal		Light
	Target	Core	Light	Core	Informal	Informal		Light
Data Architecture	Baseline	Informal	Core	Core	Informal	Informal		Light
	Target	Core	Light	Core	Informal	Informal		Light
Technology Architecture	Baseline	Informal	Core	Core	Informal	Informal		Light
	Target	Core	Light	Core	Informal	Informal		Light
Opportunities and Solutions		Light	Light	Light	Core	Core	Informal	Informal
Migration Planning		Light	Light	Light	Core	Core	Informal	Informal
Implementation Governance					Informal	Informal	Core	Core
Change Management		Informal	Informal	Informal	Informal	Informal	Core	Core

- Core: primary focus activity for the iteration
- Light: secondary focus activity for the iteration
- Informal: potential activity for the iteration, not formally mentioned in the method

Figure 19: Activity by Iteration for Target First Architecture Definition

The suggested iteration cycles mapped to the TOGAF phases are described in the following sections.

14.6.2.1 *Architecture Development Iteration (Baseline First)*

Iteration 1 – Define the Baseline Architecture

This iteration comprises a pass through the Business Architecture, Information Systems Architecture, and Technology Architecture phases of the ADM, focusing on definition of the Baseline Architecture. Opportunities, solutions, and migration plans are also considered to identify the focus for change and test feasibility.

Iteration 2 – Define the Target Architecture and Gaps

This iteration comprises a pass through the Business Architecture, Information Systems Architecture, and Technology Architecture phases of the ADM, focusing on definition of the Target Architecture and analyzing gaps against the Baseline Architecture. Opportunities, solutions, and migration plans are also considered to test viability.

Iteration *n* – Refine the Baseline Architecture, Target Architecture, and Gaps

Subsequent iterations attempt to correct and refine the Baseline and Target Architectures to achieve an outcome that is beneficial, feasible, and viable.

14.6.2.2 Architecture Development Iteration (Target First)

Iteration 1 – Define the Target Architecture

This iteration comprises a pass through the Business Architecture, Information Systems Architecture, and Technology Architecture phases of the ADM, focusing on definition of the Target Architecture. Opportunities, solutions, and migration plans are also considered to identify the focus for change and test feasibility.

Iteration 2 – Define the Baseline Architecture and Gaps

This iteration comprises a pass through the Business Architecture, Information Systems Architecture, and Technology Architecture phases of the ADM, focusing on definition of the Baseline Architecture and analyzing gaps against the Target Architecture. Opportunities, solutions, and migration plans are also considered to test viability.

Iteration *n* – Refine the Baseline Architecture, Target Architecture, and Gaps

Subsequent iterations attempt to correct and refine the Baseline and Target Architectures to achieve an outcome that is beneficial, feasible, and viable.

14.6.2.3 Transition Planning Iteration

Iteration 1 – Define and Agree a Set of Improvement Opportunities

The initial iteration of transition planning seeks to gain buy-in to a portfolio of solution opportunities in the Opportunities & Solutions phase of the ADM. This iteration also delivers a provisional Implementation and Migration Plan.

Iteration *n* – Refine the Improvement Opportunities

Subsequent iterations of transition planning seek to agree on the Transition Architecture, and refine the Implementation and Migration Plan by feeding back issues into the Opportunities & Solutions phase.

14.6.2.4 Architecture Governance Iteration

Iteration 1 – Mobilize Architecture Governance and Change Management Processes

The initial Architecture Governance iteration establishes a process for the governance of change and also puts in place the appropriate people, processes, and technology to support managed access to and changes of the defined architecture.

Iteration *n* – Carry out Architecture Governance and Change Control

Subsequent iterations of the Architecture Governance cycle focus on reviews of change initiatives to resolve issues and ensure compliance. Results of a Change Request may trigger another phase to be revisited; for example, feeding back a new requirement to the Preliminary Phase to improve the Architecture Capability, or a new requirement for the architecture into the Architecture Development phases.

14.7 Applying the ADM Across the Architecture Landscape

(Syllabus Reference: Unit 23, Learning Outcome 6: You should be able to explain how the concepts of levels and the Enterprise Continuum are used to organize the Architecture Landscape.)

In a typical enterprise, multiple architectures will exist in the Architecture Landscape at any point in time. Some architectures will address very specific needs; others will be more general. Some will address detail; some will provide a big picture. To address this complexity the TOGAF standard uses the concepts of levels and the Enterprise Continuum to provide a conceptual framework for organizing the Architecture Landscape.

14.7.1 The Architecture Landscape

(Syllabus Reference: Unit 23, Learning Outcome 7: You should be able to identify the different levels of architecture that exist in an organization.)

Levels provide a framework for dividing the Architecture Landscape into three levels of granularity as shown in Figure 20, and described below.

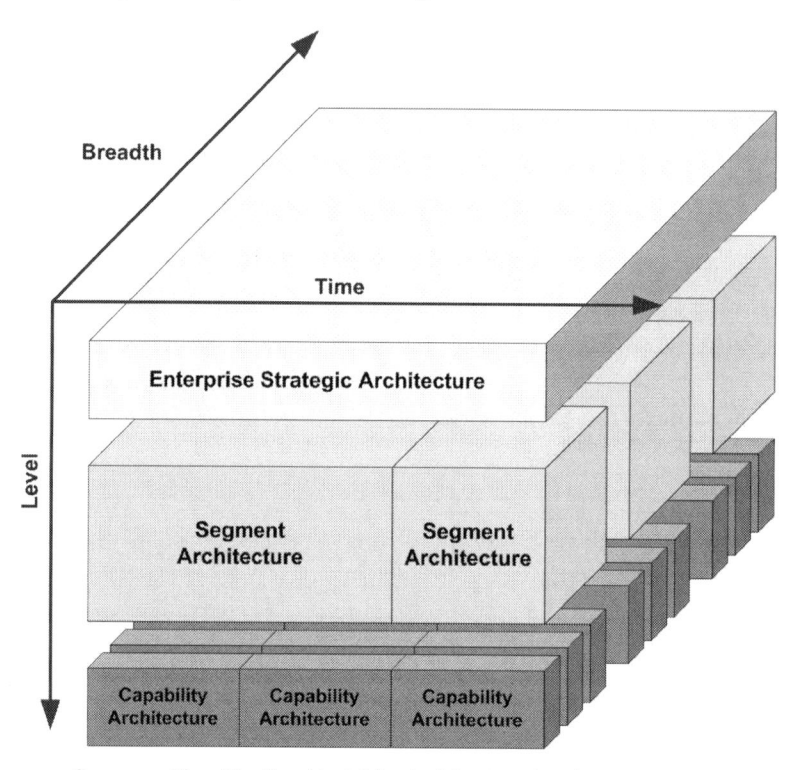

Figure 20: Summary Classification Model for Architecture Landscapes

1. Strategic Architecture provides an organizing framework for operational and change activity and allows for direction setting at an executive level.
2. Segment Architecture provides an organizing framework for operational and change activity and allows for direction setting and the development of effective architecture roadmaps at a program or portfolio level.
3. Capability Architecture provides an organizing framework for change activity and the development of effective architecture roadmaps realizing capability increments.

14.7.2 The Architecture Continuum

The Architecture Continuum provides a method of dividing each level of the Architecture Landscape by abstraction. It offers a consistent way to define and understand the generic rules, representations, and relationships in an architecture, including traceability and derivation relationships. The Architecture Continuum shows the relationships from foundation elements to organization-specific architecture, as shown in Figure 21.

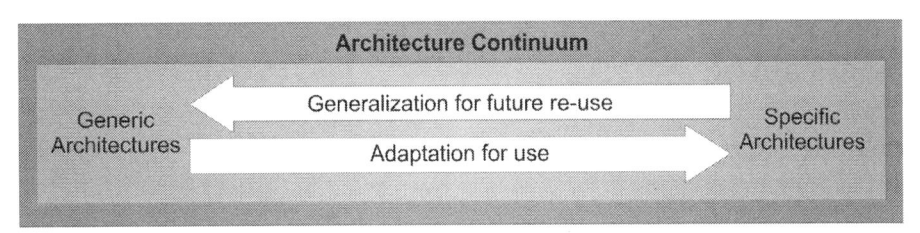

Figure 21: Summary of the Architecture Continuum

The classification methods of the Architecture Continuum can be used to partition and organize the Architecture Landscape into a set of related architectures with:

- Manageable complexity for each individual architecture or solution
- Defined groupings
- Defined hierarchies and navigation structures
- Appropriate processes, roles, and responsibilities attached to each grouping

14.7.3 Organizing the Architecture Landscape

The following characteristics can be used to organize the Architecture Landscape:

- Breadth: the breadth (subject matter) area is generally the primary organizing characteristic for describing an Architecture Landscape – architectures are functionally decomposed into a hierarchy of specific subject areas or segments
- Depth: with broader subject areas, less detail is needed to ensure that the architecture has a manageable size and complexity – more specific subject matter areas will generally permit (and require) more detailed architectures
- Time: for a specific breadth and depth an enterprise can create a Baseline Architecture and a set of Target Architectures that stretch into the future – broader and less detailed architectures will generally be valid for longer

periods of time and can provide a vision for the enterprise that stretches further into the future
- Recency: finally, each architecture view will progress through a development cycle where it increases in accuracy until finally approved After approval, an architecture will begin to decrease in accuracy if not actively maintained. In some cases recency may be used as an organizing factor for historic architectures.

Using the criteria above, architectures can be grouped into Strategic, Segment, and Capability Architecture levels, as described in Figure 20.

14.8 Summary

The TOGAF standard provides guidelines for adapting the ADM for iteration. This includes proposed iteration cycles to suit different classes of architecture engagement. Guidance is also provided on how to use levels for architecture development across the Architecture Landscape.

14.9 Exercises

Exercise 14-1
When applying iteration to the ADM it is sometimes best to produce the Baseline Architecture first. Give two examples of when a Baseline First approach to architecture development would be most appropriate.

Exercise 14-2
When applying iteration to the ADM it is sometimes best to produce the Target Architecture first. Give two examples of when a Target First approach to architecture development would be most appropriate.

Exercise 14-3
For the following example, identify a suitable class of architecture engagement, and describe the context and the approach you would take for the engagement:
- The CIO requests your advice on the following issues:
  - How to control the increasing IT operational costs
  - How to accurately forecast IT spend
  - How to remove the duplication of systems

Exercise 14-4

For the following example, identify a suitable class of architecture engagement, and describe the context and the approach you would take for the engagement:

- The CEO announces that the organization is merging with its number three competitor, and requests your advice on:
  - How to keep up with the major rivals in the industry
  - How to achieve the merger successfully in the shortest time

14.10 Recommended Reading

The following are recommended sources of further information for this chapter:

- The TOGAF Standard, Version 9.2 Part III, Applying Iteration to the ADM
- The TOGAF Standard, Version 9.2 Part III, Applying the ADM Across the Architecture Landscape

Chapter 15

Security

15.1 Key Learning Points

This chapter describes the guidelines for adapting the ADM for security. This chapter will help you understand the security considerations that need to be addressed during application of the ADM.

> **Key Points Explained**
>
> Upon completion of this chapter you should be able to:
> 1. Briefly explain Enterprise Security Architecture
> 2. Explain how security is a cross-cutting concern
> 3. Briefly explain the recommended security adaptations to the ADM

15.2 Introduction

The Open Group Guide, Integrating Risk and Security within a TOGAF® Enterprise Architecture, provides guidance for security practitioners and Enterprise Architects who need to work with the TOGAF standard to develop an Enterprise Architecture. It explains how the TOGAF method and framework can be tailored to make use of an existing Enterprise Security Architecture in order to address security and risk properly.

In this chapter, we briefly look at some high-level considerations for an Enterprise Security Architecture.

15.3 Enterprise Security Architecture

(Syllabus Reference: Unit 24, Learning Outcome 1: You should be able to briefly explain Enterprise Security Architecture.)

A Security Architecture is a structure of organizational, conceptual, logical, and physical components that interact in a coherent fashion in order to achieve and maintain a state of managed risk and security (or information security). It is both a driver and enabler of secure, safe, resilient, and reliable behavior, as well as for addressing risk areas throughout the enterprise.

An Enterprise Security Architecture does not exist in isolation. As part of the enterprise, it builds on enterprise information that is already available in the Enterprise Architecture, and it produces information that influences the Enterprise Architecture. Figure 22 shows how Enterprise Architecture and Enterprise Security Architecture relate to each other, highlighting the core security and risk concepts that are used in Information Security Management (ISM) and Enterprise Risk Management (ERM). These concepts are listed in the center column, and form a set of foundation concepts that complement and enhance the TOGAF standard. Concepts underlined in the figure are additions to the TOGAF framework and brought in by ISM or ERM.

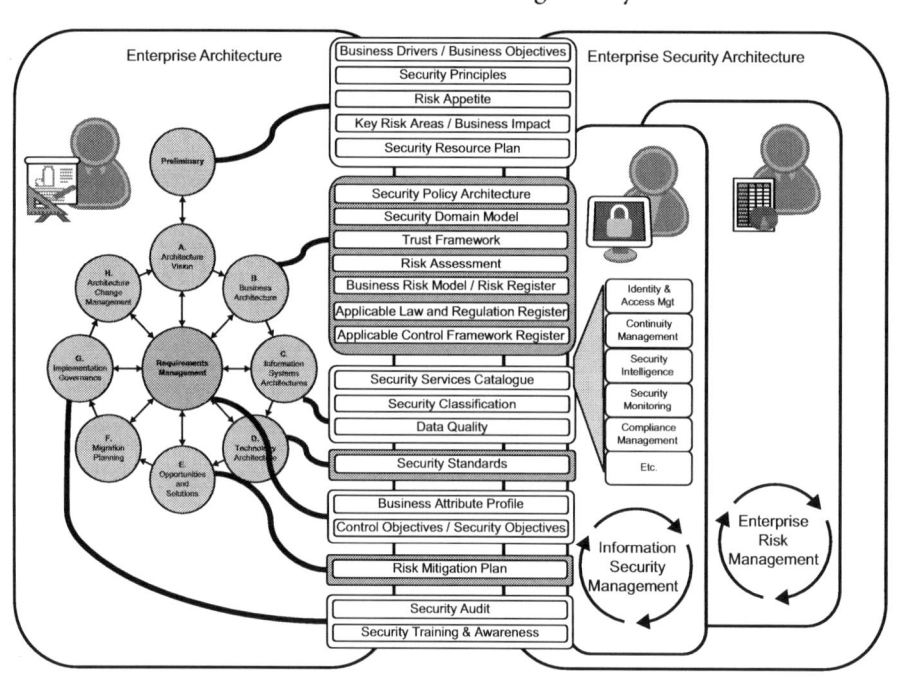

Figure 22: Essential Security and Risk Concepts and their Position in the TOGAF ADM

15.4 Security as a Cross-Cutting Concern

(Syllabus Reference: Unit 24, Learning Outcome 2: You should be able to explain how security is a cross-cutting concern.)

Security Architecture is a cross-cutting concern, pervasive through the whole Enterprise Architecture. It can be described as a coherent collection of views, viewpoints, and artifacts, including security, privacy, and operational risk perspectives, along with related topics like security objectives and security services. The Security Architecture is more than a dataset; it is based on the ISM and ERM processes.

The TOGAF ADM covers the development of the four architecture domains commonly accepted as subsets of an Enterprise Architecture: Business, Data, Application, and Technology. The Security Architecture interacts with all four of them and is therefore called cross-cutting.

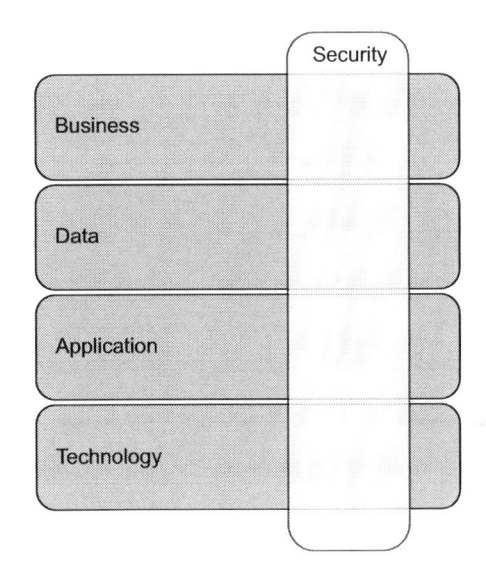

Figure 23:   Security as a Cross-Cutting Concern through the Architecture

As a cross-cutting concern, the Security Architecture impacts and informs the Business, Data, Application, and Technology Architectures. The Security Architecture may often be organized outside of the architecture scope, yet parts of it need to be developed in an integrated fashion with the architecture. These touch-points are briefly explained in the next section.

15.5 Adapting the ADM for Security

(Syllabus Reference: Unit 24, Learning Outcome 3: You should be able to briefly explain the recommended security adaptations to the ADM.)

Table 17 provides summary security guidance for adapting each phase of the ADM.

Table 17: Security Adaptations for the ADM

Phase	Guidance
ADM Requirements Management	*(Syllabus Reference: Unit 20, Learning Outcome 5: You should be able to briefly explain how Security Architecture influences this phase)* Requirements Management plays a central role in architecture work. It is recommended to use Business Attribute Profiling, a requirements engineering technique from The SABSA® Institute, which translates business goals and drivers into requirements using a risk-based approach. Advantages of this technique are: • Executive communication in non-IT terms • Traceability mapping between business drivers and requirements • Performance measurement against business-defined targets • Grouping and structuring of requirements, which facilitates understanding and oversight by architects
Preliminary Phase	*(Syllabus Reference: Unit 1, Learning Outcome 5: You should be able to briefly explain how Security Architecture influences this phase.)* The following security artifacts are recommended to be integrated into existing architecture documentation: • Business Drivers/Business Objectives affecting security • Security Principles • Risk Appetite (the enterprise's attitude towards risk that guides decision-making) • Key Risk Areas/Business Impact Analysis (the deliverable is a list of the key risk areas within the architecture scope) • Security Resource Plan (this identifies the required security resources to deliver the security elements of the architecture)
Phase A: Architecture Vision	*(Syllabus Reference: Unit 4, Learning Outcome 4: You should be able to briefly explain how Security Architecture influences this phase.)* In Phase A sufficient security-specific architecture design is carried out to: • Satisfy the security stakeholders that the end-state does not represent any unknown or unacceptable risk and aligns with corporate policies, standards, and principles • Satisfy business stakeholders – in particular those who control the budget – that the Security Architecture is instrumental in enabling and supporting the overall architecture required to deliver the business opportunities and benefits identified with the right balance between risk, compliance, and business benefits In Phase A, it is essential to identify the complete list of all stakeholders, their concerns, and associated requirements for approval of the architecture. All stakeholders will have security and risk concerns and associated requirements. Separating security stakeholders ensures that the architecture will address a subset of stakeholders and a subset of requirements.

Phase	Guidance
Phase B: Business Architecture	*(Syllabus Reference: Unit 9, Learning Outcome 5: You should be able to briefly explain how Security Architecture influences this phase.)* The security elements of Phase B: Business Architecture comprise business-level trust, risk, and controls, independent from specific IT or other systems within the specific scope of the architecture engagement. The security-related Business Architecture artifacts are as follows: • Security Policy Architecture • Security Domain Model • Trust Framework • Risk Assessment • Business Risk Model/Risk Register • Applicable Law and Regulation Register • Application Control Framework Register
Phase C: Information Systems Architectures	*(Syllabus Reference: Unit 10, Learning Outcome 5, Unit 11, Learning Outcome 4: You should be able to briefly explain how Security Architecture influences this phase.)* The security elements of Phase C: Information Systems Architectures comprise functional security services and their security classification. The artifacts are as follows: • Security Services Catalog • Security Classification • Data Quality
Phase D: Technology Architecture	*(Syllabus Reference: Unit 14, Learning Outcome 4: You should be able to briefly explain how Security Architecture influences this phase.)* In most cases, the development of specific Technology Architecture security artifacts is not necessary, as long as it incorporates the relevant security controls and mechanisms defined in earlier phases. The Security Architect must ensure that the required controls are included in the Technology Architecture and verify whether the controls are used in an effective and efficient way. A security stakeholder may request the creation of a specific Technology Architecture security view or deliverable that describes all security-related technology components and how they inter-relate. This view should explain which business risks are mitigated by what technology, providing justification for the technology.
Phase E: Opportunities & Solutions	*(Syllabus Reference: Unit 16, Learning Outcome 6: You should be able to briefly explain how Security Architecture influences this phase.)* In defining the roadmap, where the sequence of gaps to be addressed is determined, it is imperative that security and risk are evaluated. The value that is to be delivered by work packages should include measures related to security and risk value to ensure the roadmap addresses the complete set of business goals and drivers. The security building blocks defined in the previous phases become SBBs in this phase so that more specific implementation-oriented requirements and specifications are defined. The Security Services Catalog of the Baseline

Phase	Guidance
	Security Architecture probably contains existing security services or security building blocks that meet the requirements. This phase should include a Risk Mitigation Plan, that contains activities to mitigate risks. It is the implementation of the risk mitigation strategy, which could aim to increase the level of control, transfer the risk to another party, avoid the risk by changing the business activity, delay the risk, compensate for the risk, etc.
Phase F: Migration Planning	*(Syllabus Reference: Unit 17, Learning Outcome 6: You should be able to briefly explain how Security Architecture influences this phase.)* Migration is itself a business process that needs to be secured. The migration strategy should include a risk assessment and a Risk Mitigation Plan. In Phase F, the Risk Mitigation Plan is limited to the transition. These concepts have already been mentioned in earlier phases of the ADM. Migration of live environments should always include regression planning so that there is a way to reverse out a failed migration. This is an essential part of risk management. In addition, migration planning should include a security impact analysis to understand any security impacts of the target state of the change.
Phase G: Implementation Governance	*(Syllabus Reference: Unit 18, Learning Outcome 4: You should be able to briefly explain how Security Architecture influences this phase.)* Security Architecture implementation governance provides assurance that the detailed design and implemented processes and systems adhere to the overall Security Architecture. This ensures that deviations from Architecture Principles and implementation guidelines don't create any unacceptable risk. The following are relevant in this phase: • Security Audit • Security Training and Awareness
Phase H: Architecture Change Management	*(Syllabus Reference: Unit 19, Learning Outcome 4: You should be able to briefly explain how Security Architecture influences this phase.)* Phase H does not produce tangible security outputs but defines two processes essential for continued alignment between the business requirements and the architecture: risk management and Architecture Governance. Even though they are not formal artifacts, they are included here to emphasize their importance. Risk management is the process in which the existing architecture is continuously evaluated regarding changes to business opportunity and security threat. Based on the results of this process, the current architecture might deem it unsuitable to mitigate changed or new risks, or it might constrain the business too much in exploiting new opportunities. In that case, a decision on architecture change must be made. Architecture Governance is the process in which decisions are made on changes to the existing architecture, either by minor changes in the current iteration or by means of a completely new iteration. This is explained in the TOGAF Architecture Governance Framework. Changes related to risk and security should be an explicit part of that framework. Large changes to the architecture should include a security impact analysis.

15.6 Summary

The Open Group Guide, Integrating Risk and Security within a TOGAF® Enterprise Architecture, provides guidance for security practitioners and Enterprise Architects who need to work with the TOGAF standard to develop an Enterprise Architecture. It explains how the TOGAF method and framework can be tailored to make use of an existing Enterprise Security Architecture in order to address security and risk properly.

15.7 Exercises

Exercise 15-1
A new regulation regarding security compliance of e-commerce systems is being introduced. Describe the high-level approach you would take to manage its introduction using the TOGAF ADM.

15.8 Recommended Reading

The following are recommended sources of further information for this chapter:
- The Open Group Guide, Integrating Risk and Security within a TOGAF® Enterprise Architecture

PART 3
The Architecture Content Framework

In this Part, we introduce the Architecture Content Framework and high-level concepts of the TOGAF Content Metamodel. The Content Framework describes the relationships between all the concepts in an Enterprise Architecture.

Chapter 16
Architecture Content Framework

16.1 Key Learning Points

This chapter will help you understand the TOGAF Architecture Content Framework and the high-level concepts of the TOGAF Content Metamodel.

> **Key Points Explained**
>
> Upon completion of this chapter you should be able to:
> 1. Explain the purpose of the Architecture Content Framework
> 2. Describe the relationship between the Architecture Content Framework and the TOGAF ADM
> 3. Describe the main components of the TOGAF Content Metamodel
> 4. Describe the core metamodel concepts
> 5. Explain the purpose of dividing the metamodel into core and extensions
> 6. Describe the key concepts related to the core metamodel entities

16.2 Introduction

(Syllabus Reference: Unit 5, Learning Outcome 1: You should be able to explain the purpose of the Architecture Content Framework.)

The Architecture Content Framework provides a detailed model of architectural work products, including deliverables, artifacts within deliverables, and the Architecture Building Blocks (ABBs) that artifacts represent. It helps to improve the consistency of the TOGAF outputs by presenting outputs in a consistent and structured way, and also helps to reference and classify them.

The benefits of using the Architecture Content Framework include that it provides a comprehensive checklist of architecture outputs, it promotes better integration of work products, and it provides a detailed open standard for how architectures should be described.

> **Using the TOGAF Architecture Content Framework with Other Content Frameworks**
>
> The Architecture Content Framework allows the TOGAF framework to be used as a stand-alone framework for architecture within an enterprise. However, other content frameworks exist and it is expected that some enterprises may opt to use an external framework in conjunction with the TOGAF ADM instead. In these cases, the TOGAF Architecture Content Framework provides a useful reference and starting point for TOGAF content to be mapped to the metamodels of other frameworks.

16.3 The Content Framework and the TOGAF ADM

(Syllabus Reference: Unit 5, Learning Outcome 3: You should be able to describe the relationship between the Architecture Content Framework and the TOGAF ADM.)

The ADM addresses a business need through a process of vision, definition, planning, and governance. At each stage the ADM takes information as inputs and creates outputs. The content framework provides a structure for the ADM that defines inputs and outputs in detail and puts each deliverable into the context of the architecture. So the content framework is a companion to the ADM. The ADM describes what needs to be done to create an architecture and the content framework describes what it should look like in the end.

16.4 Why do we Need a Metamodel?

The use of models helps to simplify complex subjects, such as an enterprise, to make them simpler to understand. A content metamodel is used to formalize the definition of an Enterprise Architecture, structuring architectural information in an ordered way so that it can be processed to meet the stakeholder needs, which aids communication and understanding.

The majority of architecture stakeholders do not actually need to know what the architecture metamodel is and are only concerned with specific issues, such as the functionality that the application supports, or the processes which will be impacted by the project. In order to meet the needs of these stakeholders, the TOGAF standard concepts of building blocks, catalogs, matrices, and diagrams are used. A content metamodel can also formalize the relationship between objects, allowing for traceability. Most importantly it can be used as a data schema mapping for Enterprise Architecture tools.

> **What is a Metamodel?**
> A model that describes how and with what the architecture will be described in a structured way.
> [Source: The TOGAF Standard, Version 9.2 Part I, Definitions]

16.5 Components of the Content Metamodel

(Syllabus Reference: Unit 5, Learning Outcome 2: You should be able to describe the main components of the Content Metamodel.)

The Architecture Content Framework is based on a standard content metamodel that defines all the types of building blocks in an architecture, showing how these building blocks can be described and how they relate to one another. For example, when creating an architecture, an architect will identify applications, data entities held within applications, and technologies that implement those applications. These applications will in turn support particular groups of business users or actors, and will be used to fulfill business services. The content metamodel identifies all of these entities (i.e., application, data entity, technology, actor, and business service), shows the relationships that are possible between them (e.g., actors consume business services), and identifies artifacts that can be used to represent them.

Figure 24 shows the highest level abstraction of the TOGAF Content Metamodel, which closely corresponds to the ADM.

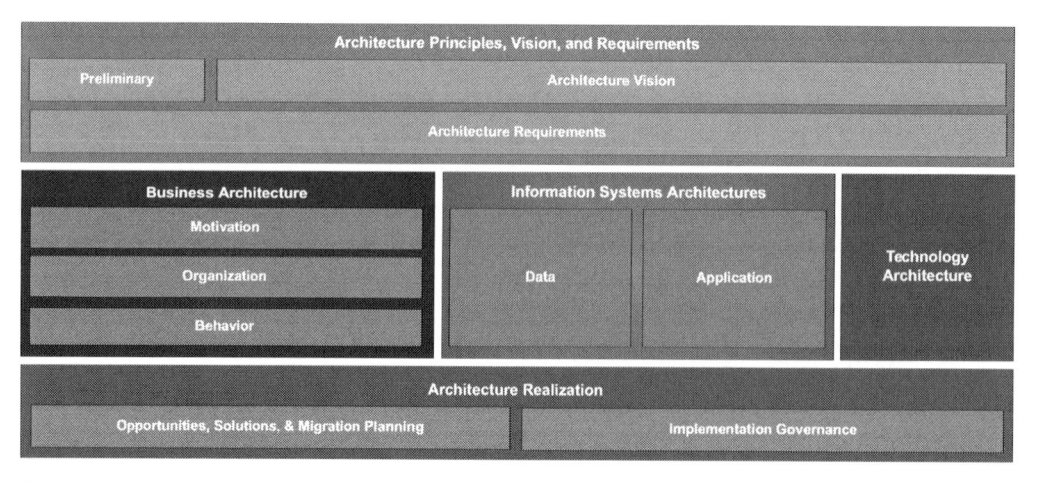

Figure 24: Content Metamodel Simplified

The metamodel can be thought of as having three layers as follows:

Layer 1: Architecture Principles, Vision, and Requirements
The entities in this layer are intended to capture the surrounding context of formal architecture models, including general Architecture Principles, strategic context that forms input for architecture modeling, and requirements generated from the architecture. The architecture context is typically collected in the Preliminary and Architecture Vision phases.

Layer 2: The Architecture Domains
Business Architecture entities capture architectural models of business operation, looking specifically at factors that motivate the enterprise, how the enterprise is organizationally structured, and also what functional capabilities the enterprise has.

Information Systems Architecture entities capture architecture models of IT systems, looking at applications and data in line with the TOGAF ADM phases.

Technology Architecture entities capture procured technology assets that are used to implement and realize information system solutions.

Layer 3: Architecture Realization
The entities in this layer capture change roadmaps showing the transition between architecture states and binding statements that are used to steer and govern an implementation of the architecture.

Figure 25 shows a more detailed representation of the content metamodel. Further detailed diagrams including the detailed relationships are provided in Part IV: Architecture Content Framework.

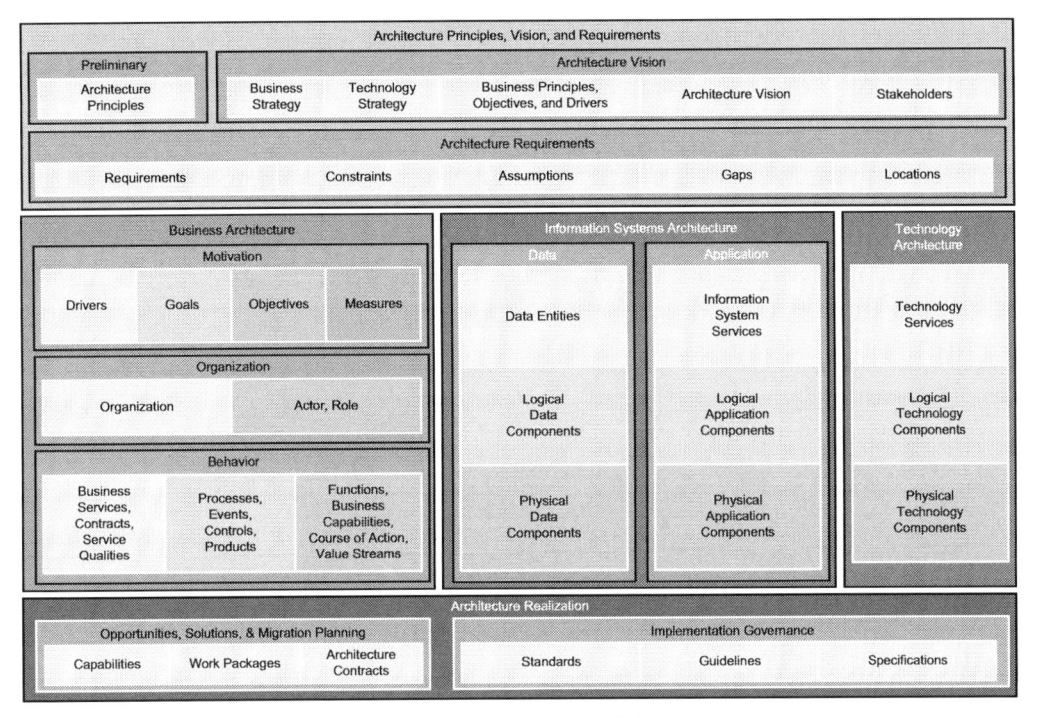

Figure 25: Detailed Representation of the Content Metamodel

16.6 Core Metamodel Concepts

(Syllabus Reference: Unit 7, Learning Outcome 1: You should be able to describe the Core Metamodel Concepts.)

A TOGAF architecture is based on defining ABBs within architecture catalogs, specifying the relationships between those building blocks in architecture matrices, and presenting communication diagrams that show in a precise way what the architecture is. The core concepts that make up the content metamodel are described in the following subsections.

16.6.1 Core and Extension Content

(Syllabus Reference: Unit 7, Learning Outcome 2: You should be able to describe the purpose of dividing the metamodel into core and extensions.)

In order for the TOGAF standard to be usable in many different scenarios and situations, it is necessary to provide both a fully featured Enterprise Architecture metamodel for content and also the ability to avoid carrying out unnecessary activities. The metamodel supports this through partitioning into Core and Extension content, as shown in Figure 26, with the Core Content designed not to be altered.

Extension to support in-depth, operational governance	Extension to support definition of discrete business and application services	Extension to support process modeling	Extension to support data modeling	Extension to support consolidation of applications and technology across locations	Extension to support linkage of drivers, goals, and objectives to organizations and services
Governance Extensions	Services Extensions	Process Modeling Extensions	Data Extensions	Infrastructure Consolidation Extensions	Motivation Extensions

Core Content Metamodel

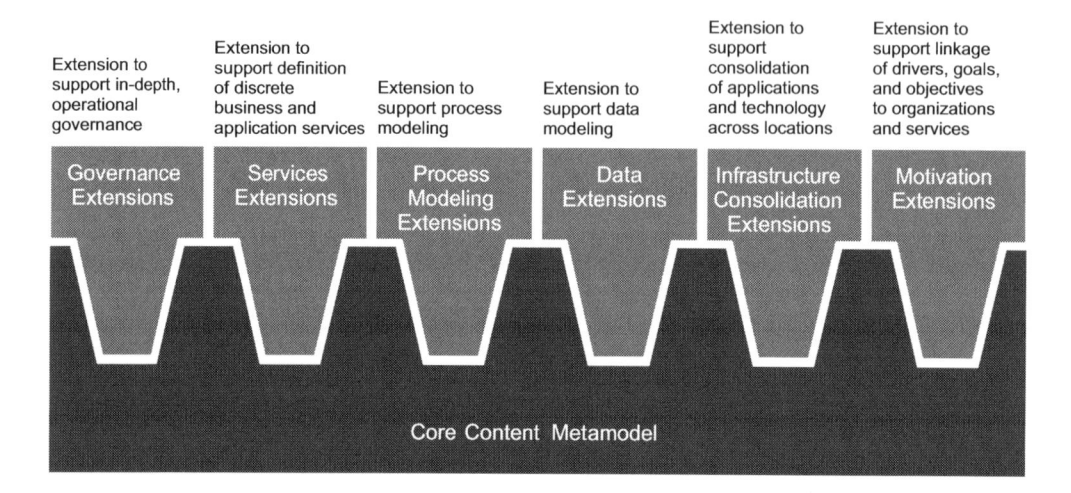

Figure 26: Core Content Metamodel and its Extensions

The Core Content Metamodel provides a minimum set of architectural content to support traceability across artifacts. Additional metamodel concepts to support more specific or more in-depth modeling are contained within a set of extensions that logically group together extension catalogs, matrices, and diagrams.

All extension modules are optional and should be selected during the Preliminary Phase of the architecture development to meet the needs of the organization. Additionally, the extension groupings described by the content metamodel are only a suggestion and further tailoring may be carried out to suit specific needs at the discretion of the architects.

This Core Content and Extension concept is intended as a move towards supporting formal method extension approaches within the TOGAF standard, such as the method plug-in concept found within the Software Process Engineering Metamodel (SPEM™) developed by the Object Management Group (OMG).

16.6.2 Core Metamodel Entities

(Syllabus Reference: Unit 7, Learning Outcome 3: You should be able to describe the key concepts related to the core metamodel entities.)

The content metamodel uses the core terms listed in Table 18 to describe metamodel entities.

Table 18: Core Metamodel Entities

Entity	Description
Actor	A person, organization, or system that is outside the consideration of the architecture model, but interacts with it.
Application Component	An encapsulation of application functionality that is aligned to implementation structure.
Business Capability	A particular ability that a business may possess or exchange to achieve a specific purpose.
Business Service	Supports business capabilities through an explicitly defined interface and is explicitly governed by an organization.
Course of Action	Direction and focus provided by strategic goals and objectives, often to deliver the value proposition characterized in the business model.
Data Entity	An encapsulation of data that is recognized by a business domain expert as a discrete concept. Data entities can be tied to applications, repositories, and services and may be structured according to implementation considerations.
Function	Delivers business capabilities closely aligned to an organization, but not explicitly governed by the organization.
Information System Service	The automated elements of a business service. An information system service may deliver or support part or all of one or more business services.
Organization Unit	A self-contained unit of resources with goals, objectives, and measures. Organization units may include external parties and business partner organizations.
Role	An actor assumes a role to perform a task.
Technology Component	An encapsulation of technology infrastructure that represents a class of technology product or specific technology product.
Technology Service	A technical capability required to provide enabling infrastructure that supports the delivery of applications.
Value Stream	A representation of an end-to-end collection of value-adding activities that create an overall result for a customer, stakeholder, or end-user.

The relationships between these core metamodel entities are summarized as follows:

- **Process should normally be used to describe flow**
  A process is a flow of interactions between functions and services and cannot be physically deployed. All processes should describe the flow of execution for a function and therefore the deployment of a process is through the function it supports; i.e., an application implements a function that has a process.
- **Function describes units of business capability at all levels of granularity**
  The term *function* is used to describe a unit of business capability at all levels of granularity, encapsulating terms such as value chain, process area, capability, business function, etc. Any bounded unit of business function should be described as a function.
- **Business services support organizational objectives and are defined at a level of granularity consistent with the level of governance needed**
  A business service operates as a boundary for one or more functions. The granularity of business services is dependent on the focus and emphasis of the business (as reflected by its drivers, goals, and objectives). A service in Service Oriented Architecture (SOA) terminology (i.e., a deployable unit of application functionality) is actually much closer to an application service, application component, or technology component, which may implement or support a business service.
- **Business services are deployed onto application components**
  Business services may be realized by business activity that does not relate to IT, or may be realized through IT. Business services that are realized through IT are implemented onto application components. Application components can be hierarchically decomposed and may support one or more business services. It is possible for a business service to be supported by multiple application components, but this is problematic from a governance standpoint and is symptomatic of business services that are too coarse-grained, or application components that are too fine-grained.
- **Application components are deployed onto technology components**
  An application component is implemented by a suite of technology components. For example, an application, such as "HR System", would typically be implemented on several technology components, including hardware, application server software, and application services.

16.6.3 Building Blocks, Catalogs, Matrices, and Diagrams

In order to meet the needs of most stakeholders who do not need to know what the TOGAF Content Metamodel is, the TOGAF concepts of building blocks, catalogs, matrices, and diagrams are used.

Building blocks are entities of a particular type within the metamodel (for example, a business service called "Purchase Order"). Building blocks carry metadata according to the metamodel, which supports query and analysis. For example, business services have a metadata attribute for *owner*, which allows a stakeholder to query all business services owned by a particular organization. Building blocks may also include dependent or contained entities as appropriate to the context of the architecture (e.g., a business service called "Purchase Order" may implicitly include a number of processes, data entities, application components, etc.).

Catalogs are lists of building blocks of a specific type, or of related types, that are used for governance or reference purposes (e.g., an organization chart, showing locations and actors). As with building blocks, catalogs carry metadata according to the metamodel, which supports query and analysis.

Matrices are grids that show relationships between two or more model entities. Matrices are used to represent relationships that are list-based rather than graphical (e.g., a CRUD matrix showing which applications Create, Read, Update, and Delete a particular type of data is difficult to represent visually).

Diagrams are renderings of architectural content in a graphical format. Diagrams can be used as a technique for graphically populating architecture content or for checking the completeness of information that has been collected. The TOGAF standard defines a set of architecture diagrams to be created (e.g., organization chart). Each of these diagrams may be created several times for an architecture with different styles or content coverage to suit stakeholder concerns.

Building blocks, catalogs, matrices, and diagrams are all concepts that are well supported by leading Enterprise Architecture tools. In environments where tools are used to model the architecture, such tools typically support mechanisms to search, filter, and query the Architecture Repository. The interactions are summarized in Figure 27.

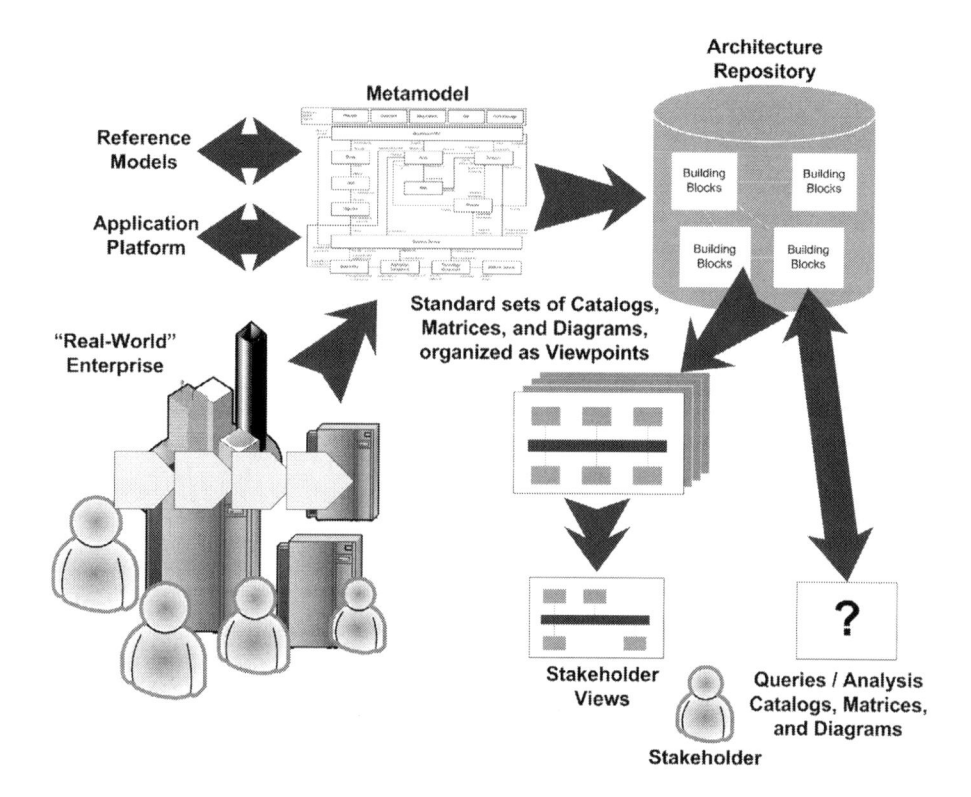

Figure 27: Interactions between Metamodel, Building Blocks, Matrices, Diagrams, and Stakeholders

16.7 Summary

The Architecture Content Framework presents outputs in a consistent and structured way. It has three categories of work products: deliverables, artifacts, and building blocks. There is a mapping from the Architecture Content Framework to the TOGAF ADM phases.

The TOGAF Content Metamodel is used to structure architectural information in a particular way. A metamodel is a precise definition of the constructs and rules needed for creating models. The TOGAF Metamodel has both a core and a set of extension modules.

16.8 Exercises

Exercise 17-1

You are establishing a content metamodel for your organization based on the TOGAF Content Framework. Which extensions would be most appropriate for the following scenarios:
- The organization has to comply with several statutory regulations on how it handles customer data
- The organization is taking its first steps to develop an Enterprise Architecture
- The organization is merging with a competitor and needs to consolidate its service offerings

16.9 Recommended Reading

The following are recommended sources of further information for this chapter:
- The TOGAF Standard, Version 9.2 Part IV, Introduction
- The TOGAF Standard, Version 9.2 Part IV, Content Metamodel
- The TOGAF Standard, Version 9.2 Architecture Content Metamodel Overview presentation: www.togaf.info/sg04

PART 4
The Enterprise Continuum

In this Part, we examine the Enterprise Continuum in more depth:
- Chapter 17 describes Architecture Partitioning
- Chapter 18 describes the Architecture Repository, which is a model for a physical instance of the Enterprise Continuum

Recommended reading before commencing this Part of the Study Guide includes:
- TOGAF 9 Foundation Study Guide, Chapter 6, The Enterprise Continuum and Tools

Chapter 17
Architecture Partitioning

17.1 Key Learning Points

The purpose of this chapter is to help you understand how Architecture Partitioning can be used to simplify the development and maintenance of an Enterprise Architecture.

> **Key Points Explained**
>
> Upon completion of this chapter you should be able to:
> 1. Describe the purpose of Architecture Partitioning
> 2. Describe the classification criteria for solutions and architectures when considering partitioning
> 3. Describe how Architecture Partitioning can be employed in the Preliminary Phase of the ADM

17.2 Introduction

(Syllabus Reference: Unit 21, Learning Outcome 1: You should be able to describe the purpose of Architecture Partitioning.)

The main purpose of Architecture Partitioning is to manage complexity by simplifying the development and management of the Enterprise Architecture. Architectures are partitioned in order to:

- **Manage Complexity**: addressing all problems within a single architecture can be too complicated
- **Manage Conflicts**: different organizational unit architectures conflict with one another
- **Manage Parallel Developments**: different teams need to work on different elements of architecture at the same time and partitions allow for specific groups of architects to own and develop specific segments of the architecture

- **Manage Re-use**: effective architecture re-use requires modular architecture segments that can be taken and incorporated into broader architectures and solutions

17.3 Applying Classification to Partitioned Architectures

(Syllabus Reference: Unit 21, Learning Outcome 2: You should be able to describe the classification criteria for solutions and architectures when considering partitioning.)

The following classification criteria can be used to support solution partitioning:

- **Subject Matter (Breadth)**: solutions are naturally organized into groups to support operational management and control
  Examples of solution partitions according to subject matter would include applications, departments, divisions, products, services, service centers, sites, etc. Solution decomposition by subject matter is typically the fundamental technique for structuring both solutions and the architectures that represent them.
- **Time**: solution lifecycles are typically organized around a timeline, which allows the impact of solution development, introduction, operation, and retirement to be managed against other business activity occurring in similar time periods
- **Maturity/Volatility**: the maturity and volatility of a solution will typically impact the speed of execution required for the solution lifecycle
  Additionally, volatility and maturity will shape investment priorities. Solutions existing in highly volatile environments may be better suited to rapid, agile development techniques.

The following classification criteria can be used to support partitioning of architectures:

- **Depth**: the level of detail within an architecture has a strong correlation to the stakeholder groups that will be interested in the architecture
  Typically less detailed architectures will be of interest to executive stakeholders. As architectures increase in detail, their relevance to implementation and operational personnel will also increase.

The following characteristics are generally not used to partition an Architecture Landscape:

- Architectures used to describe the Architecture Landscape are generally not abstract
- Solution volatility generally prevents architectures from being defined that are far in the future; volatility also reduces the accuracy of historic architectures over time, as the organization changes and adapts to new circumstances

Using the classification criteria above, architectures can be grouped into partitions.

17.4 Applying Partitioning to the ADM
(Syllabus Reference: Unit 21, Learning Outcome 3: You should be able to describe how Architecture Partitioning can be employed in the Preliminary Phase of the ADM.)

The key objective of the Preliminary Phase is to establish the Architecture Capability for the enterprise. In practical terms this activity will require the establishment of a number of architecture partitions, with defined boundaries and ownership.

Generally speaking, each team carrying out architecture activity within the enterprise will own one or more architecture partitions and will execute the ADM to define, govern, and realize their architectures. If more than one team is expected to work on a single architecture, this can become problematic, as the precise responsibilities of each team are difficult to establish. For this reason, it is preferable to apply partitioning to the architecture until each architecture has one owning team.

Steps within the Preliminary Phase to support Architecture Partitioning are as follows:
- Determine the organization structure for architecture within the enterprise and identify the teams
  For each team, establish appropriate boundaries including:
  - Subject matter areas
  - Level of detail
  - Time periods
  - Stakeholders

- Determine the responsibilities for each architecture team
  This step applies partitioning logic to the Enterprise Architecture in order to firstly identify the scope of each team and secondly to partition the architecture under the remit of a single team. Once complete, this step should have partitioned the entire scope of the enterprise and should have assigned responsibility for each partitioned architecture to a single team. Partitioning should create a definition of each architecture that includes:
  - Subject matter areas
  - Level of detail
  - Time period
  - Stakeholders
- Determine the relationships between architectures by considering where the architectures overlap and the compliance requirements between architectures
  This step allows governance relationships to be formalized and also shows where artifacts from an architecture are expected to be re-used within other architectures.

Once the Preliminary Phase is complete, the teams conducting the architecture should be defined. Each team should have a defined scope and the relationships between teams and architecture should be understood. An example of an allocation of teams to architecture is shown in Figure 28.

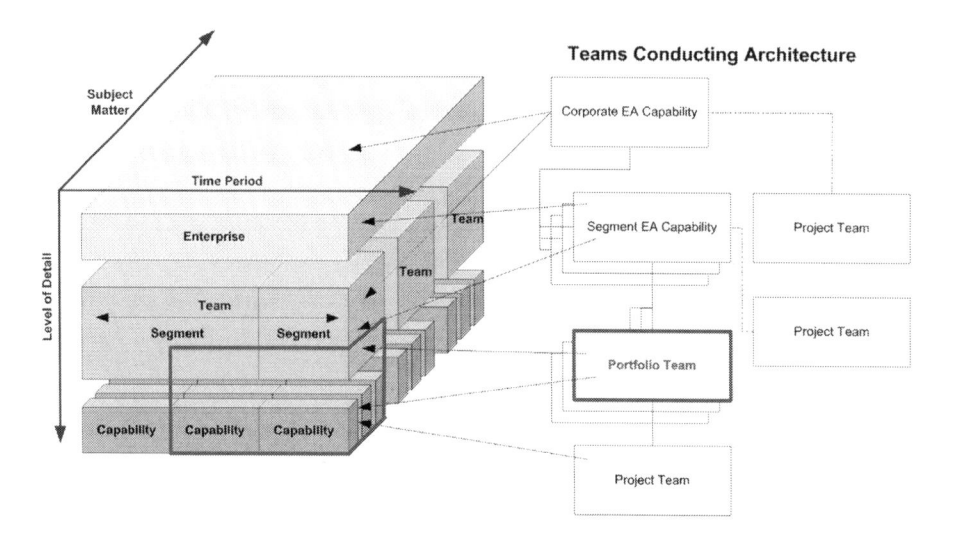

Figure 28:   Allocation of Teams to Architecture Scope

17.5 Summary

The TOGAF standard provides guidance on classifying and partitioning architectures. The use of partitioning can be beneficial to manage complexity, allow for parallel developments, and facilitate re-use.

17.6 Recommended Reading

The following are recommended sources of further information for this chapter:
- The TOGAF Standard, Version 9.2 Part V, Architecture Partitioning

Chapter 18
Architecture Repository

18.1 Key Learning Points

The purpose of this chapter is to help you understand the Architecture Repository, its constituent parts, and its relationship to other parts of the TOGAF standard.

> **Key Points Explained**
>
> Upon completion of this chapter you should be able to:
> 1. Explain the relationship between the Architecture Repository and the Enterprise Repository
> 2. Describe the purpose of the repository areas that hold the outputs of projects, specifically:
>   - Architecture Landscape
>   - Reference Library
>   - Standards Information Base
>   - Governance Log
>   - Architecture Requirements Repository
>   - Solutions Landscape
>   - Enterprise Repository

18.2 Introduction

(Syllabus Reference: Unit 22, Learning Outcome 1: You should be able to explain the relationship between the Architecture Repository and the Enterprise Repository.)

Operating a mature Architecture Capability within a large enterprise creates a huge volume of architectural output. Effective management and leverage of these architectural products requires a formal taxonomy for different types of architectural assets, alongside dedicated processes and tools for architectural content storage.

This section of the TOGAF standard provides a structural framework for an Architecture Repository that allows an enterprise to distinguish between different types of architectural assets that exist at different levels of abstraction in the organization.

This Architecture Repository is one part of the wider Enterprise Repository. While the Architecture Repository holds information concerning the Enterprise Architecture and associated artifacts, there are a number of enterprise repositories that support the architecture. The Architecture Repository also provides the capability to link architectural assets to components of the Detailed Design, Deployment, and Service Management Repositories.

18.3 The Repository in Detail

(Syllabus Reference: Unit 22, Learning Outcome 2: You should be able to describe the purpose of the repository areas that hold outputs of projects.)

The Architecture Repository is a logical information store for outputs of executing the ADM and is shown in Figure 29.

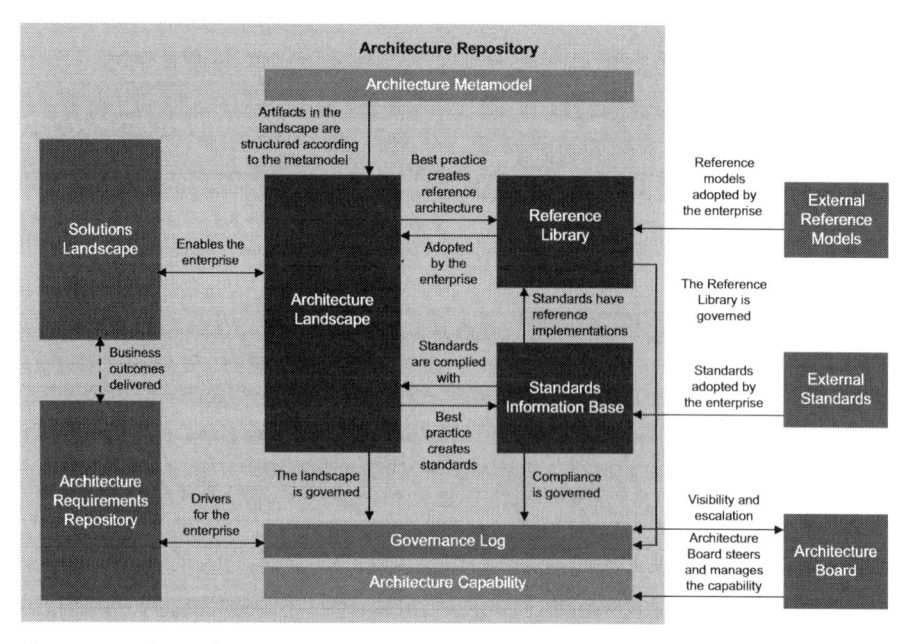

Figure 29: The Architecture Repository

18.3.1 Architecture Metamodel

The Architecture Metamodel describes the architecture framework in use within the enterprise.

18.3.2 Architecture Landscape

(Syllabus Reference: Unit 22, Learning Outcome 2.1: You should be able to describe the purpose of the Architecture Landscape.)

The Architecture Landscape shows the state of the operating enterprise at particular points in time. Due to the sheer volume and the diverse stakeholder needs throughout an entire enterprise, the Architecture Landscape is divided into three levels of granularity:

1. **Strategic Architectures** show a long-term summary view of the entire enterprise. Strategic Architectures provide an organizing framework for operational and change activity and allow for direction setting at an executive level.
2. **Segment Architectures** provide more detailed operating models for areas within an enterprise. Segment Architectures can be used at the program or portfolio level to organize and operationally align more detailed change activity.
3. **Capability Architectures** show in a more detailed fashion how the enterprise can support a particular unit of capability. Capability Architectures are used to provide an overview of current capability, target capability, and capability increments and allow for individual work packages and projects to be grouped within managed portfolios and programs.

18.3.3 Reference Library

(Syllabus Reference: Unit 22, Learning Outcome 2.2: You should be able to describe the purpose of the Reference Library.)

The Reference Library contains re-usable architecture work products. The Reference Library provides a repository area to hold reference materials that should be used to develop architectures. Reference materials held may be obtained from a variety of sources, including standards bodies, product and service vendors, industry communities or forums, standard templates, and enterprise best practice. The Reference Library should contain reference architectures, reference models, a viewpoint library, and templates.

In order to segregate different classes of architecture reference materials, the Reference Library can use the Architecture Continuum as a method for classification.

18.3.4 Standards Information Base

(Syllabus Reference: Unit 22, Learning Outcome 2.3: You should be able to describe the purpose of the Standards Information Base.)

The Standards Information Base defines the compliance criteria for work governed by architecture. It is a repository area to hold the set of specifications to which architectures must conform.

Establishment of a Standards Information Base provides an unambiguous basis for architectural governance since the standards are easily accessible to projects and therefore the obligations of the project can be understood and planned for. Also standards are stated in a clear and unambiguous manner, so that compliance can be objectively assessed.

18.3.5 Governance Log

(Syllabus Reference: Unit 22, Learning Outcome 2.4: You should be able to describe the purpose of the Governance Log.)

The Governance Log is a repository area for holding shared information relating to the ongoing governance of projects, capturing results of governance activity such as compliance assessments. Maintaining a shared repository of governance information is important because decisions made during projects (such as standards deviations or the rationale for a particular architectural approach) need to be accessed on an ongoing basis. For example, if a system is to be replaced, having sight of the key architectural decisions that shaped the initial implementation is highly valuable, as it will highlight constraints that may otherwise be obscured. Also, many stakeholders are interested in the outcome of project governance (e.g., other projects, customers of the project, the Architecture Board, etc.).

18.3.6 Architecture Requirements Repository

(Syllabus Reference: Unit 22, Learning Outcome 2.5: You should be able to describe the purpose of the Architecture Requirements Repository.)

The Architecture Requirements Repository is used by all phases of the ADM to record and manage all information relevant to the architecture requirements. The requirements address the many types of architecture requirements; i.e., strategic, segment, and capability requirements which are the major drivers for the Enterprise Architecture.

The Requirements Management phase is responsible for the management of the contents of the Architecture Requirements Repository and ensuring the integrity of all requirements and their availability for access by all phases.

18.3.7 Solutions Landscape
(Syllabus Reference: Unit 22, Learning Outcome 2.5: You should be able to describe the purpose of the Solutions Landscape.)

The Solutions Landscape holds the Solution Building Blocks (SBBs), which support the Architecture Building Blocks (ABBs) specified, developed, and deployed. The building blocks may be products or services, which may be, categorized according to the Enterprise Continuum categorization and/or the ABB specifications as Strategic, Segment, or Capability SBBs.

SBBs may also include tools, systems, services, and information, which describe the actual solutions that may be selected and their operation. For example, vendor-specific reference models or vendor-specific levels 4 and 5 of the IT4IT™ Reference Architecture would be defined here. The Solutions Landscape does not include the information and data content produced by the solutions selected; that is the responsibility of the solutions themselves.

18.3.8 Enterprise Repository
(Syllabus Reference: Unit 22, Learning Outcome 2.5: You should be able to describe the purpose of the Enterprise Repository.)

The Architecture Repository is one part of the wider Enterprise Repository. While the Architecture Repository holds information concerning the Enterprise Architecture and associated artifacts, there are a considerable number of enterprise repositories that support the architecture. These can include development repositories, specific operating environments, instructions, and configuration management repositories.

18.3.9 Architecture Capability

The Architecture Capability describes the organization, roles, skills, and responsibilities of the Enterprise Architecture practice.

18.4 Relationship to Other Parts of the TOGAF Standard

The ADM has reminders regarding when to use assets from the Architecture Repository. The Architecture Repository is a model for an implementation of the Enterprise Continuum.

18.5 Summary

The TOGAF standard provides a structural framework for a repository that is one part of a wider Enterprise IT Repository. The Architecture Repository is a logical information store for the outputs which result from executing the ADM and for inputs to it. It is a model for a physical instance of the Enterprise Continuum.

18.6 Recommended Reading

The following are recommended sources of further information for this chapter:

- The TOGAF Standard, Version 9.2 Part V, Architecture Repository

PART 5
TOGAF Reference Models

In this Part, we describe two example reference models provided with the TOGAF Library: the Technical Reference Model and the Integrated Information Infrastructure Reference Model.

Recommended reading before commencing this Part of the Study Guide includes:
- TOGAF 9 Foundation Study Guide, Chapter 13, TOGAF Reference Models

Chapter 19

The TOGAF Technical Reference Model (TRM)

19.1 Key Learning Points

This chapter describes the TOGAF Technical Reference Model (TRM) in detail.

> **Key Points Explained**
>
> Upon completion of this chapter you should be able to:
> 1. Explain the TRM graphic, including the following key elements:
>   - Application Software Categories
>   - Application Platform Interface
>   - Application Platform
>   - Communications Infrastructure Interface
>   - Qualities
> 2. Briefly describe the structure of the TRM
> 3. Briefly explain the main architecture objectives of using the TRM
> 4. Explain what the Platform Services Taxonomy is
> 5. Explain what the Service Quality Taxonomy is

19.2 Structure of the TRM

(Syllabus Reference: Unit 12, Learning Outcome 2: You should be able to briefly describe the structure of the TRM.)

The TRM has two main components:
1. A *taxonomy* that defines terminology, and provides a coherent description of the components and conceptual structure of an information system
2. A model, with an associated *TRM graphic*, that provides a visual representation of the taxonomy, as an aid to understanding

Figure 30 shows the high-level model of the TRM. The three main parts of the TRM (Application Software, Application Platform, and Communications Infrastructure) are connected by two interfaces (Application Platform Interface and Communications Infrastructure Interface).

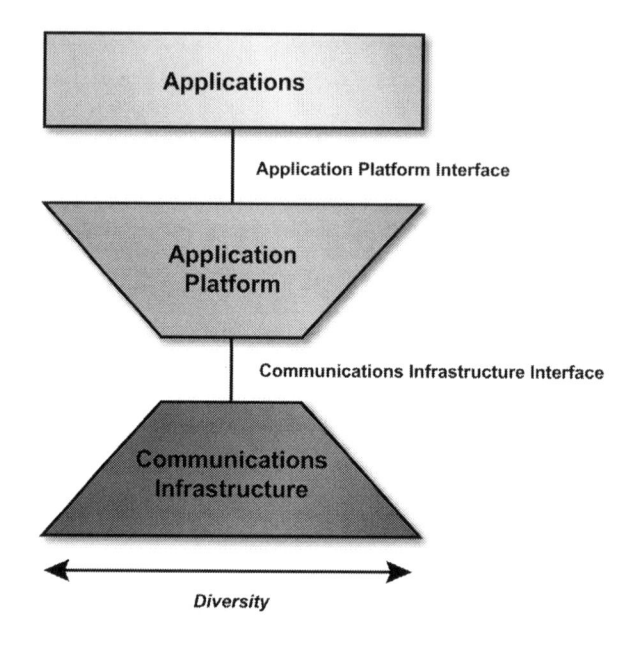

Figure 30: Technical Reference Model – High-Level Model View

(Syllabus Reference: Unit 12, Learning Outcome 3: You should be able to briefly explain the main architectural objectives of using the TRM.)

The use of the TRM emphasizes two major common architecture objectives:
1. **Application Portability**, via the Application Platform Interface, identifying the set of services that are to be made available in a standard way to applications via the platform
2. **Interoperability**, via the Communications Infrastructure Interface, identifying the set of Communications Infrastructure services that are to be built on in a standard way

19.3 The TRM in Detail

(Syllabus Reference: Unit 12, Learning Outcome 1: You should be able to explain the TRM graphic.)

Figure 31 shows the detail of the TRM. This highlights the platform service categories together with the external environment entities, such as Applications and Communications Infrastructure.

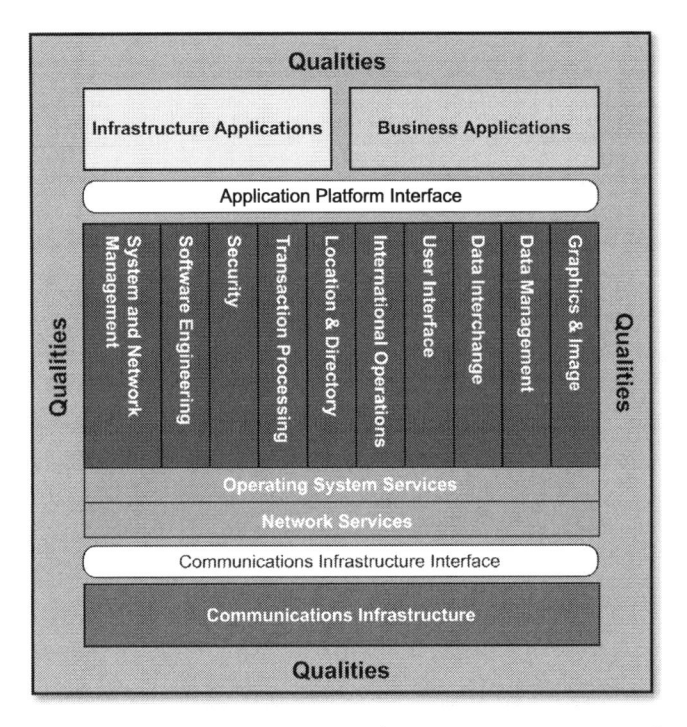

Figure 31: Detailed Technical Reference Model (Showing Service Categories)

The following sections look at various elements from the TRM.

19.3.1 Application Software

(Syllabus Reference: Unit 12, Learning Outcome 1.1: You should be able to explain Application Software Categories within the TRM.)

The TRM recognizes two categories of Application Software:
1. **Business Applications**, which implement business processes for an enterprise or vertical industry. These are specific to the enterprise or vertical industry. The internal structure of business applications relates closely to the specific Application Software configuration selected by an organization. Examples of business applications include patient record management services used in the medical industry, inventory management services used in the retail industry, geological data modeling services used in the petroleum industry, etc.

2. **Infrastructure Applications**, which provide general-purpose business functionality, based on infrastructure services. This is usually widespread Commercial Off-The-Shelf (COTS) software, where it is uneconomic to consider custom implementation. Examples of applications in this category include electronic payment and funds transfer services, electronic mail client services, calendaring and scheduling services, spreadsheet, presentation and document editing software, etc.

19.3.2 Application Platform Interface

(Syllabus Reference: Unit 12, Learning Outcome 1.2: You should be able to explain the Application Software Interface within the TRM.)

The Application Platform Interface specifies a complete interface between the Application Software and the underlying Application Platform across which all services are provided. A rigorous definition of the interface results in application portability, provided that both platform and application conform to it. For this to work, the API definition must include the syntax and semantics of not just the programmatic interface, but also all necessary protocol and data structure definitions.

19.3.3 Application Platform

(Syllabus Reference: Unit 12, Learning Outcome 1.3: You should be able to explain the Application Platform within the TRM.)

The Application Platform is a single conceptual entity that includes Operating System Services, Network Services, and a generic set of platform services. This is the set of all possible services. A specific Target Architecture will contain only those services needed to support the required function. A typical architecture will also contain several Application Platforms; for example, a desktop client, file server, print server, Internet server, database server, etc, each of which comprises a specific set of services to support the defined functionality.

19.3.4 Interfaces between Services

In addition to supporting Application Software through the Application Platform Interface (API), services in the Application Platform may support each other, either by openly specified interfaces or by private, unexposed interfaces. A key goal of architecture development is for service modules to be capable of replacement by other modules providing the same service functionality via the same service API.

19.3.5 Communications Infrastructure

The Communications Infrastructure provides the basic services to interconnect systems and provide the basic mechanisms for opaque transfer of data. It contains the hardware and software elements which make up the networking and physical communications links used by a system, and all the other systems connected to the network. It deals with the complex world of networks and the physical Communications Infrastructure, including switches, service providers, and the physical transmission media.

19.3.6 Communications Infrastructure Interface

(Syllabus Reference: Unit 12, Learning Outcome 1.4: You should be able to explain the Communications Infrastructure Interface within the TRM.)

The Communications Infrastructure Interface is the interface between the Application Platform and the Communications Infrastructure.

19.3.7 Qualities

(Syllabus Reference: Unit 12, Learning Outcome 1.5: You should be able to explain Qualities within the TRM.)

Besides the set of components making up the TRM, there is also a set of attributes that are termed "qualities" that apply across all components. Examples of qualities, which typically must apply through all elements of an architecture, include manageability and security. Qualities are specified in detail during the development of a Target Architecture. Some qualities are easier than others to describe in terms of standards. For instance, support for a set of locales can be defined to be part of the specification for the international operation quality. Other qualities can better be specified in terms of measures rather than standards (e.g., performance).

19.4 Taxonomy of Application Platform Services

(Syllabus Reference: Unit 12, Learning Outcome 4: You should be able to explain what the Platform Services Taxonomy is.)

The taxonomy of Platform Services provides a coherent description of an information system and is widely accepted as a useful, consistent structured definition of the Application Platform entity. It consists of a number of components termed "service categories", with further services defined within each category (see Table 19).

The taxonomy of the TOGAF TRM can be used in structuring a Standards Information Base, and is used in the database of standards maintained by The Open Group.[8]

Table 19: TRM Service Categories

Service Category	Description
Data Interchange Services	Data Interchange Services provide specialized support for the interchange of information between applications and the external environment. These services are designed to handle data interchange between applications on the same platform and applications on different (heterogeneous) platforms.
Data Management Services	Data Management Services provide for the management of data independently of the processes that create or use it, allow data to be maintained indefinitely, and shared among many processes.
Graphics and Imaging Services	Graphics and Imaging Services provide functions required for creating, storing, retrieving, and manipulating images.
International Operation Services	International Operation Services provide a set of services and interfaces that allow a user to define, select, and change between different culturally-related application environments supported by the particular implementation.
Location and Directory Services	Location and Directory Services provide specialized support for locating required resources and for mediation between service consumers and service providers.

---

8   Refer to www.opengroup.org/sib.

Service Category	Description
Network Services	Network Services are provided to support distributed applications requiring data access and applications interoperability in heterogeneous or homogeneous networked environments.
Object-Oriented Provision of Services	This section shows how services are provided in an object-oriented manner. "Object Services" does not appear as a category in the TRM since all the individual object services are incorporated as appropriate in the other service categories.
Operating System Services	Operating System Services are responsible for the management of platform resources, including the processor, memory, files, and input and output. They generally shield applications from the implementation details of the machine.
Security Services	Security Services are necessary to protect sensitive information in the information system. The appropriate level of protection is determined based upon the value of the information to the business end users and the perception of threats to it.
Software Engineering Services	Software Engineering Services provide the tools for professional system developers appropriate to the development and maintenance of applications.
System and Network Management Services	System and Network Management Services provide for managing a wide variety of diverse resources of information systems.
Transaction Processing Services	Transaction Processing Services provide support for the online processing of information in discrete units called transactions, with assurance of the state of the information at the end of the transaction.
User Interface Services	User Interface Services define how users may interact with an application.

A detailed description of the Service Categories and services within each is given in the TOGAF® Series Guide: The TOGAF Technical Reference Model (TRM).

19.5 Taxonomy of Application Platform Service Qualities

((Syllabus Reference: Unit 12, Learning Outcome 5: You should be able to explain what the Service Quality Taxonomy is.)

A service quality describes behaviour such as adaptability or manageability. Service qualities have a pervasive effect on the operation of most or all of the functional service categories.

> **Qualities**
> Qualities are referred to as "non-functional requirements" elsewhere. During the process of architecture development, the architect must be aware of the required or desired qualities and the extent of their influence on the choice of software building blocks used in implementing the architecture. The best way of making sure that qualities are not forgotten is to create a quality matrix, describing the relationships between each functional service and the qualities that influence it.

The service qualities presently identified in the TRM taxonomy are:
- **Availability** (the degree to which something is available for use), including:
    - **Manageability**, the ability to gather information about the state of something and to control it
    - **Serviceability**, the ability to identify problems and take corrective action, such as to repair or upgrade a component in a running system
    - **Performance**, the ability of a component to perform its tasks in an appropriate time
    - **Reliability**, resistance to failure
    - **Recoverability**, the ability to restore a system to a working state after an interruption
    - **Locatability**, the ability of a system to be found when needed
- **Assurance**, including:
    - **Security**, the protection of information from unauthorized access
    - **Integrity**, the assurance that data has not been corrupted
    - **Credibility**, the level of trust in the integrity of the system and its data

- **Usability** (ease-of-operation by users), including:
  - **International Operation**, including multi-lingual and multi-cultural abilities
- **Adaptability**, including:
  - **Interoperability**, whether within or outside the organization (for instance, interoperability of calendaring or scheduling functions may be key to the usefulness of a system)
  - **Scalability**, the ability of a component to grow or shrink its performance or capacity appropriately to the demands of the environment in which it operates
  - **Portability**, of data, people, applications, and components
  - **Extensibility**, the ability to accept new functionality
  - The ability to offer access to services in new paradigms such as object-orientation, or web-services

19.6 Summary

The TOGAF Technical Reference Model (TRM) provides a model and core taxonomy of generic platform-centric services. It can be used to build any system architecture. The taxonomy of platform services defines terminology and provides a coherent description of an information system. Few enterprises now face the challenge of building their own application platforms, taking it for granted that system and service providers deliver integrated platforms which conform to an established set of standards. As a result, other reference models – taxonomies and/or graphics – not only are possible, but may be preferable for the majority of enterprises. The TOGAF ADM is not dependent on the TOGAF TRM and can be used without reference to it or with alternative taxonomies.

19.7 Exercises

Exercise 20-1
Describe how you would adapt the TRM for your organization.

19.8 Recommended Reading

The following are recommended sources of further information for this chapter:

- TOGAF® Series Guide: The TOGAF Technical Reference Model (TRM)

Chapter 20
Integrated Information Infrastructure Reference Model (III-RM)

20.1 Key Learning Points

This chapter takes a detailed look at the Integration Information Infrastructure Reference Model (III-RM). This chapter builds on the information contained in the TOGAF 9 Foundation Study Guide.

> **Key Points Explained**
>
> Upon completion of this chapter you should be able to:
>
> 1. Describe the business and technical drivers for Boundaryless Information Flow
> 2. Explain how the III-RM fulfills the solution space for Boundaryless Information Flow
> 3. Briefly describe the high-level structure of the III-RM
> 4. Explain the III-RM graphic, including the following components:
>   - Business Applications
>   - Infrastructure Applications
>   - Application Platform
>   - Interfaces
>   - Qualities

20.2 Drivers for Boundaryless Information Flow

(Syllabus Reference: Unit 13, Learning Outcome 1: You should be able to describe the business and technical drivers for Boundaryless Information Flow.)

The key driver for Boundaryless Information Flow is the problem of supplying information to the right people at the right time, in a secure reliable manner. Readers are referred to Section 13.4 of the TOGAF 9 Foundation Study Guide for more information.

20.3 How the III-RM Fulfills the Solution Space

(Syllabus Reference: Unit 13, Learning Outcome 2: You should be able to explain how the III-RM fulfills the solution space for Boundaryless Information Flow.)

The III-RM addresses the solution space for Boundaryless Information Flow by providing a reference model for an implementation addressing this problem space.

20.4 The High-Level Structure of the III-RM

(Syllabus Reference: Unit 13, Learning Outcome 3: You should be able to briefly describe the high-level structure of the III-RM.)

The model includes the key components for developing, managing, and operating an integrated information infrastructure. It also models a set of applications that sit on top of an application platform.

The III-RM is a subset of the TOGAF TRM which uses a slightly different orientation from the one usually presented. This relationship is depicted in Figure 32. The left side is the familiar view of the TOGAF TRM; it is a side view, where we look at the model as if looking at a house from the side, revealing the contents of the "floors". The top-down view on the right-hand side depicts what one might see if looking at a house from the "roof" down.

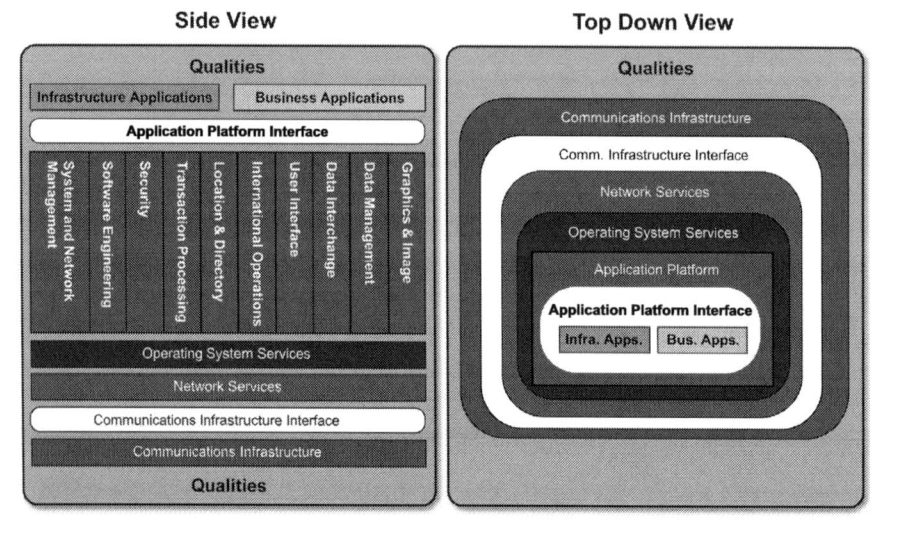

Figure 32: TOGAF TRM Orientation Views

The subset of the TRM that comprises the III-RM is contained within the "Application Platform" box in the center. This shows that the resulting focus is on the Application Software, Application Platform, and Qualities subset of the TOGAF TRM.

The resulting model is shown in Figure 33.

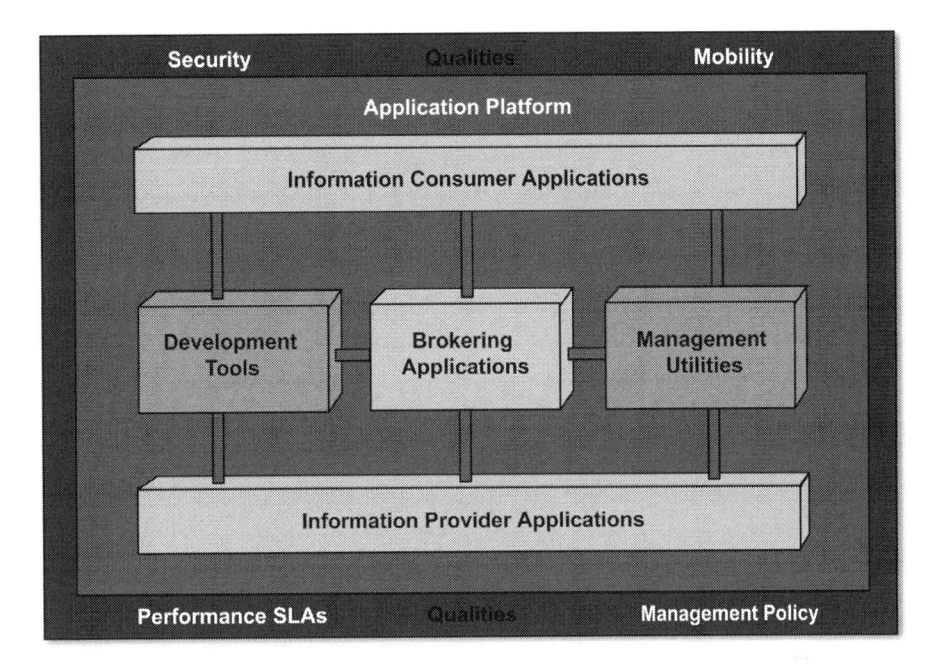

Figure 33: III-RM – High Level

The III-RM is fundamentally an Application Architecture reference model; that is, a model of the application components and application services software essential for an integrated information infrastructure. There are more business applications and infrastructure applications than these in the environment, but these are the subsets relevant to the Boundaryless Information Flow problem space. Also, the model assumes the underlying existence of a computing and network platform, and does not depict them explicitly.

20.5 Components of the III-RM

(Syllabus Reference: Unit 13, Learning Outcome 4: You should be able to explain the III-RM graphic.)

The detailed III-RM graphic is shown in Figure 34.

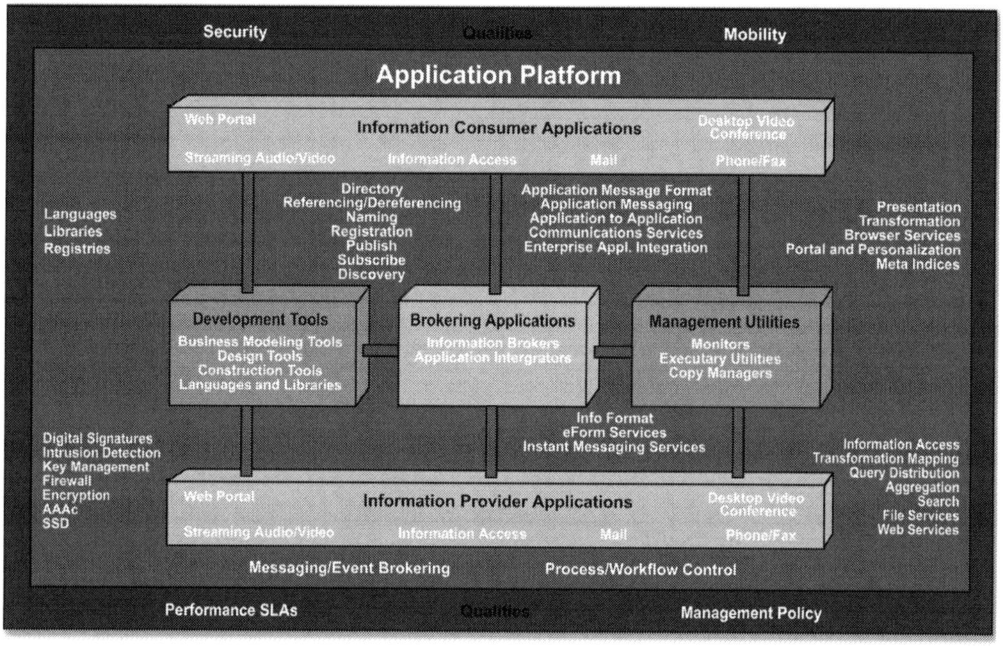

Figure 34: III-RM – Detailed

There are human and computing actors in the business environment that need information, called information consumers. There are human and computing actors that have information, called information providers. Information consumers need technology services to help them request information. Information providers need services to help them liberate the information in their control.

There are numerous types of information consumer and information providers, as in the stock market where brokers help information consumers get the information they need. Thus, we have Brokering services in the reference model.

In the business environment there are development organizations and management organizations. These organizations are supported by tools and utilities to develop and manage the information services.

In the business environment people and information are spread out and mobile. So there is a need for a directory. This is provided to the tools, utilities, and services through the directory services in the reference model.

Finally, the business environment must be secure, mobile, manageable, and must meet business needs. This is depicted by the qualities that the reference model must support.

(Syllabus Reference: Unit 13, Learning Outcome 4.1: You should be able to explain the following component of the III-RM graphic: Business Applications.)

There are three types of Business Applications in the model:
1. **Brokering Applications**, which manage the requests from any number of clients to and across any number of Information Provider Applications
2. **Information Provider Applications**, which provide responses to client requests and rudimentary access to data managed by a particular server
3. **Information Consumer Applications**, which deliver content to the user of the system, and provide services to request access to information in the system on the user's behalf

The overall set of Information Provider, Information Consumer, and Brokerage Applications collectively creates an environment that provides a rich set of end-user services for transparently accessing heterogeneous systems, databases, and file systems.

(Syllabus Reference: Unit 13, Learning Outcome 4.2: You should be able to explain the following component of the III-RM graphic: Infrastructure Applications.)

There are two types of Infrastructure Application in the model:
1. **Development Tools**, which provide all the necessary modeling, design, and construction capabilities to develop and deploy applications that require access to the integrated information infrastructure, in a manner consistent with the standards of the environment
2. **Management Utilities**, which provide all the necessary utilities to understand, operate, tune, and manage the run-time system in order to meet the demands of an ever-changing business, in a manner consistent with the standards of the environment

(Syllabus Reference: Unit 13, Learning Outcome 4.3: You should be able to explain the following component of the III-RM graphic: Application Platform.)

The Application Platform provides supporting services to all the above applications – in areas such as location, directory, workflow, data management, data interchange, etc. – and thereby provides the ability to locate, access, and move information within the environment. This set of services constitutes a subset of the total set of services of the TRM Application Platform.

The services of the Application Platform component can be used to support conventional applications as well as Brokerage, Information Consumer, and Information Provider applications. When used as part of an overall Application Architecture in this way, such an approach enables maximum leverage of a single operational environment that is designed to ensure effective and consistent transfer of data between processes, and to support fast and efficient development, deployment, and management of applications.

(Syllabus Reference: Unit 13, Learning Outcome 4.4: You should be able to explain the following component of the III-RM graphic: Interfaces.)

The Interfaces used between the components include formats and protocols, APIs, switches, data values, etc.

(Syllabus Reference: Unit 13, Learning Outcome 4.5: You should be able to explain the following component of the III-RM graphic: Qualities.)

The Application Software and Application Platform must adhere to the policies and requirements depicted by the Qualities. The Qualities component of the model is supported by services required to maintain the quality of the system as specified in Service Level Agreements (SLAs).

20.6 Summary

The III-RM is an Application Architecture reference model; that is, a model of the application components and application services. The III-RM provides help in addressing one of the key challenges facing the Enterprise Architect today: the need to design an integrated information infrastructure to enable Boundaryless Information Flow.

20.7 Recommended Reading

The following are recommended sources of further information for this chapter:

- TOGAF® Series Guide: The TOGAF Integrated Information Infrastructure Reference Model (III- RM)

PART 6
Architecture Capability

In this Part, we look at three aspects of Architecture Capability:
- Chapter 21 describes the relationship between Architecture Governance and the ADM; it also describes how to establish and operate an Architecture Board
- Chapter 22 describes Architecture Maturity Models
- Chapter 23 describes the Architecture Skills Framework

Recommended reading before commencing this Part of the Study Guide includes:
- TOGAF 9 Foundation Study Guide, Chapter 9, Architecture Governance

Chapter 21
Architecture Governance

21.1 Key Learning Points

The purpose of this chapter is to help you understand how to apply Architecture Governance in development of an Enterprise Architecture. This chapter builds on the Architecture Governance chapter contained in the TOGAF 9 Foundation Study Guide.

> **Key Points Explained**
> Upon completion of this chapter you should be able to:
> 1. Explain how Architecture Governance fits within the ADM cycle
> 2. Discuss the key success factors for putting Architecture Governance into practice
> 3. Discuss the factors that should be considered when setting up an Architecture Board
> 4. Explain how to operate an Architecture Board

21.2 Architecture Governance and the ADM

(Syllabus Reference: Unit 2, Learning Outcome 1: You should be able to explain how Architecture Governance fits within the ADM cycle.)

The TOGAF standard defines Architecture Governance as follows:
"The practice of monitoring and directing architecture-related work. The goal is to deliver desired outcomes and adhere to relevant principles, standards, and roadmaps."

[Source: The TOGAF Standard, Version 9.2 Part I, Definitions]

In the Preliminary Phase, decisions are made on how to govern the architecture framework, and how to integrate it with the existing governance and support models for the organization. Decisions are also taken as to the type of governance repository characteristics required.

In Phase F, the Implementation Governance Model produced ensures that a project transitioning into implementation smoothly transitions into the appropriate Architecture Governance for Phase G.

Phase G includes production of the Architecture Contract which features prominently in Architecture Governance as a means to ensure compliance and drive change. Periodic compliance reviews of projects are held to review progress and ensure that the design and implementation are in-line with the strategic and architectural objectives. Risk monitoring should also occur in this phase.

Phase H manages the governance process and framework for the architecture. This includes scheduling and holding meetings of the Architecture Board. The purpose of these meetings is to decide how to handle requests for change to the architecture. These can arise either from issues found in the original Architecture Definition and requirements, or from external factors such as business strategy changes and new technology opportunities. The Architecture Board should also ensure that the ADM is being applied correctly to ensure that all considerations are made and all required deliverables are produced.

21.3 Key Success Factors

(Syllabus Reference: Unit 2, Learning Outcome 2: You should be able to discuss the key success factors for putting Architecture Governance into practice.)

It is important to consider the following to ensure a successful approach to Architecture Governance, and effective management of the Architecture Contract:
- Establishment and operation of best practices for submission, adoption, re-use, reporting, and retirement of architecture policies, procedures, roles, skills, organizational structures, and support services
- Establishment of correct organizational responsibilities and structures to support Architecture Governance processes and reporting requirements

- Integration of tools and processes to facilitate take-up of processes (both procedural and cultural)
- Management of criteria for control of Architecture Governance processes, dispensations, compliance assessments, Service Level Agreements (SLAs), and Operational Level Agreements (OLAs)
- Meeting internal and external requirements for effectiveness, efficiency, confidentiality, integrity, availability, compliance, and reliability of Architecture Governance-related information, services, and processes

21.4 Setting up the Architecture Board

(Syllabus Reference: Unit 2, Learning Outcome 3: You should be able to discuss the factors that should be considered when setting up an Architecture Board.)

Factors to consider include identification of the executive sponsor, the size of the board, the structure of the board, and its relationship to other organizational groups and responsibilities.

In many companies, the executive sponsor of the initial architecture effort is the CIO (or other senior executive). However, to gain broad corporate support, a sponsoring body can have more influence. This sponsoring body is called an Architecture Board. The Architecture Board is the sponsor of the architecture within the enterprise, but the Architecture Board itself needs an executive sponsor from the highest level of the corporation. This commitment must span the planning process and continue into the maintenance phase of the architecture project. In many companies that fail in an architecture planning effort, there is a notable lack of executive participation and encouragement for the project.

The recommended size for an Architecture Board is four or five permanent members and the recommended upper limit is ten. A technique to manage the size of the board is to rotate the membership. This may be required due to some Architecture Board members finding that time constraints prevent long-term active participation. However, some continuity must exist on the Architecture Board, to prevent the corporate architecture from fluctuating from one set of ideas to another. One technique for ensuring rotation with continuity is to have set terms for the members, and to have the terms expire at different times.

The TOGAF Architecture Governance Framework provides a generic organizational framework that positions the Architecture Board in the context of the broader governance structures of the enterprise. This structure identifies the major organizational groups and responsibilities, as well as the relationship between each group. This is a best practice structure, and may be subject to change depending on the organization's form and existing structures.

The structure of the Architecture Board should reflect the form of the organization. The Architecture Governance structure required may well go beyond the generic structures outlined in the TOGAF Architecture Governance Framework. The organization may need to define a combination of the IT governance process and the existing organizational structures and capabilities, which typically may include a global governance board, local governance board, design authorities, and working parties.

21.5 Operating an Architecture Board

(Syllabus Reference: Unit 2, Learning Outcome 4: You should be able to explain how to operate an Architecture Board.)

The TOGAF standard provides guidance on the operation of the Architecture Board, particularly from the governance perspective. This focuses primarily on how to prepare and conduct meetings and is summarized below.

21.5.1 General

Architecture Board meetings should be conducted with clearly identified agendas with explicit objectives, content coverage, and defined actions. These meetings will provide key direction in:

- Supporting the production of quality governance material and activities
- Providing a mechanism for formal acceptance through consensus and authorized publication
- Providing a fundamental control mechanism for ensuring the effective implementation of the architectures
- Establishing and maintaining the link between the implementation of the architectures and the stated strategy and objectives of the organization (business and IT)
- Identifying divergence from the contract and planning activities to realign with the contract through dispensations or policy updates

21.5.2 Preparation

Prior to a meeting, each participant should receive an agenda and any supporting documentation (e.g., dispensation requests, performance management reports, etc.). Each participant is expected to be familiar with the contents of each. Where actions have been allocated to an individual, it is that person's responsibility to report on progress against these. Each participant must confirm their availability and attendance at the Architecture Board meeting.

21.5.3 Agenda

The TOGAF standard provides an outline set of contents for an Architecture Board meeting agenda. Each agenda item is described in terms of its content only.

Minutes of Previous Meeting

Minutes contain the details of the previous Architecture Board meeting as per standard organizational protocol.

Requests for Change

Items under this heading are normally Change Requests for amendments to architectures, principles, etc., but may also include business control with regard to Architecture Contracts; e.g., ensure that voice traffic to premium numbers, such as weather reports, are barred and data traffic to certain websites is controlled.

Any request for change is made within agreed authority levels and parameters defined by the Architecture Contract.

Dispensations

A dispensation is used as the mechanism to request a change to the existing architectures, contracts, principles, etc. outside of normal operating parameters; e.g., exclude provision of service to a subsidiary, request for unusual service levels for specific business reasons, deploy non-standard technology or products to support specific business initiatives.

Dispensations are granted for a given time period and set of identified services and operational criteria that must be enforced during the lifespan of the dispensation. Dispensations are not granted indefinitely, but are used as a mechanism to ensure that service levels and operational levels, etc. are met while providing a level flexibility in their implementation and timing. The time-bound nature of dispensations ensures that they are a trigger to the Architecture Compliance activity.

Compliance Assessments
Compliance is assessed against Service Level Agreements (SLAs), Operational Level Agreements (OLAs), cost targets, and required architecture refreshes. These assessments will be reviewed and either accepted or rejected depending on the criteria defined within the Architecture Governance Framework. The Architecture Compliance assessment report will include details as described.

Dispute Resolution
Disputes that have not been resolved through the Architecture Compliance and dispensation processes are identified here for further action and are documented through the Architecture Compliance assessments and dispensation documentation.

Architecture Strategy and Direction Documentation
This describes the architecture strategies, direction, and priorities and will only be formulated by the global Architecture Board. It should take the form of standard architecture documentation.

Actions Assigned
This is a report on the actions assigned at previous Architecture Board meetings. An action tracker is used to document and keep the status of all actions assigned during the Architecture Board meetings and should consist of at least the following information:
- Reference
- Priority
- Action description
- Action owner
- Action details
- Date raised
- Due date
- Status
- Type
- Resolution date

Contract Documentation Management
This is a formal acceptance of updates and changes to architecture documentation for onward publication.

Any Other Business (AOB)
Description of issues not directly covered under any of the above. These may not be described in the agenda but should be raised at the beginning of the meeting. Any supporting documentation must be managed as per all Architecture Governance documentation.

Schedule of Meetings
All meeting dates should be detailed and published.

21.6 Summary

Architecture Governance is the practice and orientation by which Enterprise Architectures and other architectures are managed and controlled at an enterprise-wide level. The TOGAF standard provides guidance on aspects of Architecture Governance in the Architecture Capability Framework.

21.7 Exercises

Exercise 22-1
You have been asked to establish an Architecture Board for your organization. Draw up a list of the candidates with explanation of why they should be included, and set the agenda for the first meeting.

21.8 Recommended Reading

The following are recommended sources of further information for this chapter:
- The TOGAF Standard, Version 9.2 Part VI, Architecture Board
- The TOGAF Standard, Version 9.2 Part VI, Architecture Governance
- TOGAF 9 Foundation Study Guide, Chapter 9, Architecture Governance

Chapter 22

Architecture Maturity Models

22.1 Key Learning Points

This chapter introduces Architecture Maturity Models. The purpose of this chapter is to help you understand their role in enabling an enterprise to determine the state of the Enterprise Architecture and to evaluate risks and options during the development of the Enterprise Architecture.

> **Key Points Explained**
>
> Upon completion of this chapter you should be able to:
> 1. Explain the role of a Capability Maturity Model
> 2. Explain the CMMI® process improvement approach development by Carnegie Mellon University (CMU)
> 3. Describe the structure and levels of the ACMM developed by CMU for the US Department of Commerce
> 4. Explain the role of Maturity Assessments in the ADM

22.2 Capability Maturity Models

(Syllabus Reference: Unit 25, Learning Outcome 1: You should be able to explain the role of a Capability Maturity Model.)

Organizations that can manage change effectively are generally more successful than those that cannot. Many organizations know that they need to improve their processes in order to successfully manage change, but don't know how. Such organizations typically either spend very little on process improvement, because they are unsure how best to proceed; or spend a lot, on a number of parallel and unfocused efforts with mixed results.

Capability Maturity Models (CMMs) address this problem by providing an effective method for an organization to gradually gain control over and improve its change processes. Benefits of such models include:

- They describe the practices that any organization must perform in order to improve its processes
- They provide measures for improvement
- They constitute a proven framework within which to manage the improvement efforts
- They organize the various practices into levels, each level representing an increased ability to control and manage the development environment

An evaluation of the organization's practices against the model – called an "assessment" – determines the level at which the organization currently stands. It indicates the organization's ability to execute in the area concerned, and the practices on which the organization needs to focus in order to see the greatest improvement and the highest return on investment. The benefits of CMMs to effectively direct effort are well documented.

The models have been used for assessment in different domains including e-commerce maturity, process implementation and audit, quality measurements, people competencies, and investment management.

The methods involve using several models, and focus in particular on measuring business benefits and return-on-investment. Another key driver is the increasing use of outsourcing. The CMM is increasingly the standard by which outsourcers are being evaluated.

> **Capability Maturity Models**
>
> The original CMM was developed in the early 1990s by Carnegie Mellon University and is still widely used today. CMMs have also been developed for other areas such as:
> - People: the P-CMM® (People Capability Maturity Model), and the IDEAL Life Cycle Model for Improvement
> - Systems Engineering: the SE-CMM® (Systems Engineering Capability Maturity Model)
> - Software Acquisition: the SA-CMM® (Software Acquisition Capability Maturity Model)
> - CMMI: Capability Maturity Model Integration

The increasing interest in applying CMMs to the IT architecture and Enterprise Architecture fields has resulted in a series of templates which can be used to assess the state of the IT architecture process, the IT architecture, and the organization's buy-in to both.

22.3 Capability Maturity Model Integration (CMMI)

(Syllabus Reference: Unit 25, Learning Outcome 2: You should be able to explain the CMMI process improvement approach developed by CMU.)

In recent years, the industry has witnessed significant growth in the area of maturity models. The multiplicity of models available has led to problems of its own, in terms of how to integrate all the different models to produce meaningful measures for overall process maturity. In response to this need, Carnegie Mellon University (CMU) developed a framework called Capability Maturity Model Integration (CMMI), to provide a means of managing the complexity.

According to the developers, the use of the CMMI models improves on the best practices of previous models in many important ways, in particular enabling organizations to:
- More explicitly link management and engineering activities to business objectives
- Expand the scope of and visibility into the product lifecycle and engineering activities to ensure that the product or service meets customer expectations
- Incorporate lessons learned from additional areas of best practice (e.g., measurement, risk management, and supplier management)
- Implement more robust high-maturity practices
- Address additional organizational functions critical to products and services
- More fully comply with relevant ISO standards

22.4 ACMM

(Syllabus Reference: Unit 25, Learning Outcome 3: You should be able to describe the structure and levels of the ACMM developed by CMU for the US Department of Commerce.)

The US Department of Commerce (DoC) has developed an IT Architecture Capability Maturity Model (ACMM) to facilitate internal assessments. The goal is to identify weak areas and provide a way to improve the overall architecture process. The ACMM has three sections:
- The architecture maturity model
- The characteristics of processes at different maturity levels
- The architecture CMM scorecard

The ACMM has six maturity levels:
1. None
2. Initial
3. Under development
4. Defined
5. Managed
6. Measured

The ACMM also has nine architecture characteristics:
1. IT architecture process
2. IT architecture development
3. Business linkage
4. Senior management involvement
5. Operating unit participation
6. Architecture communication
7. IT security
8. Architecture Governance
9. IT investment and acquisition strategy

Two methods are used in the ACMM to calculate a maturity rating. The first method obtains a weighted mean IT architecture maturity level. The second shows the percentage achieved at each maturity level for the nine architecture characteristics.

22.5 Maturity Assessments and the ADM

(Syllabus Reference: Unit 25, Learning Outcome 4: You should be able to explain the role of Maturity Assessments in the ADM.)

Maturity assessments are referred to in the Preliminary Phase, Phase A, and Phase E of the ADM. The approach to the Preliminary Phase recommends their use as part of developing the Organizational Model for Enterprise Architecture. In Phase A, a maturity assessment is part of the Capability Assessment used to determine the baseline and target capability of the enterprise. This Capability Assessment is also revisited in Phase E, when preparing the Implementation and Migration Plan.

When using CMMs with the ADM, it is recommended that they be customized and discussed in workshops involving the major stakeholders within the organization. The actual levels of maturity can provide a strategic measure of the organization's ability to change, as well as a series of sequential steps to improve that ability.

22.6 Summary

Architecture Maturity Models can be used to assess the maturity of the process of Enterprise Architecture. The CMMI framework provides a set of models that incorporate best practice for process assessment. A maturity assessment can be used as a business tool and can provide executives with an insight into how to pragmatically move forward when developing an Enterprise Architecture.

22.7 Exercises

Exercise 23-1

Provide a list of questions which could be used to determine the maturity of the nine architecture characteristics within a particular Enterprise Architecture. Use the US Department of Commerce ACMM document as a guide.

Exercise 23-2

Provide an assessment of your own organization's Enterprise Architecture process maturity, on a scale from Level 0 to Level 5 using the templates provided with the US Department of Commerce ACMM document.

22.8 Recommended Reading

The following are recommended sources of further information for this chapter:

- The TOGAF Standard, Version 9.2 Part VI, Architecture Maturity Models

Chapter 23
Architecture Skills Framework

23.1 Key Learning Points

This chapter introduces the Architecture Skills Framework. The purpose of this chapter is to help you understand the Architecture Skills Framework, which is a classification model for architect roles.

> **Key Points Explained**
>
> Upon completion of this chapter you should be able to:
> 1. Explain the purpose of the Architecture Skills Framework and why it is needed
> 2. Describe the benefits of using the Architecture Skills Framework
> 3. Describe the structure of the Architecture Skills Framework, including roles, skills, and proficiency levels

23.2 Purpose

(Syllabus Reference: Unit 26, Learning Outcome 1: You should be able to explain the purpose of the Architecture Skills Framework and why it is needed.)

The purpose of the TOGAF Architecture Skills Framework is to help organizations seeking to establish an Enterprise Architecture practice to reduce the time, cost, and risk involved in training, recruiting, and managing Enterprise Architecture professionals, and at the same time enable and encourage more organizations to institute an internal Enterprise Architecture practice, based on the role and skill definitions provided.

An Enterprise Architecture practice is both difficult and costly to establish. To address this, the Architecture Skills Framework provides a standard set of definitions of the architecting skills and proficiency levels required of personnel – internal or external – who are to perform the various architecting roles defined within the TOGAF framework.

23.3 Benefits

(Syllabus Reference: Unit 26, Learning Outcome 2: You should be able to describe the benefits of using the Architecture Skills Framework.)

The benefits of using the Architecture Skills Framework are summarized in Table 20.

Table 20: Benefits of Using the Architecture Skills Framework

Benefit	Rationale
Reduced time, cost, and risk in training, hiring, and managing architecture professionals, both internal and external	Simplifies communication between recruiting organizations, consultancies, and employment agencies. Avoids wasting resources interviewing staff who may have applied in good faith, but lack the skills and/or experience required by the employer. Avoids staff who are capable of filling architecture roles being overlooked, or not identifying themselves with advertised positions and hence not applying.
Reduced time and cost to set up an internal architecture practice	Many enterprises do not have an internal architecture practice due to the complexity involved in setting one up, preferring instead to simply interview and recruit architecture staff on an *ad hoc* basis. By providing definitions of the architecting skills and proficiency levels required of personnel who are to perform the various architecting roles defined within the TOGAF standard, the Architecture Skills Framework greatly reduces the time, cost, and risk of setting up a practice for the first time, and avoids "re-inventing the wheel". Enterprises that already have an internal architecture practice are able to set enterprise-wide norms, but still experience difficulties as outlined above in recruiting staff, or engaging consultants, from external sources, due to the lack of uniformity between different enterprises. By aligning its existing skills framework with an industry-accepted definition, an enterprise can greatly simplify these problems.
Reduced time, cost, and risk of overall solution development	Enterprises that do not have an internal architecture practice run the risk of unsuitable personnel being employed or engaged. The resultant time and cost penalties far outweigh the time and cost of having an internal architecture practice: • Personnel costs are increased, through the need to rehire or reassign staff • Even more important is the adverse impact on the time, cost, and quality of operational IT systems, and the projects to deliver them, resulting from poor staff assignments

23.4 Enterprise Architecture Roles, Skills Categories, and Proficiency Levels

(Syllabus Reference: Unit 26, Learning Outcome 3: You should be able to describe the structure of the Architecture Skills Framework, including roles, skills, and proficiency level.)

The TOGAF Architecture Skills Framework defines the competency levels for specific roles within the Enterprise Architecture team. This includes:
- The roles within an Enterprise Architecture work area
- The skills required by those roles
- The depth of knowledge required to fulfill each role successfully

This provides value by enabling a rapid means of identifying skills and gaps. Successfully applied, the framework can be used as a measure for:
- Staff development
- Ensuring the right person does the right job

23.4.1 TOGAF Roles

The framework defines the following roles for a team undertaking the development of an Enterprise Architecture:
- Architecture Board Members
- Architecture Sponsor
- Architecture Manager
- Architects for Enterprise Architecture, Business Architecture, Data Architecture, Application Architecture, and Technology Architecture
- Program and/or Project Managers
- IT Designer

23.4.2 Skills Categories

The framework defines the skills categories for a TOGAF team as shown in Table 21.

Table 21: Skills Categories

Skill	Description
Generic Skills	Leadership, team-working, inter-personal skills, etc.
Business Skills & Methods	Business cases, business process, strategic planning, etc.
Enterprise Architecture Skills	Modeling, building block design, applications and role design, systems integration, etc.
Program or Project Management Skills	Managing business change, project management methods and tools, etc.
IT General Knowledge Skills	Brokering applications, asset management, migration planning, Service Level Agreements (SLAs), etc.
Technical IT Skills	Software engineering, security, data interchange, data management, etc.
Legal Environment	Data protection laws, contract law, procurement law, fraud, etc.

23.4.3 Proficiency Levels

The framework defines four levels of knowledge or proficiency in any area, as shown in Table 22.

Table 22: Proficiency Levels

Level	Achievement	Description
1	Background	Not a required skill though should be able to define and manage skill if required.
2	Awareness	Understands the background, issues, and implications sufficiently to be able to understand how to proceed further and advise client accordingly.
3	Knowledge	Detailed knowledge of subject area and capable of providing professional advice and guidance. Ability to integrate capability into architecture design.
4	Expert	Extensive and substantial practical experience and applied knowledge on the subject.

23.4.4 Example Role and Skill Definitions

The framework also includes a number of tables matching roles with skills and proficiency levels within each skill category. A single table is shown in Table 23 as an illustration, showing the definition of Enterprise Architecture skills by role.

Table 23: Example Role and Skill Definition

Roles	Architecture Board Member	Architecture Sponsor	Enterprise Architecture Manager	Enterprise Architecture Technology	Enterprise Architecture Data	Enterprise Architecture Applications	Enterprise Architecture Business	Program/Project Manager	IT Designer
Enterprise Architecture Skills									
Business Modeling	2	2	4	3	3	4	4	2	2
Business Process Design	1	1	4	3	3	4	4	2	2
Role Design	2	2	4	3	3	4	4	2	2
Organization Design	2	2	4	3	3	4	4	2	2
Data Design	1	1	3	3	4	3	3	2	3
Application Design	1	1	3	3	3	4	3	2	3
Systems Integration	1	1	4	4	3	3	3	2	2
IT Industry Standards	1	1	4	4	4	4	3	2	3
Services Design	2	2	4	4	3	4	3	2	2
Architecture Principles Design	2	2	4	4	4	4	4	2	2
Architecture Views & Viewpoints Design	2	2	4	4	4	4	4	2	2
Building Block Design	1	1	4	4	4	4	4	2	3
Solutions Modeling	1	1	4	4	4	4	4	2	3
Benefits Analysis	2	2	4	4	4	4	4	4	2
Business Interworking	3	3	4	3	3	4	4	3	1
Systems Behavior	1	1	4	4	4	4	3	3	2
Project Management	1	1	3	3	3	3	3	4	2

Key: 1 = Background, 2 = Awareness, 3 = Knowledge, 4 = Expert

23.5 Summary

The Architecture Skills Framework is a classification model for architecture roles. It has a number of benefits which have been described in this chapter. The structure of the Architecture Skills Framework stipulates roles, skills, and proficiency levels.

23.6 Exercises

Exercise 24-1

Place yourself within the Architecture Skills Framework and write a brief summary of your role, your skills, and proficiency level.

Exercise 24-2

The director of the human resources department has requested your assistance with recruitment for a new Enterprise Architecture project. She has asked you to write summary job descriptions for the following roles aligned with the Architecture Skills Framework:
- Enterprise Architecture Manager
- A Project Manager

23.7 Recommended Reading

The following are recommended sources of further information for this chapter:
- The TOGAF Standard, Version 9.2 Part VI, Architecture Skills Framework

Appendix A
Test Yourself Examination Paper

A.1 Introduction

> This examination paper is for candidates who are taking the TOGAF 9 Part 2 Examination.
>
> This is an open-book examination. You may need to refer to sections of the TOGAF standard in order to answer the questions.
>
> Please note that when taking the examination a PDF version of the TOGAF standard is provided built into the test and available on the REFERENCE button.

A.2 Instructions

This section consists of eight gradient scored, multiple-choice, single response questions. In order to answer each question you will need to read the related scenario fully. On the basis of the information provided in the scenario, and the guidance in the TOGAF standard, which one of the four possible answers is the best answer?

There is a maximum of five (5) points per question.
The CORRECT answer scores five (5) points.
The SECOND BEST answer scores three (3) points.
The THIRD BEST answer scores one (1) point.
The DISTRACTER (the incorrect answer) scores zero (0) points.

In order to pass this section, you must achieve a total of 28[9] points or more out of a maximum of 40 points (70%).

You should spend no more than 90 minutes on this examination.

---

[9] Note that this pass mark may differ from the live TOGAF 9 Part 2 Examination. Consult The Open Group certification website for the latest information on pass marks.

A.3 Questions

Question 1

SCENARIO 1

You are serving as the Lead Architect in a multi-national company that operates production facilities in 24 countries and sells its products in over 100 countries. It has three sectors: Transportation, Energy Systems, and Automation. Each sector has several business units that operate independently. An Executive Vice President heads each of the business units. Traditionally, each business unit has acted independently with few shared customers or suppliers. They were expected to share financial and human resource information from the corporate headquarters.

A consultancy firm has recommended a realignment that will enhance sharing of product information across business units. The implementation of this strategic realignment will require the development of integrated customer information systems and product information systems.

The company has a mature Enterprise Architecture practice and uses the TOGAF standard for the basis for its method and deliverables. An architecture development program has been created to address the development of these capabilities and is about to commence. The Enterprise Architecture program is sponsored by the CIO.

At the most recent meeting of the Corporate Board, the Chairman of the Board expressed a concern about the risk to the business while a potentially disruptive program is being rolled out across the company. He noted that several competitors had tried similar initiatives with poor results. The Corporate Board agreed that this concern must be satisfactorily addressed before this program can commence.

(Refer to the scenario)

You have been asked to recommend an approach to address the concerns raised.

Based on the TOGAF standard, which of the following is the best answer?

Answers

A. You recommend that a Risk Aversion Assessment be conducted in the Implementation Governance phase to determine the implementation organization's degree of risk aversion with regard to the proposed business transformation. Based on that, if the Corporate Board is not willing to accept a reasonable amount of risk, then you recommend they put in place a set of parallel systems to mitigate the risks.

B. You recommend that techniques be used throughout the program to manage risk including risk monitoring. This will enable you to identify, classify, and mitigate the risks associated with the proposed transformation and ensure suitable business continuity plans are in place. In the Implementation Governance phase, you ensure a residual risk assessment is conducted to determine the best way to manage risks that cannot be mitigated.

C. You recommend classifying the risks in terms of time, cost, and scope during the Architecture Vision phase. This will enable you to ensure that certain risks with certain types of impact are managed by the right individuals. You would then ensure that the Architecture Contracts issued in the Implementation Governance phase address those initial risks and include adequate risk monitoring actions to confirm that they have been addressed.

D. You recommend that a risk management framework is used in Phase G, the Implementation Governance phase. This would include a risk classification scheme and completion of worksheets for risk assessment. This will enable you to assess the risks associated with the proposed business transformation. You then ensure that the initial level of risk is well understood before issuing the Architecture Contracts.

Question 2

SCENARIO 2

You are serving as a consultant to the Chief Architect of a low-cost airline. The airline was formed in 2002 and its main base is a major international airport on the east coast of North America. It currently serves 65 destinations in 20 US states, and nine countries in the Caribbean, South America, and Latin America.

The airline has received approval to acquire a smaller regional carrier that will extend the market it reaches and enable it to feed its primary routes with connecting flights from smaller cities.

In order to integrate the new acquisition, an Enterprise Architecture program has been initiated, using the TOGAF standard as the method and guiding framework. The CIO is the sponsor of the activity. The Chief Architect has indicated that this program should make use of iteration with the ADM.

As the program moves into Phase A within the initial iteration of an Architecture Capability cycle, the CIO has emphasized the need to ensure that the architecture is embraced across the enterprise.

(Refer to the scenario)

You have been asked to explain how you would identify and engage the stakeholders at this stage of the program.

Based on the TOGAF standard, which of the following is the best answer?

Answers

A. You would conduct a series of business scenarios with the stakeholders impacted by the acquisition, and determine which stakeholders are likely to block the initiative and which are likely to support it. You would identify the most relevant architecture viewpoints and validate with the stakeholders.

B. You would focus on communications with the stakeholders at the regional carrier as effective communication of targeted information to the right stakeholders at the right time is a Critical Success Factor (CSF) for such a merger. You would develop a Communications Plan to ensure they are aware of the key features of the architecture and have the opportunity to comment.

C. You would conduct a pilot project in Phase A to demonstrate to the stakeholders the technical feasibility of the approaches that are available from your preferred suppliers. Once the stakeholders confirm that the approach meets their requirements you would then complete a Statement of Work and issue an Architecture Contract to your suppliers.

D. You would identify key stakeholders across both the current airline and the new acquisition. You would classify their positions and influence, recording the results in a Stakeholder Map. You would then focus on key stakeholders ensuring that you identify the most relevant viewpoints for each stakeholder and validate that their concerns are being addressed.

Question 3

SCENARIO 3

You are serving as the Lead Enterprise Architect for a major bank, leading a group of domain architects as well as working with the corporate project management office, strategic planners, and operations management planners. The bank has been in business for over 60 years, growing through a series of acquisitions with other financial institutions. It has a large IT service department and routinely has over 100 infrastructure and service projects in progress. The Governing Board has decided that a more structured approach to its infrastructure and services is necessary to safeguard the business, especially given the recent turmoil in the financial markets.

As a result, the CIO has sponsored the creation of an Enterprise Architecture group. This group has adopted the TOGAF 9 standard as the basis for its Enterprise Architecture, developed an Architecture Vision, which has been approved, and defined a set of domain architectures. The time has come to consolidate the domain architectures and review the current initiatives and projects in the corporate portfolio as well as potentially create new projects in order to realize the vision.

The CIO has stated that the implementation approach must accommodate the constantly occurring changes to the technology and business landscapes. Shareholders want to see not just a vision but want to know that there is a flexible, integrated Implementation and Migration Plan that has the best chance of realizing the vision in these uncertain times.

(Refer to the scenario)

A meeting has been scheduled with the stakeholders and you have been asked to recommend the best approach to address the concerns raised.

Based on the TOGAF standard, which of the following is the best answer?

Answers

A. You recommend that the Enterprise Architecture team leverage all of the existing projects and their deliverables to address the findings from the gap analysis results for the architecture domains. The Enterprise Architecture team will request from the stakeholders all of the existing project charters and architectures so that the architects can integrate them together in a coherent manner. They will inform the operations management staff of their plans so that they can prepare to support the deliverables. Each of the domain architects will then come up with specific projects to address their gaps and then consider whether existing projects need to have their scope revised. The sum of the work required in each one of the domains will then be consolidated into the Implementation and Migration Plan. The timeline for progression of the deliverables will be documented in the Architecture Roadmap.

B. You recommend that the domain architectures are implemented immediately and all ongoing projects have their scopes revised to align with the new architectures. In order to save time you will then take the requirements from Phases B through D and create new IT projects for each one of the requirements that will enable the projects to create their individual requirements-based project architectures. The projects will work together through the creation of new point-to-point interfaces following defined interoperability architecture guidelines.

C. You recommend development of a series of Transition Architectures. This can then deliver continuous business value in an incremental manner, achieved by all the projects delivering their increments in a coordinated approach based on capability planning. You will consolidate the gap analysis results from each of the domain architectures and analyze the dependencies so as to come up with a work-breakdown structure. You will examine what is achievable and identify logical work packages that can become the basis for projects or the leveraging of existing projects. You will then hold a series of facilitated sessions to seek consensus on the Implementation and Migration Strategy.

D. You recommend that the stakeholders provide input on what has to be done to implement the defined domain architectures. The intent is to ensure that all stakeholders will be allowed to contribute to the Enterprise Architecture planning. The joint analysis will then result in a detailed list of work activities that will be rolled into an IT portfolio plan that will eventually give rise to a series of projects. The intent is to create a comprehensive Target Architecture that will include the detailed technology choices for the organization for the next five years. A full report will be completed highlighting what was done including a detailed dependencies and factors assessment.

Question 4

SCENARIO 4

You are working as the Lead Enterprise Architect for a global manufacturing firm. The firm has decided to improve the efficiency of its sales force by replacing its legacy fax and paper-based configuration and ordering systems with a hand-held device solution. This will impact both the firm and its suppliers.

The firm uses the TOGAF framework for their internal Enterprise Architecture and uses an iterative approach to applying the ADM. The Enterprise Architecture team has established the Architecture Capability for this project and also completed the first iteration of the Architecture Definition cycle, using a Baseline First approach. The CIO is the sponsor of the Enterprise Architecture program.

The initial iteration has established the approach, the scope, and vision for the project. A set of Architecture Principles has been established based on the set provided in the TOGAF standard. The CIO has highlighted the importance of adhering to the following principles:
- Data is an asset
- Data is shared
- Data is accessible

The initial iteration has also established a number of business goals and objectives for the new target system. The principal goal is to give the sales force in the field direct access to the sales process, allowing sales staff to create and verify product configurations, check pricing and availability, and to place an order while still on the client site with the customer.

As part of achieving this goal, the architectures developed will need to address the following stakeholder concerns:
- What changes to existing business processes are needed?
- What data will need to be shared?
- How will distributed data be secured?
- What non-sales applications will need to be integrated with any new sales applications?

(Refer to the scenario)

You have been asked to identify the most appropriate artifacts (catalogs, matrices, and diagrams) for the second iteration of the Architecture Development Cycle.

Based on the TOGAF standard, which of the following is the best answer?

Answers

A. Describe the Business Architecture with a Process/Event/Control/Product catalog and Role catalog.
Describe the Data Architecture with a Data Entity/Data Component catalog, Application/Data matrix, and Data Security diagram.
Describe the Application Architecture with an Interface catalog.
Describe the Technology Architecture with a Networked Computing/ Hardware diagram.

B. Describe the Business Architecture with a Location catalog and Business Interaction matrix.
Describe the Data Architecture with a Data Migration diagram and Data Lifecycle diagram.
Describe the Application Architecture with a Software Engineering diagram.
Describe the Technology Architecture with a Processing diagram.

C. Describe the Business Architecture with a Location catalog and Business Footprint diagram.
Describe the Data Architecture with a Application/Data matrix, Data Migration diagram, and Data Lifecycle diagram.
Describe the Application Architecture with an Application Communication diagram.
Describe the Technology Architecture with a Networked Computing/Hardware diagram.

D. Describe the Business Architecture with a Location catalog and Role catalog.
Describe the Data Architecture with a Data Entity/Business Function matrix, Application/Data matrix, and Data Security diagram.
Describe the Application Architecture with an Application Interaction matrix.
Describe the Technology Architecture with a Networked Computing/Hardware diagram.

Question 5

SCENARIO 5

You are serving as the Lead Architect for a European Insurance company. The company has grown substantially over the last 15 years. Due to the many mergers and acquisitions, the application portfolio of the enterprise has grown significantly with little consideration for consolidation or rationalization. Each business unit has managed its own applications, with no coordination between them. In the last two years the competition in the insurance industry has increased with the advent of many Internet-based comparison sites leading to increased pressure to reduce the operational expenses including IT.

The Corporate Board has approved the directive to establish an Enterprise Architecture program within the company to integrate and rationalize the application portfolio and introduce a company-wide customer information management system. The Corporate Board has also given a strategic direction that the company should expand its markets significantly to cover all the member country states of the European Union in the next 24 months.

The company has no existing Enterprise Architecture. The CIO is the sponsor of the program and has mandated the TOGAF standard for the architecture method and deliverables. The CIO has established an Architecture Board and called the first meeting.

(Refer to the scenario)

You have been asked how you will establish the Enterprise Architecture program.

Based on the TOGAF standard, which of the following is the best answer?

Answers

A. You work with the Architecture Board to develop and tailor the TOGAF framework, so it can be integrated with the existing procedures established by the Program Management Office. In addition, you examine the relationship to other processes and frameworks for systems development, operations management, and governance. You then conduct a study to determine the footprint of the Enterprise Architecture.

B. You issue a Request for Architecture Work so that the necessary resources needed to define an Architecture Vision can be allocated. You then conduct a business scenario that addresses the Board's mandate upon expansion. Based on that, you define a Common Systems Architecture that will guide the selection of Solution Building Blocks (SBBs) for integrating the systems across business units.

C. You ensure that there is agreement on the scope of the Enterprise Architecture, and identify the key business drivers. You document and validate the requirements for architecture work. You develop a set of Architecture Principles with the Architecture Board to guide the architecture work. You then consider how to best tailor the TOGAF framework for use, and identify tools for supporting the program.

D. You start by conducting an Architecture Maturity Assessment to assess the ability of the organization to undergo change. Using that input you then apply the TOGAF ADM to define the overall requirements for integrating a new company information management system into the enterprise. You then work with the Architecture Board to define the business goals that will drive the Enterprise Architecture program.

Question 6

SCENARIO 6

You are serving as the Lead Architect for a telecommunications company that recently formed through the merging of three other telecommunication companies. The business operating model has been unified, and an Enterprise Architecture program has been put in place as part of the integration of the three organizations.

The company has adopted the TOGAF 9 Architecture Development Method. The Architecture Board has approved the outline Implementation and Migration Plan and they are now at the stage of conducting detailed migration planning. A working group has been formed that involves all the key architects and the stakeholders from the corporate matrix (those who will work on the project).

It is recognized that others outside the Enterprise Architecture team will have the responsibility to fund, build, support, and use what is put in place based on the Enterprise Architecture. For the company, getting this right is critical especially as the competition in the marketplace has been fierce and the lines of business have been resistant to implementing any new business model. The CIO is the sponsor of the program and has mandated an incremental approach to rollout the integration program.

(Refer to the scenario)

You have been asked to describe:
- How you would conduct migration planning
- What you would be implementing
- Who you would involve
- What would be the major deliverable(s)

Based on the TOGAF standard, which of the following is the best answer?

Answers

A. Migration planning should be conducted by the Chief Architect, his direct reports, and shared with the domain architects. When complete the Implementation and Migration Plan will be sent to the Architecture Board secretariat for circulation before the next meeting. The plan will include a prioritized list of projects, their approximate cost, and the recommended way ahead. Comments from the Board (and their staff) would be incorporated into the plan and then the individual projects would have to go in front of the board to secure approval for project resources for the next project increment. The Implementation and Migration Plan would include a high-level GANNT chart that could be used as the Architecture Roadmap.

B. Migration planning should be conducted by the Enterprise Architecture team. The approach should be confirmed and coordinated with the corporate management frameworks involved. Detailed resource estimates should be created for the work to be completed and the business value identified for all deliverables. A series of Transition Architectures should be planned that take into account the priorities. When this is completed the Implementation and Migration Plan can be finalized. The Business Planning, Portfolio Management, and Operations Management groups should all be involved in the development of the major deliverables. Once the deliverables have been completed, the Architecture Development Cycle should be completed.

C. Migration planning should be conducted by the Project Managers using the Implementation and Migration Strategy from Phase E to create project plans focusing on scope, budget, and time. Project Management best practices can then be used to conduct more detailed analysis and come up with business value on a project by project basis. Project Managers will assign business value and prepare submissions to the IT governance Board for funding. The Chief Architect will sit as a member of the Board and advise members with respect to the criticality of the project and its relative importance. Over time the projects will continuously come forward for renewed funding and approval to proceed. The sum of the project plans and roadmaps will serve as the detailed Implementation and Migration Plan.

D. Migration planning should be conducted by the Enterprise Architecture team, in particular the domain (Business, Application, Data, Technology, and Security) architects who would look at implementing a series of Transition Architectures using sound project management techniques. The Enterprise Architecture team will then create a prioritized list of activities and place the high-level Architecture Building Blocks (ABBs) in an Implementation and Migration Plan and Architecture Roadmap. These deliverables would be circulated around the organization for comments that would be selectively integrated. The circulation would be to the lines of business and the members of the Executive Board so that they would be ready to fund the proposed Enterprise Architecture work.

Question 7

SCENARIO 7

You are serving as the Lead Architect for a business unit within a major logistics company. The business unit has selected a Commercial Off-the-Shelf (COTS) Market Analytics solution in order to improve its capability to respond to market demands for its new rail-based freight delivery service. It has identified that the current system does not provide the required functionality to support the marketing activities. Its performance limitations cause unacceptable delays and missed opportunities to meet market targets. Clearly, the current system is costing the unit in terms of lost revenue.

The company has a mature Enterprise Architecture Capability spanning all of its business units and has adapted the TOGAF framework as the basis for its ongoing program. The CIO is the sponsor of the Enterprise Architecture practice.

The Enterprise Architecture team initiated a project with the business unit that has defined the business vision and requirements for the new system. It includes a detailed business process analysis. A solution has been proposed that can support the existing applications and technologies currently in place. The proposed solution requires a non-standard operating system platform to support the business application and also requires different web server software to the current supported web server solutions. The Architecture Board has held a review, and it was noted that some of these project requirements were not consistent with the firm's current infrastructure standards.

After discussions with several senior executives, the CIO feels that he must support the business unit's urgent need to deploy the Market Analytics package. He has approved the implementation. A project manager has been chosen, and a feasibility meeting has been held with a decision to move forward. The project is critical and must be completed as quickly as possible; a contract has been signed with the software vendor to implement the solution.

The vendor has provided a Statement of Work that has passed through the migration planning phase, and major impacts to existing systems and the infrastructure have been documented.

The CIO has asked the Enterprise Architecture team to prepare for Phase G, ensuring that the Key Performance Indicators (KPIs) for system performance and security are met, and the project remains within budget.

(Refer to the scenario)

You have been asked to recommend a plan to implement the direction from the CIO.

Based on the TOGAF standard, which of the following is the best answer?

Answers

A. Based on the review held by the Architecture Board, you recommend the vendor modify the web server software and hardware components in the product so they can meet the current infrastructure standards. You recommend development of an in-house prototype of the product to investigate coding change options.

You would then obtain the approval of the development leads for supporting the development effort, develop an Architecture Contract, and provide the project plan to the project manager, emphasizing adherence to schedule.

After implementation, you schedule frequent operational reviews to monitor performance of the solution.

B. You review the output from the Architecture Board and recommend the co-existence of a second web server standard, noting the additional hardware and support skills issues. You add this technology to the currently supported inventory of standard products in the company Standards Information Base.

You direct the project architects to construct an Architecture Contract with the development team. You emphasize the importance of using appropriate Architecture Compliance Reviews in addition to the test plans required for performance, and monitor the testing results. You establish agreements with the business unit for Service Level Agreements (SLAs) and delivery dates. After implementation, you identify re-usable objects and procedures.

C. Based on the recommendations of the Architecture Board, you would eliminate the non-standard web server from the solution. You create a revised plan and Architecture Contract for the development of a replacement application and server environment using standard re-usable components and internal development resources.

You would inform the CIO that in the long term the development of this standardized version is the lower-cost option. You ensure that the budget implications to these recommendations are presented to the finance committee. You hold frequent project management meetings to monitor compliance to standards and the revised schedule.

D. You prepare an expanded risk analysis and inform the development team of the required deliverables and the dates. You prepare a detailed impact analysis of the use of a "non-standard" web and hardware solution. You construct an Architecture Contract. You obtain approval from the CIO prior to implementation.

You schedule a test of the solution just prior to implementation according to user performance requirements. You deliver the required artifacts and archive them when implementation is completed.

Question 8

SCENARIO 8

You are serving as the Chief Architect for an online grocer, headquartered in Los Angeles, California. After several years of continued profitable operations, the Board of Directors has approved a strategic plan to expand operations to major cities in the Southwestern United States.

To realize this strategy, management has an Enterprise Architecture program in place to plan and implement the rollout which is estimated to take five years to complete. The program needs to consider how to take the current organization, physical plant, and information systems and transform them to support expanded operations.

The TOGAF standard has been adopted as the methodology and framework for the Enterprise Architecture program. The CIO is the sponsor.

A major concern that must be addressed is how to migrate from a "best-of-breed" logistics system that was built in the early days. It is not expected that this system will be able to scale to support the expanded operations. The CIO recognizes this and has an option to purchase a packaged solution from an industry leader in online sales and fulfillment. One disadvantage of this solution is that the terminology and definitions of its services do not align well to the current Enterprise Architecture.

This is now being piloted in a major fulfillment center in Southern California. It is a large-scale project and members of your Enterprise Architecture team have been deeply involved with the pilot program. As part of the pilot program, the Architecture Board has requested a compliance review be held at the fulfillment center to determine the status of the implementation. The timing of the compliance review is such that there is still time to correct any major shortcomings with the proposed solution.

(Refer to the scenario)

What approach should you adopt to ensure that the compliance reviews are conducted successfully?

Based on the TOGAF standard, which of the following is the best answer?

Answers

A. You delegate the review to the lead Enterprise Architect. You request that she organizes, leads, and conducts the review. Where possible she should involve the appropriate business domain experts. The review should follow the established 12-step process and deliver an assessment report at completion.

B. You meet with the project architect and check she clearly understands the purpose of the review. You ask her to run a lightweight review process where the architects and team leaders pose a series of questions to themselves highlighting their observations on the performance and scalability of the pilot system. The responses should be aggregated into a report.

C. You assign the Enterprise Architecture team to manage the review. You request they ensure that the review covers the development methods. You ask them to identify where any modifications are needed to the standards being used in the project. You ask them to document the strategies being used by the implementation team for collaboration with the external supplier.

D. You assign the lead Enterprise Architect to coordinate the review. You request that she assemble a team of business and domain experts to conduct the interviews for the review. The checklists that the team has prepared for the interviews should be reviewed to ensure they meet the criteria for the program and the business objectives. The responses to the interviews should be compiled into a formal report.

Appendix B
Bonus Questions

B.1 Introduction

> This appendix contains four bonus questions derived from the scenarios and questions used in Appendix A.
>
> These should be taken as an open-book examination. The questions are scored the same as the questions in Appendix A. You should spend no more than 45 minutes on these four questions. You may need to refer to sections of the TOGAF standard in order to answer the questions. An alternative technique when using these questions for practice purposes is to place the four answers in order of correctness from best answer to worst answer.

B.2 Questions

Question 9

SCENARIO 9

You are serving as the Lead Architect for a European Insurance company. The company has grown substantially over the last 15 years. Due to the many mergers and acquisitions, the application portfolio of the enterprise has grown with little consideration for consolidation or rationalization. Each business unit has managed its own applications, with no coordination between them. In the last two years the competition in the insurance industry has increased with the advent of many Internet-based comparison sites leading to increased pressure to reduce the operational expenses, including IT.

An Enterprise Architecture program has been underway within the company to integrate and rationalize the application portfolio and introduce a company-wide customer information management system. A recent review has identified shortcomings within the Enterprise Architecture practice at the company. This has highlighted concerns about the lack of buy-in to the architecture processes and the Enterprise Architecture program. Concerns have also been raised about lack of appropriate staff skills and experience in key roles.

The CIO is the sponsor of the Enterprise Architecture program and the TOGAF framework has been adopted for the architecture method and deliverables. It has been tailored by the Enterprise Architecture team.

(Refer to the scenario)

The CIO has asked you to recommend an approach to improve the performance of the Enterprise Architecture practice within the company.

Based on the TOGAF standard, which of the following is the best answer?

Answers

A. You would ensure that the IT vision, principles, business linkages, and Baseline and Target Architectures are identified and that a set of Architecture Standards is being followed. You would recommend that the senior management team are briefed regularly and support the Enterprise Architecture processes. You would ensure that performance metrics associated with the Enterprise Architecture practice are captured and analyzed regularly.

B. You recommend conducting an Architecture Maturity Assessment as this will identify the practices on which the company should focus to see the greatest improvement. You also recommend that a skills framework be introduced, based on that of the TOGAF Architecture Skills Framework. This will provide a clear definition of skills and proficiency levels for roles within the team.

C. You recommend developing an automated Skills Assessment Tool based on the TOGAF Architecture Skills Framework. The tool will provide a rapid means of identifying skills and gaps. The results from running the tool can then be used to determine the training and development needs of the Enterprise Architecture team members and also used when recruiting new team members.

D. You recommend engaging the services of an external consultant to evaluate the tailored Architecture Development Method to ensure that it is fit for purpose. A set of interviews should then be held with the Lead Enterprise Architect and other architects. A report should then be prepared and presented to the Architecture Board detailing the actions necessary to improve the performance of the Enterprise Architecture practice.

Question 10

SCENARIO 10

You are serving as the Lead Architect for a telecommunications company that recently formed through the merging of three other telecommunications companies. The business operating model has been unified, and an Enterprise Architecture program has been put in place to manage the integration of the three organizations.

The company has adopted the TOGAF 9 Architecture Development Method. It has successfully completed the Architecture Definition phases of an ADM cycle and has identified a large collection of candidate roadmap components. The CIO is the sponsor of the program. She is concerned about the risks to the existing revenue lines and would also like to ensure that the most cost-beneficial projects are undertaken first.

The Architecture Board has approved the draft Architecture Definition Document and they are now at the stage of conducting migration planning. A working group has been formed that involves all the key architects and the stakeholders from the corporate matrix (those who will work on the project).

(Refer to the scenario)

You have been asked to recommend how they can identify and prioritize the projects from these roadmap components, taking account of the CIO's concerns.

Based on the TOGAF standard, which of the following is the best answer?

Answers

A. Use the Implementation Factor Assessment and Deduction Matrix to document factors impacting the Migration Plan; use the Consolidated Gaps, Solutions, and Dependencies Matrix to consolidate the gaps from Phases B, C, and D; use the Transition Architecture State Evolution Table to show the proposed state of the architectures at various levels; use the Business Value Assessment Technique to analyze the relative value and risk of each proposed project; and use the Architecture Definition Increments Table to show the proposed series of Transition Architectures.

B. Determine the key corporate change attributes; determine the business constraints; review and consolidate gap analysis results from Phases B, C, and D; review requirements; consolidate interoperability requirements; refine and validate dependencies; confirm readiness and risk for business transformation; formulate the Implementation and Migration Strategy; identify and group major work packages; identify Transition Architectures; create roadmap and plan.

C. Review and consolidate the gap analysis results from Phases B, C, and D by making use of the Consolidated Gaps, Solutions, and Dependencies Matrix. Rationalize the gap analysis and identify dependencies. Group the activities into a coherent set of projects. Use the Business Value Assessment Technique to assign a business value to each project, taking account of value and risk factors. Prioritize the projects into a Migration Plan taking account of dependencies, cost/benefit analysis, and risk.

D. Create a list of all possible projects from the gap analysis results of Phases B, C, and D. Use the Business Value Assessment Technique to assign a business value to each project, taking account of value and risk factors. Prioritize the projects into a Migration Plan, taking account of dependencies, cost/benefit analysis, and risk. Create an Architecture Definition Increments Table showing how a series of Transition Architectures may be implemented to achieve the Migration Plan.

Question 11

SCENARIO 11

You are serving as a consultant to the Chief Architect of a low-cost airline. The airline was formed in 2002 and has its main base at a major international airport on the east coast of North America. It currently serves 65 destinations in 20 US states, and nine countries in the Caribbean, South America, and Latin America.

The airline has received approval to acquire a smaller regional carrier that will extend the market it reaches and enable it to feed its primary routes with connecting flights from smaller cities.

In order to integrate the new acquisition, an Enterprise Architecture program has been initiated to manage the restructuring of the organization, using the TOGAF standard as the method and guiding framework. The CIO is the sponsor of the activity.

The CIO has stated that the following need to be addressed in the restructuring:
- The airline needs to provide a seamless travel experience for customers
- The airline needs low operating costs
- The airline needs increased revenue and optimized resources
- The airline needs a business-driven integration approach rather than simply integrating the IT systems

The Chief Architect has indicated that, as this is the first acquisition, a review should be undertaken of the Architecture Principles.

(Refer to the scenario)

Note: You should assume that the company has adopted the example set of principles that are listed and defined in the Architecture Principles chapter of the TOGAF standard.

You have been asked to identify the most relevant Architecture Principles for this situation.

Based on the TOGAF standard, which of the following is the best answer?

Answers

A. Common Use Applications, Service-Orientation, Responsive Change Management, Information Management is Everybody's Business

B. Compliance with Law, Protection of Intellectual Property, Technology Independence, Data is Accessible

C. Common Vocabulary and Data Definitions, Data Security, Requirements-based Change, IT Responsibility

D. Control Technical Diversity, Interoperability, Ease-of-Use, Maximize Benefit to the Enterprise

Question 12

SCENARIO 12

You are serving as the Lead Architect to a multi-national coffeehouse company. The company is the second largest coffeehouse chain in the world and the largest in the United Kingdom. It currently has over 10,000 stores in 31 countries. The company has a long tradition of innovation, offering its customers a wide range of products and services to attract them to stay longer in their stores. They were one of the first stores to offer Free Wi-Fi internet access across their whole chain.

The company has recently received approval to acquire the fourth largest coffeehouse chain. In order to integrate the new acquisition, an Enterprise Architecture program has been initiated, using the TOGAF 9 standard as the method and guiding framework.

The CIO is the sponsor of the activity. The Chief Architect has indicated that this program should make use of iteration with the ADM. As the program moves into Phase A within the initial iteration of an Architecture Capability cycle, the CIO has emphasized the need to ensure that the architecture is embraced across the enterprise, especially amongst powerful stakeholders across both organizations.

(Refer to the scenario)

You have been asked to explain how you would ensure that the Architecture Vision responds to the requirements of the stakeholders.

Based on the TOGAF standard, which of the following is the best answer?

Answers

A. You would identify all the stakeholders involved in the merger activity, their concerns, and any cultural factors. You would classify their positions and influence, recording the results in a Stakeholder Map. You would then focus on the most influential stakeholders ensuring that you identify the most relevant viewpoints for each stakeholder and validate that their concerns are being addressed.

B. The effective communication of targeted information to the powerful stakeholders at the right time is a Critical Success Factor (CSF) for such a merger. Therefore, you would develop a Communications Plan to ensure that they are engaged in the program, are made aware of the key features of the architecture, and have the opportunity to check that their requirements are being addressed.

C. You would select one area of the business affected by the merger and conduct a pilot project to demonstrate to the stakeholders the technical feasibility of the approaches that are available. Once all stakeholders confirm the approach meets their requirements you would then complete a Statement of Work and issue an Architecture Contract to your suppliers.

D. You would conduct a series of business scenarios with the stakeholders impacted by the acquisition. This will enable you to discover and document the business requirements for the merger activity and determine which stakeholders are likely to support or block the initiative. It will also enable validation of the scope for the activity. Based on the input you would develop a high-level description of the Baseline and Target Architectures.

Appendix C
Test Yourself Examination Answers

C.1 Question 1

Topic	TOGAF 9: Risk Assessment
Scenario	1
Subjects	15.4, 31.7-1
Rationale	It is important that the candidate understands how the risks associated with an architecture activity can be identified, categorized, and mitigated.
Most Correct — B	This is the best answer. It summarizes the approach recommended in the TOGAF chapter on Risk Management. It recognizes that risk has to be managed through all phases, and that you need to identify, classify, and mitigate risk before starting a transformation. In the Implementation Governance Phase, those residual risks should be understood and managed to the extent possible.
Second Best — D	This choice is less correct since it performs no Risk Assessment prior to the Implementation Governance phase. It provides good guidance on managing the risks using worksheets. However, this answer does not address risk monitoring or the management of residual risks.
Third Best — C	The TOGAF standard does recommend conducting risk classification in Phase A; however, the classifications being proposed do not address the concerns being put forward. Also this answer does not address the mitigation of risks or residual risk assessment.
Distracter — A	This answer is incorrect. There is no such thing as a Risk Aversion Assessment in the TOGAF standard. Putting in place a parallel solution would seem excessive and have its own risks.

C.2 Question 2

Topic	TOGAF 9: Stakeholder Analysis
Scenario	2
Subjects	24-1
Rationale	It is important for the candidate to be able to describe the TOGAF approach to Stakeholder Management and recognize that it is a key technique for engaging stakeholders.
Most Correct — D	This is the best answer. Stakeholder analysis and the development of a Stakeholder Map is the technique that the TOGAF standard recommends for identifying and engaging the key stakeholders in Phase A. The Stakeholder Map is a major product output and used to support other outputs in this phase.
Second Best — A	This answer is less correct since it omits the Stakeholder Map approach recommended by the TOGAF standard to explicitly identify stakeholders. Business scenarios are an appropriate technique to develop the Architecture Vision and can accomplish some of the engagement. This answer also lacks the identification of key players and the active engagement policy of stakeholder analysis.
Third Best — B	This answer is less correct since it focuses on stakeholders at the regional carrier only, thus omitting key stakeholders that should be involved. The Communications Plan is produced from the work done by the Stakeholder Management approach suggested in answer A.
Distracter — C	This answer is incorrect. The TOGAF standard does not recommend implementing pilot projects in Phase A to assess solution feasibility. This also does not follow the recommended approach for creation and approval of a Statement of Architecture Work.

C.3 Question 3

Topic	TOGAF 9 Level 2: ADM Phases Architecture Definition; Phase E: Opportunities and Solutions
Scenario	3
Subjects	13.*
Rationale	This question determines whether the candidate understands the implications of architecture transformation especially in an existing environment
Most Correct — C	This is the best answer. It recommends the use of Transition Architectures and capability increments to deliver business value which addresses the concern that the implementation has the ability to accommodate changes to technology and business landscape. It describes the migration planning techniques to deliver Transition Architectures, as well as seeking consensus input on the Implementation and Migration Strategy rather than going straight to an Implementation and Migration Plan.
Second Best — A	This is a less correct approach that addresses the deliverables of the architectures but in an uncoordinated way. It looks at rolling up the work in each domain rather than consolidating the gaps and creating projects as a function of capability management. It also does not directly describe the use of Transition Architectures. It does describe the role of the Implementation and Migration Plan and the Architecture Roadmap accurately.
Third Best — D	This is less correct as it focuses on a detailed technology-based Implementation and Migration Plan, negating the impact of using Transition Architectures to deliver incremental business value that could absorb technology and business environment change.
Distracter — B	This answer is incorrect. This approach does not address the concerns, nor follow TOGAF guidance. Most likely it would produce IT-centric architectures and plans that ignore proper documentation and coordination with other stakeholders in order to deliver IT infrastructure as soon as possible.

C.4 Question 4

Topic	TOGAF 9: Viewpoint Selection
Scenario	4
Subjects	35, 19
Rationale	This question tests the ability of the candidate to reference the TOGAF standard in order to select appropriate artifacts to address specific concerns.
Most Correct — A	This is the best answer. The Process/Event/Control/Product catalog allows an enterprise to identify the full chain of impacts resulting from changing a high-level process (addressing concern 1). The Data Entity/Data Component catalog and Application/Data matrix address concern 2 (the sharing of data). The Data Security diagram and Networked Computing/Hardware diagram would address concern 3 (securing of distributed data). A Role catalog can be used also to support the security definition for the enterprise (addressing concern 3). The Interface catalog allows the interaction between applications to be developed and so will address concern 4.
Second Best — D	This choice is less good since it does not address concern 1 explicitly. The viewpoints selected address the other concerns. Note that the Application Interaction matrix is the matrix equivalent of the Interface catalog.
Third Best — C	This choice as well as not addressing concern 1, falls short on defining roles to aid security (concern 3), Data Sharing (concern 2), and Data Security (concern 3) compared to the most correct answer.
Distracter — B	This answer is incorrect as it does not directly address the concerns.

C.5 Question 5

Topic		TOGAF 9: ADM Preliminary Phase
Scenario		5
Subjects		6.4-1
Rationale		This question checks that the candidate understands that the TOGAF standard has a Preliminary Phase and that they can identify the appropriate procedures and steps given the situation.
Most Correct	C	This is the best answer. It follows the procedures outlined in the Preliminary Phase. As this is establishing the program, these are the key steps for this phase.
Second Best	A	This choice is less correct as it misses out scoping, identifying drivers, and developing principles that would be very much needed in this establishment situation.
Third Best	D	This choice can be performed as part of the Preliminary Phase, but it is not the immediate priority as the scenario is program establishment. This omits key items, such as scoping the enterprise and establishing principles, and moves forward to apply the ADM before that program establishment is completed.
Distracter	B	This answer is incorrect because it skips past the program establishment that would be provided in the Preliminary Phase into Phase A activities, and begins execution of an architecture project focused on the Solution Architecture.

C.6 Question 6

Topic	TOGAF 9 Level 2: ADM Phases Architecture Definition Phase F: Migration Planning
Scenario	6
Subjects	14.*, 28.*
Rationale	This question determines whether the candidate understands the implications of architecture transformation especially in an existing environment in Phase F: Migration Planning.
Most Correct	B	This is the best answer. The answer is concise and complete as per Phase F, with an emphasis on building corporate consensus and ensuring that the Transition Architectures are solidly based upon business value.
Second Best	D	This is a less correct approach, as it is incomplete, missing key steps of Phase F. This also lacks the collaborative planning in close cooperation with the stakeholders within and outside of the organization.
Third Best	A	The approach is also incomplete. Phase F emphasizes collaborative planning in close cooperation with the stakeholders within and outside of the organization, and this lacks that approach.
Distracter	C	This is a wrong answer. The intent of Enterprise Architecture using the TOGAF standard is to provide detailed guidance to the projects so that they can focus on operational design issues rather than strategic ones.

C.7 Question 7

Topic	TOGAF 9 Level 2 ADM Phases: Governance (Phase G)
Scenario	7
Subjects	Implementation Governance
Rationale	This question deals with the need for Implementation Governance of development projects.
Most Correct	B	This is the best answer. All of the criteria fall within Phase G. The architect accepts the mandate of the CIO and decides that a second standard is an acceptable compromise, since time is of the essence and a contract has already been signed with the vendor per his product design. The architect then works with the development team to draw up an Architecture Contract. The architect emphasizes use of compliance reviews, the testing of the performance as the solution is developed (a critical user requirement), and gets buy-in and visibility of Service Level Agreements (SLAs) and schedule with the business unit. Finally, after implementation, re-useable artifacts and objects are collected and are available for future projects.
Second Best	A	This answer is less correct as the response (to recommend the vendor change the product) may take time and, as noted in the scenario, this is a time-critical project. Performing a prototype would reduce the risk, but again at the expense of time and perhaps budget. The project plan should be drawn up by the project manager not the architect. Finally, performance is paramount, yet the architect is suggesting monitoring the performance after implementation, rather than testing the product's performance before implementation.
Third Best	D	This approach follows the CIO direction but focuses on risk rather than co-existence. There is no negotiation with the implementation team – just a handover of schedules – or with the business unit regarding service levels. The suggestion to test the solution just prior to implementation is too late, since the solution has already been constructed and any surprises will likely impact schedule and budget. The attention to artifacts is superfluous.

Distracter	C	This answer is incorrect. The scenario states that the decision has already been made, and a contract put in place. This proposed solution does not address the CIO mandate which stated that this is time-critical and approval had been given to move ahead with the selected vendor. The consultation with the finance committee is irrelevant. Holding frequent project management meetings is not the Enterprise Architect's job, but the job of the project manager.

C.8 Question 8

Topic		TOGAF 9: Conducting Compliance Reviews
Scenario		8
Subjects		15.4, 48.6
Rationale		It is important for the candidate to be able to manage the process of conducting compliance reviews that are appropriate to the situation.
Most Correct	D	This is the best answer. It is most appropriate to the situation – it is a large-scale project and the Enterprise Architects have been heavily involved. In this approach the lead Enterprise Architect coordinates the review and assembles domain experts to manage the reviews. This response includes the mention of checklists and them being reviewed as well as a formal report being produced.
Second Best	A	This answer is less correct. This is a reasonable approach, usually best done when the architects are not involved in the project; however, in this case they are. It also omits specific mention of the checklists.
Third Best	B	This answer is less correct. This approach is more suited to smaller-scale projects and the informality is not suitable to such an important project. The aggregation of responses to create the report is incorrect.
Distracter	C	This answer is incorrect. It fails to appoint a specific coordinator, and asks that the review focus on the development methods being used, rather than whether the solution meets any business criteria. It also focuses on collaboration and standards which are not of prime concern.

Appendix D
Bonus Answers

D.1 Question 9

Topic		Architecture Maturity and Skills Framework
Scenario		9
Subjects		KLP 51.3-*, 52.4-1
Rationale		The candidate should be able to identify techniques in the TOGAF standard that can be used to properly manage the Enterprise Architecture Capability.
Most Correct	B	This answer is best because it examines the Enterprise Architecture using a technique explicitly designed for assessing process improvement for Enterprise Architectures. Second, it focuses on assessing the skill levels of the staff by creating an organization-specific skills inventory.
Second Best	C	This answer is less correct, as it only examines the staff skill levels.
Third Best	A	This answer is less correct because it focuses on specific actions to address improving the architecture processes, but lacks application of any techniques to evaluate the processes. It also fails to address staff skills.
Distracter	D	This answer is incorrect. The TOGAF standard does not recommend the proposed course of action.

D.2 Question 10

Topic	TOGAF 9: Use of Migration Planning Techniques
Scenario	10
Subjects	28.2, 28.5, 13.4, 13.5, 14.4
Rationale	To show that the candidate understands how to use some of the TOGAF migration planning techniques to prioritize projects.
Most Correct	C	This is the most straightforward approach, selecting just two of the migration planning techniques, relevant to project identification and prioritization, risk, and cost/benefit analysis. This most addresses the CIO concern of risk and cost/benefit.
Second Best	D	This is similar to answer C; C is slightly better because the Consolidated Gaps, Solutions, and Dependencies Matrix identifies possible duplicated projects earlier and is a more rigorous approach than just creating a list of the projects. It also addresses the concerns of risk and cost/benefit analysis.
Third Best	A	This is less correct – it uses all the migration planning techniques available but without showing understanding of what each technique is used for. It is just a list of the techniques.
Distracter	B	This is incorrect. It is just a list of the steps of Phase E but fails to demonstrate application to the specific scenario which requires use of techniques from Phase F as well as Phase E.

D.3 Question 11

Topic	TOGAF 9: Applying Principles
Scenario	11
Subjects	6.4.4-1, 23.4-1, 23.5-1, 23.6-1, 36.2-2
Rationale	The candidate should be able to apply Architecture Principles, such as the example ones that are provided in the TOGAF standard.
Most Correct — D	This is the most appropriate set of principles. Those selected match specific concerns: Control Technical Diversity can help in reducing costs and optimizing resources as will the principle of Interoperability. Ease-of-Use can help address the aim to provide a seamless user experience. Maximize Benefit to the Enterprise addresses ensuring that a business-driven approach is taken.
Second Best — A	This is less correct. Information Management is Everybody's Business will help to ensure that efforts are aligned with the business. The other principles do not directly address the scenario but may help.
Third Best — B	This set of principles is less correct. Compliance with Law, Protection of Intellectual Property, and Data is Accessible are good practice but do not directly address the scenario. It is possible that Technology Independence will increase running costs and lead to less than optimal resources.
Distracter — C	This set of principles is incorrect as they are primarily IT-focused and do not address the scenario.

D.4 Question 12

Topic	TOGAF 9: Business Scenarios
Scenario	12
Subjects	Business Scenarios
Rationale	The candidate should be able to describe the TOGAF technique of business scenarios and recognize that it is a key technique for identifying and validating requirements with key stakeholders.
Most Correct — D	This is the best answer. Business scenarios are the recommended technique for developing the Architecture Vision and ensuring that requirements are identified and validated.
Second Best — A	This is less correct. Stakeholder analysis and the development of a Stakeholder Map is the technique that the TOGAF standard recommends for identifying and engaging the key stakeholders in Phase A. However, running a business scenario would then enable identification and validation of requirements from the stakeholders.
Third Best — B	This answer is less correct since it focuses only on the powerful stakeholders, and thus could omit key stakeholders that should be involved. The Communications Plan is produced from the work done by the Stakeholder Management approach suggested in answer A.
Distracter — C	This answer is incorrect. The TOGAF standard does not recommend implementing pilot projects in Phase A to assess solution feasibility. This also does not follow the recommended approach for creation and approval of a Statement of Architecture Work.

Appendix E
TOGAF 9 Certified Syllabus

This appendix provides a copy of the Level 2 Learning Units that comprise the Level 2 Syllabus for the TOGAF 9 Certified qualification. Each learning outcome is phrased in terms of what the candidate should have learned. In addition, candidates for Level 2 are assumed to have the knowledge of the Level 1 Syllabus (documented in the TOGAF 9 Foundation Study Guide). The Key Learning Point (KLP) references in the tables can be used to trace the requirements back to sections of the TOGAF 9.2 document.

E.1 Preliminary Phase

UNIT 1	Preliminary Phase
Purpose	The purpose of this Learning Unit is to help the Candidate understand how to apply the Preliminary Phase in development of an Enterprise Architecture.
KLP Reference	5-*, 20-*, SEC.5-1, 32.2
Learning Outcome	The Candidate must be able to: 1. Understand the inputs to the phase (KLP 5.2-1), and be able to explain the following key elements:<ul><li>Architecture Frameworks</li><li>Business principles, business goals, and business drivers</li></ul>2. Explain the influence of pre-existing architectural inputs on the phase (KLP 5.2-1) 3. Understand the steps (KLP 5.3-1, 5.3.3), and be able to:<ul><li>Describe how to establish an Enterprise Architecture team and organization</li><li>Identify and establish a set of Architecture Principles for a given scenario (KLP 5.3.4-1, 20.4-1, 20.5-1)</li><li>Discuss the appropriate considerations for tailoring the TOGAF framework (KLP 5.3.5-1)</li></ul>4. Understand the outputs (KLP 5.4-1), and be able to explain the following key elements (KLP 32.2-2):<ul><li>Architecture Principles</li><li>Architecture Governance Framework</li><li>Request for Architecture Work</li></ul>5. Briefly explain how Security Architecture influences this phase (KLP SEC.5-1)

E.2 Architecture Governance (Level 2)

UNIT 2	Architecture Governance (Level 2)
Purpose	The purpose of this Learning Unit is to help the Candidate understand how to apply Architecture Governance in development of an Enterprise Architecture.
KLP Reference	5-*, 13-*, 14-*, 41-*, 44-*
Learning Outcome	The Candidate must be able to: 1. Explain how Architecture Governance fits within the ADM cycle (KLP 5.4-1, 13.2-1, 14.4-1) 2. Discuss the key success factors for putting Architecture Governance into practice (KLP 44.3-1) 3. Discuss the factors that should be considered when setting up an Architecture Board (KLP 41.3-1) 4. Explain how to operate an Architecture Board (KLP 41.4-1) Note: There is expected to be some overlap with the Learning Unit covering Phase G.

E.3 Business Scenarios Technique

UNIT 3	Business Scenarios Technique
Purpose	The purpose of this Learning Unit is to help the Candidate understand how to apply the Business Scenarios technique.
KLP Reference	BS-*
Learning Outcome	The Candidate must be able to 1. Describe the properties of a good Business Scenario (KLP BS.1-1, BS.7-1, BS.9-1) 2. Explain how to develop and validate a Business Scenario (KLP BS.3-1, BS.7-1, BS.9-1)

E.4 Phase A: Architecture Vision

UNIT 4	Phase A: Architecture Vision
Purpose	The purpose of this Learning Unit is to help the Candidate understand how to apply Phase A in development of an Enterprise Architecture.
KLP Reference	6-*, SEC.5-1, 26-*, 27-*, 32.2
Learning Outcome	The Candidate must be able to: 1. Understand the inputs to the phase (KLP 6.2-1), and be able to: • Describe the typical contents of the Architecture Repository at this point 2. Understand the steps (KLP 6.3-1), and be able to: • Describe how to identify stakeholders, their concerns, and business requirements • Explain the purpose of a Business Transformation Readiness Assessment • Describe the risk assessment approach taken in this phase 3. Understand the outputs (KLP 6.4-1), and be able to explain the following key elements including their purpose (KLP 32.2-2): • Statement of Architecture Work • Capability Assessment • Architecture Vision • Communications Plan 4. Explain the Security Architecture influences on this phase (KLP SEC.5-1)

E.5 Architecture Content Framework

UNIT 5	Architecture Content Framework
Purpose	The purpose of this Learning Unit is to help the Candidate understand the TOGAF Architecture Content Framework.
KLP Reference	29-*
Learning Outcome	The Candidate must be able to: 1. Explain the purpose of the Architecture Content Framework (KLP 29.2-1) 2. Describe the main components of the Content Metamodel (KLP 29.2-1) 3. Describe the relationship between the Architecture Content Framework and the TOGAF ADM (KLP 29.3-1)

E.6 Stakeholder Management

UNIT 6	Stakeholder Management
Purpose	The purpose of this Learning Unit is to help the Candidate understand how to apply the Stakeholder Management technique.
KLP Reference	21-*, 31-*
Learning Outcome	The Candidate must be able to: 1. Describe the Stakeholder Management process (KLP 21.1-1, 21.2-1, 21.3-1, 21.4-1) 2. Explain the benefits of creating architecture views (KLP 31.2-1) 3. For the example architecture view described in Section 31.4.1: • Describe the stakeholders and their concerns • Define a Stakeholder Map

E.7 TOGAF Content Metamodel

UNIT 7	TOGAF Content Metamodel
Purpose	The purpose of this Learning Unit is to help the Candidate understand the TOGAF Content Metamodel.
KLP Reference	30.1-*, 30.2-*
Learning Outcome	The Candidate must be able to: 1. Describe the core metamodel concepts (KLP 30.2-1) 2. Explain the purpose of dividing the metamodel into core and extensions (KLP 30.2-1) 3. Describe the key concepts related to the core metamodel entities (KLP 30.2-3)

E.8 Architecture Implementation Support Techniques

UNIT 8	Architecture Implementation Support Techniques
Purpose	The purpose of this Learning Unit is to help the Candidate understand how to apply different techniques that will assist with the implementation of the architectures defined in the coming phases.
KLP Reference	6.3-*, 25-*, 26-*, 27-*, 28-*
Learning Outcome	The Candidate must be able to: 1. Explain how to reconcile Interoperability Requirements with potential solutions (KLP 25.6-1) 2. Explain the factors that influence Business Transformation Readiness (KLP 26.2-1) 3. Explain how to determine requirements for risk assessments (KLP 27.4-1) 4. Explain how Capability-Based Planning is applied in an Enterprise Architecture context (KLP 28.4-2) Note: There is expected to be some overlap with the Phase A Learning Unit.

E.9 Phase B: Business Architecture

UNIT 9	Phase B: Business Architecture
Purpose	The purpose of this Learning Unit is to help the Candidate understand how to apply Phase B in development of an Enterprise Architecture.
KLP Reference	7-*, SEC.5-1, 23-*
Learning Outcome	The Candidate must be able to: 1. Understand the inputs to the phase (KLP 7.2-1), and explain the following key elements: • Business principles, business goals, and business drivers 2. Understand the steps (KLP 7.3-1), and be able to: • Describe techniques for business modeling • Explain the considerations for selecting reference models, viewpoints, and tools (KLP 7.3.1-1) • Explain the technique of Gap Analysis (KLP 23.1, 23.2) 3. Explain how building blocks are used in the development of the Business Architecture (KLP 7.3.1-1) 4. Understand the outputs (KLP 7.4-1), and be able to explain the following key elements: • Business Architecture components of the Architecture Definition Document • Business Architecture components of the Architecture Requirements Specification 5. Briefly explain the Security Architecture influences on this phase (KLP SEC.5-1)

E.10 Phase C: Information Systems Architectures – Data Architecture

UNIT 10	Phase C: Information Systems Architectures – Data Architecture
Purpose	The purpose of this Learning Unit is to help the Candidate understand how to apply Phase C (Data Architecture) in development of an Enterprise Architecture.
KLP Reference	9-*, SEC.5-1
Learning Outcome	The Candidate must be able to: 1. Explain the considerations for the implementation order of the Data and Application Architectures (KLP 8.2-1) 2. Understand the inputs to the phase (KLP 9.2-1), and explain the following key elements: • Data Principles 3. Understand the steps (KLP 9.3-1), and be able to: • Explain the considerations for selecting reference models, viewpoints, and tools 4. Understand the outputs (KLP 9.4-1), and be able to explain the following key elements: • Data Architecture components of the Architecture Definition Document • Data Architecture components of the Architecture Requirements Specification 5. Briefly explain the Security Architecture influences on this phase (KLP SEC.5-1)

E.11 Phase C: Information Systems Architectures – Application Architecture

UNIT 11	Phase C: Information Systems Architectures – Application Architecture
Purpose	The purpose of this Learning Unit is to help the Candidate understand how to apply Phase C (Application Architecture) in development of an Enterprise Architecture.
KLP Reference	10-*, SEC.5-1
Learning Outcome	The Candidate must be able to: 1. Understand the inputs to the phase (KLP 10.2-1), and explain the following key elements: 　• Application Principles 2. Understand the steps (KLP 10.3-1), and be able to: 　• Explain the considerations for selecting reference models, viewpoints, and tools 3. Understand the outputs (KLP 10.4-1), and be able to explain the following key elements: 　• Application Architecture components of the Architecture Definition Document 　• Application Architecture components of the Architecture Requirements Specification 4. Briefly explain the Security Architecture influences on this phase (KLP SEC.5-1)

E.12 TOGAF Foundation Architecture: Technical Reference Model (Level 2)

UNIT 12	TOGAF Foundation Architecture: Technical Reference Model (Level 2)
Purpose	The purpose of this Learning Unit is to help the Candidate have a detailed understanding of the TOGAF Technical Reference Model (TRM).
KLP Reference	TRM-*
Learning Outcome	The Candidate must be able to: 1. Explain the detailed TRM graphic, including the following key elements (KLP TRM.4-2, TRM.4-3, TRM.4-4, TRM.4-5): • Application Software Categories • Application Platform Interface • Application Platform • Communications Infrastructure Interface • Qualities 2. Briefly describe the structure of the TRM components and high-level model view (KLP TRM.2-3, TRM.3-1) 3. Briefly explain the main architecture objectives of using the TRM (KLP TRM.3-2) 4. Explain what the Platform Services Taxonomy is (KLP TRM.5-1) 5. Explain what the Service Quality Taxonomy is (KLP TRM.5-2)

E.13 Integrated Information Infrastructure Reference Model (Level 2)

UNIT 13	Integrated Information Infrastructure Reference Model (Level 2)
Purpose	The purpose of this Learning Unit is to help the Candidate have a detailed understanding of the TOGAF Integrated Information Infrastructure Reference Model (III-RM).
KLP Reference	IIIRM-*
Learning Outcome	The Candidate must be able to: 1. Describe the business and technical drivers for Boundaryless Information Flow (KLP IIIRM.1.4-1) 2. Explain how the III-RM fulfills the solution space for Boundaryless Information Flow (KLP IIIRM.1.4-2) 3. Briefly describe the high-level structure of the III-RM (KLP IIIRM.2-1) 4. Explain the detailed III-RM graphic, including the following components (KLP IIIRM.3-1): • Business Applications • Infrastructure Applications • Application Platform • Interfaces • Qualities

E.14 Phase D: Technology Architecture

UNIT 14	Phase D: Technology Architecture
Purpose	The purpose of this Learning Unit is to help the Candidate understand how to apply Phase D in development of an Enterprise Architecture.
KLP Reference	11-*, SEC.5-1

Learning Outcome	The Candidate must be able to:
	1. Understand the inputs to the phase (KLP 11.2-1), and explain the following key elements:
	   • Technology Principles
	2. Understand the steps (KLP 11.3-1), and be able to:
	   • Explain how a taxonomy of technology services and technology components can be used when developing a Technology Architecture
	   • Explain the role of ABBs
	3. Understand the outputs (KLP 11.4-1), and be able to explain the following key elements:
	   • Technology Architecture components of the Architecture Definition Document
	   • Technology Architecture components of the Architecture Requirements Specification
	4. Briefly explain the Security Architecture influences on this phase (KLP SEC.5-1)

E.15 Migration Planning Techniques

UNIT 15	Migration Planning Techniques
Purpose	The purpose of this Learning Unit is to help the Candidate understand the techniques used in Phase E and F for migration planning.
KLP Reference	24-*
Learning Outcome	The Candidate must be able to: 1. Describe how the Implementation Factor Assessment and Deduction Matrix can be used to document factors impacting the Architecture Implementation and Migration Plan (KLP 24.1-1) 2. Explain the purpose of the Consolidated Gaps, Solutions, and Dependencies Matrix (KLP 24.2-1) 3. Describe the purpose of an Architecture Definition Increments Table (KLP 24.3-1) 4. Explain how the Transition Architecture State Evolution Table can be used in conjunction with a defined taxonomy such as the TOGAF TRM (KLP 24.4-1) 5. Explain how the Business Value Assessment Technique can be used in architecture development (KLP 24.5-1) Note: There is expected to be overlap with Learning Units on Phase E and F.

E.16 Phase E: Opportunities and Solutions

UNIT 16	Phase E: Opportunities and Solutions
Purpose	The purpose of this Learning Unit is to help the Candidate understand how to apply Phase E in development of an Enterprise Architecture.
KLP Reference	12-*, SEC.5-1
Learning Outcome	The Candidate must be able to: 1. Explain how migration planning techniques are used in this phase to review and consolidate the gap analysis results from earlier phases (KLP 12.3.3-1) 2. Describe the steps to create the Implementation and Migration Strategy (KLP 12.3.8-1) 3. Describe three basic approaches to implementation (KLP 12.3.8-1) 4. Explain how to identify and group work packages (KLP 12.3.9-1) 5. Explain how Transition Architectures are created and documented (KLP 12.3.10-1) 6. Briefly explain the Security Architecture influences on this phase (KLP SEC.5-1)

E.17 Phase F: Migration Planning

UNIT 17	Phase F: Migration Planning
Purpose	The purpose of this Learning Unit is to help the Candidate understand how to apply Phase F in development of an Enterprise Architecture.
KLP Reference	13-*, SEC.5-1, 24-*
Learning Outcome	The Candidate must be able to: 1. Describe the management frameworks that have to be coordinated within this phase (KLP 13.3) 2. Explain how business value is assigned to each work package (KLP 13.3.1-1) 3. Describe the steps to prioritize the migration projects (KLP 13.3.4-1) 4. Describe the steps to confirm the Architecture Roadmap (KLP 13.3.5-1) 5. Explain key outputs of this phase (KLP 13.4-1), specifically: • Implementation and Migration Plan • Architecture Definition Document, including Transition Architectures (if any) 6. Briefly explain the Security Architecture influences on this phase (KLP SEC.5-1)

E.18 Phase G: Implementation Governance

UNIT 18	Phase G: Implementation Governance
Purpose	The purpose of this Learning Unit is to help the Candidate understand how to apply Phase G in development of an Enterprise Architecture.
KLP Reference	14-*, 27-*, 42-*, 43-*, 44-*, SEC.5-1
Learning Outcome	The Candidate must be able to: 1. Understand the inputs to the phase (KLP 14.2-1) 2. Understand the steps (KLP 14.3-1), and be able to describe the following: • Explain how to tailor and conduct an Architecture Compliance Review (KLP 42.6-1) 3. Understand the outputs (KLP 14.4-1), and be able to explain the following key elements: • The contents of Architecture Contracts (KLP 43.2-1) • Their relationship to Architecture Governance (KLP 44.3-1) 4. Briefly explain the Security Architecture influences on this phase (KLP SEC.5-1) 5. Demonstrate the role that risk monitoring plays in this phase (KLP 27.7-1)

E.19 Phase H: Architecture Change Management

UNIT 19	Phase H: Architecture Change Management
Purpose	The purpose of this Learning Unit is to help the Candidate understand how to apply Phase H in development of an Enterprise Architecture.
KLP Reference	15-*, 41-*, SEC.5-1
Learning Outcome	The Candidate must be able to: 1. Understand the inputs to the phase (KLP 15.2-1), and be able to explain the following: • Change Requests 2. Understand the steps (KLP 15.3-1), and be able to describe the following: • Architecture Board meetings 3. Understand the outputs (KLP 15.4-1), and be able to explain when the following might occur: • Updated Architecture Contracts • A new Request for Architecture Work 4. Briefly explain the Security Architecture influences on this phase (KLP SEC.5-1)

E.20 ADM Architecture Requirements Management

UNIT 20	ADM Architecture Requirements Management
Purpose	The purpose of this Learning Unit is to help the Candidate understand how to apply the process of managing architecture requirements.
KLP Reference	16-*, SEC.5-1
Learning Outcome	The Candidate must be able to: 1. Understand the inputs to the phase (KLP 16.2-1) 2. Understand the steps (KLP 16.3-1) 3. Explain how the Requirements Management steps correspond to ADM phases (KLP 16.3-2) 4. Explain the purpose of the outputs of Requirements Management (KLP 16.4-1) 5. Briefly explain the Security Architecture influences on the requirements captured (KLP SEC.5-1)

E.21 Architecture Partitioning

UNIT 21	Architecture Partitioning
Purpose	The purpose of this Learning Unit is to help the Candidate understand how Architecture Partitioning can be used to simplify the development and maintenance of an Enterprise Architecture.
KLP Reference	36-*
Learning Outcome	The Candidate must be able to: 1. Describe the purpose of Architecture Partitioning (KLP 36.1) 2. Describe the classification criteria for solutions and architectures when considering partitioning (KLP 36.2-1) 3. Describe how Architecture Partitioning can be employed in the Preliminary Phase of the ADM (KLP 36.2-3)

E.22 Architecture Repository

UNIT 22	Architecture Repository
Purpose	The purpose of this Learning Unit is to help the Candidate understand the purpose of the Architecture Repository, its constituent parts, and its relationship to other parts of the TOGAF standard.
KLP Reference	37-*
Learning Outcome	The Candidate must be able to: 1. Explain the relationship between the Architecture Repository and the Enterprise Repository (KLP 37.1-1) 2. Describe the purpose of the repository areas that hold output of projects, specifically: • Architecture Landscape (KLP 37.2-1) • Reference Library (KLP 37.3-1) • Standards Information Base (KLP 37.4-2) • Governance Log (KLP 37.5-1) • Architecture Requirements Repository (KLP 37.6-1) • Solutions Landscape (KLP 37.7-1) • Enterprise Repository (KLP 37.8-1)

E.23 Guidelines for Adapting the ADM: Iteration and Levels

UNIT 23	Guidelines for Adapting the ADM: Iteration and Levels
Purpose	The purpose of this Learning Unit is to help the Candidate understand how to apply iteration and different levels of architecture with the ADM.
KLP Reference	18-*, 19-*
Learning Outcome	The Candidate must be able to: 1. Describe the concept of iteration and how it applies to the ADM (KLP 18.1-1) 2. Describe the factors influencing the use of iteration (KLP 18.6-1) 3. Describe some suggested iteration cycles (KLP 18.2-1) 4. Describe how the ADM supports different types of engagements within the organization (KLP 18.3-1, 18.4-1) 5. Explain how to apply iteration cycles to the ADM phases (KLP 18.5-1) 6. Explain how the concepts of levels and the Enterprise Continuum are used to organize the Architecture Landscape (KLP 19.1-1, 19.2-1, 19.3-1, 19.4-1) 7. Identify the different levels of architecture that exist in an organization (KLP 19.2-1)

E.24 Guidelines for Adapting the ADM: Security

UNIT 24	Guidelines for Adapting the ADM: Security
Purpose	The purpose of this Learning Unit is to help the Candidate understand the security considerations that need to be addressed during application of the ADM.
KLP Reference	SEC-*
Learning Outcome	The Candidate must be able to: 1. Briefly explain Enterprise Security Architecture (KLP SEC.1-1) 2. Explain how Security is a cross-cutting concern (KLP SEC.4-1) 3. Briefly explain the recommended security adaptations to the ADM (KLP SEC.5-1) Note: This Learning Unit overlaps with each of the ADM phases.

E.25 Architecture Maturity Models

UNIT 25	Architecture Maturity Models
Purpose	The purpose of this Learning Unit is to help the Candidate understand the role of Architecture Capability Maturity Models in enabling an enterprise to determine the state of the Enterprise Architecture and to evaluate risks and options during the development of the Enterprise Architecture.
KLP Reference	5.5-*, 6.3.4-*, 12.1-*, 45-*
Learning Outcome	The Candidate must be able to: 1. Explain the role of a Capability Maturity Model (KLP 45.1-1) 2. Explain the CMMI process improvement approach development by CMU (KLP 45.2-1) 3. Describe the structure and levels of the ACMM developed by CMU for the US DoC (KLP 45.3-1) 4. Explain the role of Maturity Assessments in the ADM (KLP 5.5-1, 6.3.4-1, 12.2-1)

E.26 Architecture Skills Framework

UNIT 26	Architecture Skills Framework
Purpose	The purpose of this Learning Unit is to help the Candidate understand the Architecture Skills Framework, a classification model for architect roles.
KLP Reference	46-*
Learning Outcome	The Candidate must be able to: 1. Explain the purpose of the Architecture Skills Framework and why it is needed (KLP 46.2-1) 2. Describe the benefits of using the Architecture Skills Framework (KLP 46.3-1) 3. Describe the structure of the Architecture Skills Framework, including roles, skills, and proficiency levels (KLP 46.4-1)

Index

–

Requirements Management 149

A

ACMM 244
Application Platform 216
Application Platform Interface 214, 216
application principles 84
Architecture Board 235
Architecture Capability 160, 210
Architecture Content Framework 185
Architecture Contracts 137
Architecture Definition Document 62
Architecture Definition Increments
    Table 124
Architecture Definition, styles 161
Architecture Development 160
architecture framework 13
architecture framework, tailoring 20
Architecture Governance 132, 160, 180, 233
Architecture Governance and the ADM 233
Architecture Governance Framework 25
Architecture Landscape 207
Architecture Maturity Models 241
Architecture Partitioning 199
Architecture Principles 16, 23
Architecture Repository 24, 206
Architecture Requirements
    Specification 64
Architecture Roadmap 65
Architecture Skills Framework 247
architecture tools 22
Architecture Vision 41, 46

B

Baseline Application Architecture
    Description 87
Baseline Business Architecture
    Description 57
Baseline Data Architecture Description 77
Baseline Technology Architecture
    Description 98
Boundaryless Information Flow 223
building blocks 61, 193
Business Architecture 63
Business Attribute Profile 178
business modeling 58
business principles 53
business principles, goals, and drivers 13, 24
business requirements 65
business scenarios 41
Business Transformation Readiness
    Assessment 38, 112
Business Value Assessment Technique 122

C

Capability Architectures 207
Capability Assessment 45
Capability-Based Planning 37, 112
catalogs 193
certification document structure 2
Change Request 143
CMMI 242
Communications Infrastructure
    Interface 214, 217
Communications Plan 47
Compliance Assessment 139

C

Compliance Reviews 135
Consolidated Gaps, Solutions, and
    Dependencies matrix 110
content tailoring 21
Core Content Metamodel 190
core metamodel concepts 189
core metamodel entities 191
cross-cutting concern 177

D

data principles 74

E

Enterprise Architecture team 16
Enterprise Risk Management 176
Enterprise Security Architecture 176
examinations 4

G

gap analysis 60, 78, 88, 100, 109
governance 180
Governance Log 208

I

III-RM 223
III-RM, components of 226
Implementation and Migration Plan 127
Implementation Factor Assessment and
    Deduction matrix 108
Implementation Governance Model 129
Information Security Management 176
Initial Level of Risk 42
interoperability requirements 111
iteration cycles 160

M

matrices 193
maturity assessment 245
migration 180

O

Organizational Model for Enterprise
    Architecture 23

P

Phase A Architecture Vision 29
Phase B Business Architecture 51
Phase B catalogs, matrices, and diagrams 57
Phase C Application Architecture 83
    Data Architecture 73
    Information Systems Architectures 69
Phase D Technology Architecture 93
Phase E Opportunities and Solutions 105
Phase F Migration Planning 117
Phase G Implementation Governance 131
Phase H Architecture Change
    Management 141, 149
Preliminary Phase 11
primacy of principles 20
process tailoring 21
proficiency levels 250

Q

qualities 220

R

Reference Library 207
Request for Architecture Work 25
Requirements Impact Assessment 153
Requirements Management 178
Residual Level of Risk 42
risk assessment 43, 180
Risk Mitigation Plan 180
risk monitoring 136
roles 249

S

security, adapting the ADM 178
Security Architecture 175, 177

Segment Architectures 207
Stakeholder Management 32
Stakeholder Map 35
Statement of Architecture Work 44
Strategic Architectures 207

T

tailored architecture framework 24
Target Application Architecture
    Description 88
Target Business Architecture Description 58
Target Data Architecture Description 78
Target Technology Architecture
    Description 99
taxonomy of Platform Services 218
technology principles 95
terminology tailoring 21
TOGAF 9 Certified 291
TOGAF 9 Foundation 3
TOGAF Content Metamodel 185
TOGAF TRM 99, 213
Transition Architecture State
    Evolution Table 126
Transition Planning 160

Printed by Amazon Italia Logistica S.r.l.
Torrazza Piemonte (TO), Italy